PRENTICE-HALL, INC. / ENGLEWOOD CLIFFS, N.J. 076

A SPECTRUM BOOK

THE SMALL BUSINESS HANDBOOK

A Comprehensive Guide to Starting and Running Your Own Business

IRVING BURSTINER

Library of Congress Cataloging in Publication Data

Burstiner, Irving.
  The small business handbook

  Includes bibliographies and index.
    1. Small business—Management—Handbooks, manuals, etc.
  2. Small business—Handbooks, manuals, etc. I.   Title.
  HD69.S6B85   658'.022   79-14647
  ISBN 0-13-814202-5
  ISBN 0-13-814194-0 pbk.

Editorial/production supervision and
    interior design by Fred Dahl
Cover design by Muriel Nasser
Manufacturing buyer: Cathie Lenard

A SPECTRUM BOOK

10 9 8 7 6 5 4 3 2 1

Printed in the United States of America

PRENTICE-HALL INTERNATIONAL, INC., *London*
PRENTICE-HALL OF AUSTRALIA PTY. LIMITED, *Sydney*
PRENTICE-HALL OF CANADA, LTD., *Toronto*
PRENTICE-HALL OF INDIA PRIVATE LIMITED, *New Delhi*
PRENTICE-HALL OF JAPAN, INC., *Tokyo*
PRENTICE-HALL OF SOUTHEAST ASIA PTE. LTD., *Singapore*
WHITEHALL BOOKS LIMITED, *Wellington, New Zealand*

With love to Razel,
    Our children: Harry and Trish, Ronald,
        Alan and Roseann,
        Our grandchildren: Joseph, Brian and David,
            and
        In memory of our son Stuart.

Contents

Preface

Relinquishing the security of a job to launch one's own business venture is partly an American tradition and partly the grand American dream. Each year, more than one-third of a million new enterprises are started up. Unfortunately, a nearly equal number annually close up shop.

The most often quoted reason for business failure is managerial ineptitude. Obviously, education and experience are fundamental. People who try business do need help. Few are expert in even a single major area, such as production, finance, or sales. Fewer still understand the details of legal requirements, tax regulations, financial and risk management, and other specialized facets of business administration.

Still, interest in owning a business grows each year. Attendance at small business shows and conventions is way up; colleges and universities show their increasing awareness of public interest by offering courses in entrepreneurship; the federal government frequently sponsors small business institutes, and new legislation encouraging small business has been enacted regularly since the 1950s. Indeed, small business *is* American business—nine out of every ten manufacturing firms, wholesale establishments, and retail stores are small enterprises as defined by the Small Business Administration—small in annual sales volume, in number of employees, and in scope of operations.

The Small Business Handbook is designed to be an informative, comprehensive, and balanced guide to small business management. Written in clear, non-technical language, it is packed with facts and techniques needed to: (1) make the initial decision to start your own business; (2) plan, organize, arrange financing for, locate, staff, and finally launch the new enterprise; (3) insure its viability, and (4) sustain both profitability and growth over the long term.

Consequently, this Handbook is useful as a basic text for academic courses in entrepreneurship at both junior and senior college levels. *The Small Business Handbook* is an invaluable reference for the dissatisfied job-holder who occasionally toys with the notion of managing a business of his or her own. For the reader with little formal business education, the ten chapters which comprise Part III furnish the would-be entrepreneur with a realistic mini-education in business fundamentals. Other sections of the book include solutions to common "starting-up" problems, methods for improvement once the business has been started, techniques for creative thinking, and pointers on planning company growth and expansion.

I wish to express my indebtedness to those who helped and encouraged me throughout this endeavor: first and foremost, my lovely wife and companion, Razel; my family; my congenial friends and colleagues at Baruch College—Professors Mel Unger, Bernard Belasco, Maurice Roth, and Martin Weiss, and Alan Goldberg, president of Parliament Brokerage, Ltd. of Commack, New York.

Finally, my sincere thanks to the editorial staff at Prentice-Hall for their guidance in this project.

IRVING BURSTINER

I

Making the Decision

Almost everyone has, at some time or other—and for one reason or another—daydreamed of going into business. Comparatively few attempt to convert this reverie into reality. Most people suppress this wondrous dream, opting instead for the fragile security of a job in someone else's business. Of those who do try, some are successful, occasionally far beyond their initial expectations. Unfortunately, though, many do not make it.

*The benefits and the drawbacks of either choice, business or job, are set forth clearly in this first section. The facts will help you make up your mind as to whether small business is for you. Venturing into a business of your own takes courage—***plus***. That "***plus***" factor—an amalgam of personality traits, aptitudes, skills, experience, financial wherewithall, and other elements—is dissected methodically in Chapter One. The same chapter also suggests that you analyze your weaknesses and strengths before proceeding.*

To aid you in your search for the kind of business that will best match your tastes, talents, capital, and investment objectives, many details are furnished regarding the basic types of opportunities available. Included are financial data for different types of businesses, based on averages and medians.

Finally, the valuable concept of "customer targeting" will help you set your sights correctly. Knowing your customer is a major avenue to success in business.

1

What It Takes to Succeed in Your Own Business

So you're thinking about going into business?

You're not alone. Each year, several hundreds of thousands of Americans try their hands at businesses of their own. Multiply that figure by five or six, and you'll probably still be far short of the number of people who *think* about going into business but who put it off to the indeterminate future.

To many, the thought of owning their own businesses has an attraction that is downright irresistible; they are drawn repeatedly to the idea. To some, it represents the kind of freedom and independence they cannot hope to find working for others—and much more money than they could ever earn on a job. Others are completely turned off by the thought, preferring the cozy security of a steady position.

In this first chapter, you will be led into exploring the pros and cons of working for other people and for yourself. You will learn some of the reasons why people go into business—and the kinds of risks they face. And—most important of all if you follow the instructions carefully—you will find out if *you* have what it takes to make a go of it.

SHOULD YOU GO INTO BUSINESS?

The decision to try your hand at business should never be approached lightly. This is a major decision. Once you have committed yourself, you can be certain that the road ahead will be long, winding, tumultuous on occasion, and blocked by obstacles. If the business fails—and it *could*—it may not only play havoc with your personal savings (and perhaps other assets as well), but it may also deal a traumatic blow to your ego. Indeed, business people who are compelled to declare bankruptcy often show severe signs of psychological strain. The question that floors many individuals after bankruptcy is, "Where do I go from here?" No, I am not attempting to frighten you away from trying your own business. Rather, I am trying to paint a realistic picture and foster caution on your part; because the majority of new businesses started up each year are nowhere to be found five years later.

If your notion of an enjoyable career encompasses being situated in an agreeable environment, working five days a week at your assigned tasks accepting only a modicum of responsibility, leaving your job promptly after eight hours, and then forgetting all about your firm till the next working day, then don't think about venturing into a business on your own. On the other hand, if you are lucky enough to possess a high level of self-confidence, if you can think positively about (and are not turned off by) the prospect of hard work, long hours, and onerous responsibility, if each new problem challenges you to tackle it with everything at your command, *then* owning your own business might be the proper route to chart.

The next two sections of this chapter may help you make up your mind one way or the other ...

What's Good About Working for Others?

Having a job isn't the worst thing in the world. Working for someone else has lots of advantages; some of the more significant ones for you to think about follow:

1. Most likely, as an employee, you work regular hours and no more

than eight each day. Your evenings and weekends remain free to enjoy family, friends, hobbies, and other leisure activities.

2. You have an occasional holiday off with pay, paid vacations after a while, and maybe some sick benefits, too, should you be laid up for a while.

3. You'll have security, in the form of a regular income that you can count on—for your rent, utility bills, groceries, clothing, transportation, and all the other expenses that characterize modern living.

4. Your personal savings will remain relatively untouched—at least, they won't be risked on a business enterprise.

5. You can expect to receive occasional pay increases as the years roll by.

6. Possibly you may be blessed with special bonuses or profit-sharing.

7. The chances are fairly good, too, that your efforts will be recognized, leading to one or more promotions.

8. Even though you may be saddled with more and more responsibilities as the years pass, the business will always remain someone else's. You will be able to spend evenings and weekends with a relatively clear head.

9. You may find that your job provides adequately for the personal needs most people want filled, such as status and belongingness, pride in your work, and the like.

But There Are Drawbacks Too!

Only a few points need to be mentioned. For one, you are subject to the vagaries of the economy. Should conditions deteriorate, your firm may have to lay off some people (including you, perhaps), close down, or make a major move to another section of the country. Also, since you are working for others, you will be subject to their whims and pleasures. For example, you may find that your supervisor is totally illogical, unfair, and highly emotional; he or she could make working conditions rather unpleasant. Or, you may find yourself quite easily replaced with a brother, friend, or cousin of the owner, despite the fact that you may have put in quite a few years on your job.

There is really no such thing as job security, no matter what you may believe. (Even civil service positions with tenure have become somewhat insecure in recent years.) Your only security, as you know, is *you*. Even though you may have moved up the ladder into the management echelons, you may be replaced if your firm is bought by another company. Should you be replaced (and thousands of people have), you will probably find securing another comparable position very difficult—despite federal laws banning discrimination because of age.

Finally, while you may indeed rise to a position where you enjoy a fine salary, your job—like most in industry—will have a "cap" or ceiling on it. Your earnings are therefore limited.

REASONS WHY SOME PEOPLE PREFER TRYING A BUSINESS

You might want to run through this list of some of the reasons as to why people go into business. (The reasons are presented in no particular order, and the list is not, of course, all-inclusive.)

1. a strong desire to be your own master, independent, not taking orders from others and relying on your own talents;
2. the chance to work at something you enjoy, instead of settling for second- or third-best because of a desire for security in the form of a regular, steady income;
3. the feeling that you would like to operate at your own pace;
4. a yearning for recognition and prestige;
5. a powerful drive to accumulate wealth—and the opportunity to earn far more than you ever could working for others;
6. the discovery of an opportunity that others have overlooked or ignored; and
7. the challenge of pitting your resources and skills against the environment.

Doubtlessly, of the many more reasons for going into business, some are thoroughly logical, others emotional, and most probably a combination of the two.

WEIGH THE DRAWBACKS TOO

Although benefits are implied in such reasoning, the disadvantages need to be borne in mind:

1. You can forget about the eight-hour day, as well as unconcerned evenings and weekends—at least for the first few months (or perhaps years) of business operation. You will put in long, irregular hours and take your business home with you religiously.
2. There is a possibility that you may lose your capital investment and, perhaps, other people's money as well.
3. You probably will not be able to count on a regular income—or any income, for that matter—at the beginning. Indeed, it may take years before you attain the same salary level you enjoyed on the job.
4. You'll carry a tremendous weight of responsibility on your shoulders. You will have to make all the decisions (unless you share them with a partner—who presents another problem completely). You will be embroiled in all phases of your business.
5. In this last connection, you may find yourself having to perform chores that you dislike or actually abhor.

6. By no means can you escape "boss-free." Your customers—and your suppliers—will, in effect, become your new bosses (in the sense that you will have to accede to their wishes and commands).

7. Like it or not, your business will tend to consume just about all your time and all your energies. You will have little time to spare for family, friends, or fun (except for the fun of running your own business!).

THE KINDS OF RISKS YOU FACE

Each new business venture represents a considerable gamble involving time, effort, and money on the part of the gambler. Moreover, the odds against surviving for even a few years are substantially stacked against the one who plunks down the stakes.

To quote from Dun & Bradstreet's *Business Failure Record* for 1976:

> Every year several hundred thousand firms are started, almost an equal number discontinued, and even more transfer ownership or control. Each business day, more than 5,000 changes are made in listings in the Dun & Bradstreet Reference Book; new names are added and discontinued businesses deleted, name styles are altered, and credit and financial ratings are revised up or down. All evidence of the dynamic change and turnover constantly taking place in the business population.[1]

In Table 1–1, 9,628 businesses that failed during the year 1976 are analyzed by both the type of business and the age of the

[1]Business Economics Division, Dun & Bradstreet, Inc., *The Business Failure Record (1976)* (New York: Dun & Bradstreet, Inc., 1977), p. 3. Used with permission.

TABLE 1–1. Ages of 9,628 businesses that failed in 1976.

		Type of Business				
Age of Business	All Types Combined	Manufacturing	Wholesale	Retail	Construction	Services
1 year or less	1.5%	1.2%	1.3%	2.0%	0.8%	1.4%
2 years	10.7	10.1	9.3	14.2	5.2	8.4
3 years	15.0	13.3	12.8	18.3	10.6	14.1
4 years	14.7	11.8	15.6	15.6	14.6	14.6
5 years	12.9	11.8	12.8	12.8	13.2	13.2
Total 5 years or less	54.8%	48.2%	49.3%	62.9%	46.3%	51.7%
6 to 10 years	26.0	26.4	24.0	22.6	30.9	31.8
Over 10 years	19.2	25.4	26.7	14.5	22.8	16.5

Source: Business Economics Division, Dun & Bradstreet, Inc., *The Business Failure Record (1976),* (New York: Dun & Bradstreet, Inc., 1977). Used with permission.

business; the results are cross-tabulated. In this context, Dun & Bradstreet wisely cautions:

> Failures do not represent total business discontinuances. As defined in Dun & Bradstreet's statistics, failures include concerns involved in court proceedings or voluntary actions involving loss to creditors. An entrepreneur may discontinue operations for a variety of reasons, such as loss of capital, inadequate profits, ill health, retirement, etc., but if his creditors are paid in full, he is not tallied as a failure by the D&B definition. Failures comprise only a small percentage of total discontinuances . . . [2]

In the table, note that across the various business types well over one-half of the failures were companies that had been in business for five or fewer years—and that the percentage of failures in the retail trades indicates that over one-third were in existence for three years or less.

Business Mortality

Regardless of your method of entry into the business fraternity (or sorority, as the case may be)—through purchasing an existing company, signing up for a franchise, or launching a brand-new enterprise—the gambling aspect is not your only concern. Any new business represents a contest—a struggle over the long term, replete with an interminable series of challenges to your knowledge and skills. Some might look at these challenges as a steady stream of small, gambling situations that must be resolved—the outcomes of which, when all totaled up, will result in a business success or demise.

Yes, businesses fail. Indeed, many knowledgeable business advisors ascribe such failures, in the main, to initial errors in judgment: selecting the wrong business location, offering the wrong product or product line, deciding to proceed with insufficient capital, ignoring the need for doing one's homework (projections and the like), or even choosing the wrong type of business to go into in the first place.

As I probe behind those initial errors, I find several major factors, such as a lack of experience in the particular field of endeavor or sheer incompetence in business management. Indeed, Dun & Bradstreet reports that this is so in its analysis of the "underlying causes" of business failures in 1976 (Table 1–2).

Clearly, before rushing into a business of your own, you owe it to yourself to increase your chances for success by:

[2]Dun & Bradstreet, Inc., *The Business Failure Record (1976)*, p. 3. Used with permission.

TABLE 1–2. Underlying causes of 9,628 business failures in 1976.

Underlying Cause	Percentage of Total Failures
Incompetence	42.3%
Unbalanced experience[a]	23.0
Lack of experience in the line	13.8
Lack of managerial experience	13.0
Disaster	0.8
Neglect	0.8
Fraud	0.5
Reason unknown	5.8

Source: Business Economics Division, Dun & Bradstreet, Inc., *The Business Failure Record (1976)* (New York: Dun & Bradstreet, Inc., 1977). Used with permission.
[a]Owner(s) or corporate officers not well rounded in sales, finance, purchasing, and production.

1. preparing for the challenge by obtaining a good education, preferably one that includes some business courses;

2. accumulating months, or even a year or more, of experience in the field you seek to enter;

3. securing a managerial post in that field in order to gain all possible exposure to the many facets of business administration: sales, purchasing, production, stock control, financial management, and so forth;

4. keeping up with change and innovation in the industry, through reading business publications and trade literature, and through personal contacts.

WHAT YOU NEED TO MAKE IT

Essentially, only four ingredients are necessary to a new business success:

- *A Qualified Entrepreneur*
- *A Potential Business Opportunity*
- *A Solid and Detailed Plan*
- *Sufficient Capital*

Upon further reflection, I'm adding a fifth element to that list: *luck.*

Of course, the biggest single factor in this recipe for success is the entrepreneur. This man or woman needs business experience plus knowledge and skills. In addition to such obvious traits as drive, willingness to take chances, and "stick-to-it-iveness," the following personal qualities characterize the individual who makes a go of his or her own business:

energy	innovativeness
health	sense of ethics
inquisitiveness	tact
confidence	adaptability
boldness	imagination
empathy	sociability
good sense of timing	consideration
independence	good judgment

Moreover, the entrepreneur:

- is willing to work hard,
- gets along well with others,
- has good communicative ability,
- knows how to organize,
- takes pride in what he or she does,
- maintains good interpersonal relations,
- is a self-starter,
- welcomes responsibility, and
- is willing and able to make decisions.

So you've checked over these characteristics and decided that they describe you very well. Moreover, you are ready, willing, and eager to go into business. Now you must discover a bona fide business opportunity and then develop a comprehensive business plan.

The next two chapters in Part I of this book, along with the five chapters that comprise Part II, will help you do just that. In addition, you can order free and helpful booklets from the Small Business Administration, such as *Checklist for Going into Business, Business Plan for Retailers,* among others.[3]

What About Money?

Yes, launching a business takes money. The days of starting out on a shoestring are long gone, although thousands of people still attempt this feat every year.

You will need different kinds of capital: *initial capital* to set up the business properly and *working capital* to keep it going until your business begins to pay. Of course, the amount of money you will need depends on the kind of business you select. There'll be rent to pay, a deposit plus one or more month's rent

[3]See "Free Materials" at end of chapter.

in advance, utility deposits and monthly bills to meet, and equipment to buy. You'll also need funds for incidentals (legal fees, permits, and insurance premiums) and, of course, initial stock to begin operations.

You'll learn more about capital—and about where to find it—in Chapter Six ("How to Estimate Your Financial Needs"), and in Chapter Seventeen ("Financial Management").

THINK BEFORE YOU LEAP—TRY SELF-ANALYSIS

Before committing yourself to the investment of extraordinary amounts of time, energy, and money, wouldn't it make sense to engage in some personal soul-searching? You ought to pause and think about the following questions:

- What am I looking for? What do I want out of life?
- Are my aspirations realistic? Attainable?
- Am I prepared to struggle and make sacrifices?
- Am I a self-starter?
- Am I blessed with plain, old-fashioned common sense?
- Can I usually control my emotions?
- Do I have self-discipline?
- How are my managerial skills?
- Do I have enough experience in this field?
- Am I more of a doer than a dreamer?

The entrepreneur *is* the business—its originator, its motivating force, its energy. Do you have what it takes to make a success of your business? Review your pluses and your minuses, your strengths and your weaknesses. *In toto,* are you a suitable match for this challenge? A few hours of introspection—with a pencil for recording your own self-portrait—is long enough to make this decision.

As a cautionary note, some individuals have difficulty seeing themselves in a realistic light. Others have overly inflated egos and believe they can do anything, even things that are definitely beyond their reach and capabilities. Such confidence is admirable when deserved; it becomes a powerful weapon in the struggle for success. On the other hand, when unreasonably egotistical people fail, they quickly blame others (competitors, luck or fate, even their spouses or close relatives).

The majority of people, however, can see themselves pretty much as they really are if they (a) make the effort and (b) proceed on an intellectual and unemotional basis. The Worksheet (Table 1–3) and Self-Rating Chart (Table 1–4) will help you with your self-analysis.

"Worksheet No. 1"

The small booklet *Checklist for Going Into Business* is distributed free-of-charge by the Small Business Administration and should be required reading for everyone thinking about starting a new enterprise. It contains extremely valuable information and the short quiz shown in Table 1–3. This quiz will help you decide whether you "have what it takes" to start a business. You have ten minutes—enjoy answering the questions!

"The Creativity/Leadership Self-Rating Chart"

I developed and copyrighted this instrument some years ago and have used it in several studies of supervisory and managerial personnel.[4] Essentially, the chart consists of two lists of characteristics—twenty-five "Creativity Traits" and twenty-five "Leadership Traits"—culled from literature and research in these two areas.

Obviously, entrepreneurs who want to be successful should have above-average scores on the list of "leadership" characteristics. Although the need for high scores on "creativity" may not be as apparent, I have no doubt that creativity is essential for the long-term success of a small business, if only to enable the owner to cope with recurring new challenges, competitive efforts, and

---

[4]Irving Burstiner, "Creative Management Training for Department Store Middle Managers: An Evaluation," *Journal of Creative Behavior,* 11 (Second Quarter, 1977), 105–8; Irving Burstiner, "Evaluation of a Mini-Workshop in 'Creative Leadership' for Educational Administrators," *Education,* 93 (September–October, 1972), 47–50.

TABLE 1–3. Worksheet No. 1.

Under each question, check the answer that says what you feel or comes closest to it. Be honest with yourself.

Are you a self-starter?
- ☑ I do things on my own. Nobody has to tell me to get going.
- ☐ If someone gets me started, I keep going all right.
- ☐ Easy does it, man. I don't put myself out until I have to.

How do you feel about other people?
- ☑ I like people. I can get along with just about anybody.
- ☐ I have plenty of friends—I don't need anyone else.
- ☐ Most people bug me.

Can you lead others?
- ☑ I can get most people to go along when I start something.
- ☐ I can give the orders if someone tells me what we should do.
- ☐ I let someone else get things moving. Then I go along if I feel like it.

Can you take responsibility?

☑ I like to take charge of things and see them through.

☐ I'll take over if I have to, but I'd rather let someone else be responsible.

☐ There's always some eager beaver around wanting to show how smart he is. I say let him.

How good an organizer are you?

☑ I like to have a plan before I start. I'm usually the one to get things lined up when the gang wants to do something.

☐ I do all right unless things get too goofed up. Then I cop out.

☐ You get all set and then something comes along and blows the whole bag. So I just take things as they come.

How good a worker are you?

☑ I can keep going as long as I need to. I don't mind working hard for something I want.

☐ I'll work hard for a while, but when I've had enough, that's it, man!

☐ I can't see that hard work gets you anywhere.

Can you make decisions?

☑ I can make up my mind in a hurry if I have to. It usually turns out O.K., too.

☐ I can if I have plenty of time. If I have to make up my mind fast, I think later I should have decided the other way.

☐ I don't like to be the one who has to decide things. I'd probably blow it.

Can people trust what you say?

☑ You bet they can. I don't say things I don't mean.

☐ I try to be on the level most of the time, but sometimes I just say what's easiest.

☐ What's the sweat if the other fellow doesn't know the difference?

Can you stick with it?

☑ If I make up my mind to do something, I don't let *anything* stop me.

☐ I usually finish what I start—if it doesn't get fouled up.

☐ If it doesn't go right away, I turn off. Why beat your brains out?

How good is your health?

☐ Man, I *never* run down!

☑ I have enough energy for most things I want to do.

☐ I run out of juice sooner than most of my friends seem to.

Now count the checks you made.

How many checks are there besides the *first* answer to each question? ___9___

How many checks are there beside the *second* answer to each question? ___1___

How many checks are there beside the *third* answer to each question? ___0___

If most of your checks are beside the first answers, you probably have what it takes to run a business. If not, you're likely to have more trouble than you can handle by yourself. Better find a partner who is strong on the points you're weak on. If many checks are beside the third answer, not even a good partner will be able to shore you up.

Source: From *Small Marketers Aid No. 71* (Washington, D.C.: Small Business Administration, 1975), pp. 4–5.

change. In fact, top executives earn comparatively high scores in both areas of the Self-Rating Chart.

Instructions.   To score the chart yourself, follow these steps:

1. Part I of the Chart lists twenty-five "Creativity Traits"; Part II lists twenty-five "Leadership Traits." Mark each half of the Chart separately.

2. Put the total number of "Xs" in Column 1/"Extremely Low" at the bottom of the first column.

3. Continue totaling Columns 2, 3, and so on, until you have totaled all seven columns.

4. (First, your various totals should add up to 25—the number of traits you've rated.) Now multiply each column total by the number at the top of the column. For example, your self-report shows the following numbers of Xs: 1, 2, 4, 8, 3, 5, and 2. Here is how you work out a sample score on Part I of the chart:

Column Number		Number of X's		Total Value
1	×	1	=	1
2	×	2	=	4
3	×	4	=	12
4	×	8	=	32
5	×	3	=	15
6	×	5	=	30
7	×	2	=	14
	Total Creativity Traits Score =			108

5. Write your Total Creativity Traits Score in the box on the Scoring Chart.

6. Repeat the entire procedure with Part II, Leadership Traits. Write your total score in the Leadership box on the Scoring Chart.

7. Add up the totals in the Scoring Chart box. Write in "Total Test."

People who see themselves as "average" in all traits (a rating of "4" multiplied by 25 traits) would earn scores of about 100 on each of the two parts. The majority of successful executives tested with this chart score in the "110 and above" range on the Creativity Traits—and even higher on the Leadership Traits. Total test scores above 240 are quite common among them.

The Chart As a Diagnostic Instrument

If you have been entirely honest with yourself—and perceive yourself clearly—an analysis of your responses on the chart will pinpoint your strengths and expose your weaknesses. Low ratings on any qualities (Xs in "Extremely Low" to "Average"

TABLE 1–4. Creativity/Leadership Self Rating-Chart*.

How well do you know yourself?

Below is a list of nouns and short phrases. You are to consider each item carefully—and then place an *X* in one of the boxes alongside of the trait you are rating. There are seven choices available to you (Columns *1* through *7*). Placing an *X* in Column *1* would indicate that you rate yourself "Extremely Low" in the particular trait; an *X* in Column *4* would signify an "Average" rating; and *X* in Column *7* would mean "Extremely High."

Forget your natural modesty, yet *do* be honest with your self-evaluation.

Part I: Creativity Traits.

Item	Extremely Low 1	Quite Low 2	Somewhat Low 3	Average 4	Somewhat High 5	Quite High 6	Extremely High 7
Ability to express oneself							X
Adaptability					X		
Awareness					X		
Curiosity						X	
Drive							X
Enthusiasm						X	
Facility with numbers						X	
Flexibility of thinking					X		
Independence of outlook							X
Lack of compulsion to conform					X		
Openmindedness				X			
Originality						X	
Positive attitude					X		
Powers of concentration				X			
Productivity						X	
Resourcefulness						X	

©Copyright Irving Burstiner 1972. *Revised, 1974.

Item	Extremely Low 1	Quite Low 2	Somewhat Low 3	Average 4	Somewhat High 5	Quite High 6	Extremely High 7
Self-confidence							X
Self-sufficiency						X	
Sense of humor							X
Sensitivity to problems				X			
"Sticktoitiveness"					X		
Wide and varied interests							X
Willingness to take chances					X		
Word fluency				X			
Zest for solving puzzles				X			
Creativity Traits Totals:	0	0	0	20	40	36	42

96

138

©Copyright Irving Burstiner 1972. *Revised, 1974.

Part II: Leadership Traits.

Item	Extremely Low 1	Quite Low 2	Somewhat Low 3	Average 4	Somewhat High 5	Quite High 6	Extremely High 7
Ability to enlist the cooperation of others							X
Ability to judge people						X	
Ability to see the whole picture						X	
Ability to set priorities					X		
Clarifying ideas for others					X		
Communication skills						X	
Decision-making capability						X	
Evaluation skills					X		
Giving credit when due						X	
Interest in people (as against things)						X	
Good judgement						X	
Knowledge of good human relations							X
Planning ability					X		
Powers of persuasion							X
Receptivity to change					X		
Self-control					X		
Sensitivity to others				X			
Skill at motivating others					X		

©Copyright Irving Burstiner 1972. *Revised, 1974.

Item	Extremely Low 1	Quite Low 2	Somewhat Low 3	Average 4	Somewhat High 5	Quite High 6	Extremely High 7
Skill in scheduling						X	
Supportive of subordinates						X	
Taking the initiative							X
Talent for analyzing situations						X	
Technical knowledge of my job							X
Warmth of personal relations						X	
Willingness to listen to subordinates							X
Leadership Traits Totals:				4	35	39 66	105 42

105   147

Scoring Chart. ──────

Creativity Traits	138
Leadership Traits	147
TOTAL TEST:	285

©Copyright Irving Burstiner 1972.
*Revised, 1974.

columns) show that you do realize your deficiencies—and that you can improve through study and effort.

Finally, many leadership qualities develop on the job, as you work hard making your own business a success.

FOR FURTHER INFORMATION

Books

Baty, Gordon B. *Entrepreneurship: Playing to Win.* Reston, Va.: Reston, 1977.

Baumbach, Clifford M. et al. *How to Organize and Operate a Small Business,* 5th ed. Englewood Cliffs, N.J.: Prentice-Hall, 1973.

Broom, Halsey N. and Longenecker, Justin G. *Small Business Management,* 4th ed. Cincinnati: South-Western, 1975.

Chapman, E. N. *Getting Into Business.* New York: Wiley, 1976.

Greene, Gardiner G. *How to Start and Manage Your Own Small Business.* New York: McGraw-Hill, 1975.

Kuriloff, Arthur H. and Hemphill, John M., Jr., *How to Start Your Own Business and Succeed.* New York: McGraw-Hill, 1978.

Mancuso, Joseph R. *How to Start, Finance, and Manage Your Own Small Business.* Englewood Cliffs, N.J.: Prentice-Hall, 1978.

MacFarlane, William N. *Principles of Small Business Management.* New York: McGraw-Hill, 1977.

Pickle, Hal B. and Abrahamson, Royce L. *Small Business Management.* New York: Wiley-Hamilton, 1976.

Steinhoff, Dan. *Small Business Management Fundamentals.* 2d ed. New York: McGraw-Hill, 1978.

Stegall, Donald P., Steinmetz, Lawrence L., and Kline, John B. *Managing the Small Business,* rev. ed. Homewood, Ill.: Irwin, 1976.

Stern, Howard H. *Running Your Own Business.* Pasadena, Cal.: Ward Ritchie, 1976.

Tate, Curtis E., Jr. et al. *Successful Small Business Management,* rev. ed. Dallas: Business Publications, 1978.

Timmons, Jeffry, Smollen, Leonard E., and Dingee, Alexander L. M., Jr. *New Venture Creation: A Guide to Small Business Development.* Homewood, Ill.: Irwin, 1977.

Free Materials from the Small Business Administration

Contact the nearest field office for a copy of Form SBA 115-A; there are ninety-five field offices throughout the country. This form lists all current free assistance publications for small business.

Management Aids:
    # 179—*Breaking the Barriers to Small Business Planning"*

218—*Business Plan for Small Manufacturers*

221—*Business Plan for Small Construction Firms*

Small Marketers Aids:

71—*Checklist for Going Into Business*

145—*Personal Qualities Needed to Manage a Store*

150—*Business Plan for Retailers*

153—*Business Plan for Small Service Firms*

Available from the Superintendent of Documents is the "Starting and Managing Series." Of particular interest is No. 1—*Starting and Managing a Small Business of Your Own* (Stock #034-000-00123-7; 97 pp.; $2.40). Send this identification information, together with check or money order for the amount indicated, to: Superintendent of Documents, Government Printing Office, Washington, D.C. 20402.

2

How to Choose the Right Business for *You*

If you have thoroughly read the introductory material in Chapter 1, and have concluded from your self-analysis that you have what it takes to succeed in your own business, the logical next step is to think about the type of business that suits your own needs better than any other.

To help you make up your mind, you should know something about the business world in general, the various types of businesses available to the new entrepreneur, and the general characteristics shared by each.

Ultimately, your choice will be influenced by a variety of variables, a few of which are listed below:

- the size of your pocketbook (how much capital you can invest)
- the potential payoff

- the nature of the work activities involved
- your past work experiences
- the objectives you set
- your attitudes and opinions
- your personality
- your knowledge and skills

THE AMERICAN BUSINESS WORLD

Ours is a vigorous economy; living standards here are among the highest in the world. In recent decades there has been infringement into the private sector by all levels of government; however, private control of business and industry is assured by custom and by statute. Ours is a capitalists' society where business is open to everyone who has what it takes—including courage.

In all, there are now around thirteen million firms in operation in the United States. Of these, well over 90 percent are considered small businesses. Most of today's giant companies (like J.C. Penney, Ford Motor Company, Woolworth's, the A & P) were once small businesses. In fact, the entire aviation industry began in a garage run by a pair of bicycle repairmen! You never know—today's small home business or part-time hobby might become tomorrow's successful corporation!

According to the Small Business Administration, the term "small business" is applied to the following: retail firms that have an annual sales volume of less than $1 million, wholesale establishments with annual volumes of under $5 million (up to $15 million in certain industries), and manufacturing companies with fewer than 250 employees (although as many as 500 or 1,000 in certain industries).

The small enterprise has the following characteristics: relatively small size in a particular industry, localized scope of operations, personal involvement of its owner or owners in operations, and comparatively limited initial investment of capital.

The law favors small business. Monopolies, unfair methods of competition, and restraint of free trade are illegal in the United States. Back in 1953, the Small Business Administration was created to "encourage, assist and protect the interests of small businesses."

The country's business structure is divided into types, according to the federal government's Standard Industrial Classification System:

- agriculture
- mining
- construction
- manufacturing
- transportation, communication, utilities, and sanitary services
- wholesale and retail trades
- finance, insurance, and real estate
- services
- government

The vast majority of new businesses that start up each year are not in the areas of agriculture, mining, or utilities. Most of them fall into four major business categories, each of which is treated in detail in the next section.

TYPES OF BUSINESSES

Chances are your new venture will be one of the following: manufacturing, wholesaling, retailing, or service. Of the four, retailing is the most favored by new entrepreneurs (possibly because it's easy to enter the field and because it's the one kind of business familiar to most consumers). On the other hand, services has been the fastest growing area in recent years.

Manufacturing

Several different types of manufacturing processes are found in the economy: the conversion of raw materials into finished products, the assembling of parts into wholes, the fabrication of machinery and equipment, and so on. (See Chapter 16.) Usually, the manufacturing enterprise involves a heavy initial investment in a plant and machinery, requires a number of specialized employees, and depends upon large purchases of raw or semi-processed materials and supplies. Depending on what you manufacture, your customers may be the public-at-large (or special segments of the consumer population), wholesalers, retailers, industry itself, commerce, the agricultural sector, or government agencies at any level.

Among the manufacturing enterprises preferred by small operators are bakeries, printing establishments, toy factories, machine shops, potteries, and apparel plants. More commonly encountered manufacturing businesses are listed in Table 2–1, along with the approximate number of firms in each category (per the 1972 Census).

Obviously of far more interest are the financial data furnished

TABLE 2-1. Manufacturing in Ameria: More frequent types (1972).

Type of Business	Approximate Number of Firms
Printing and publishing	42,100
Machinery, except electrical	40,800
Fabricated metal products	29,500
Food and kindred products	28,200
Apparel, other textile products	24,400
Stone, clay, and glass products	16,000
Electric and electronic equipment	12,300
Chemicals and allied products	11,400
Furniture and fixtures	9,200
Textile mill products	7,200
Paper and allied products	6,000

Source: Bureau of the Census, U.S. Department of Commerce, *Statistical Abstract of the United States (1977)* (Washington, D.C.: Department of Commerce, 1978).

for ten selected manufacturing businesses in Table 2-2. Note that gross profit percentages for these types run from as low as 25.9 percent (women's dresses) to a high of 36.3 percent (advertising displays and devices). The range of operating profit for this group runs from 2.6 percent to 5.4 percent before taxes.

TABLE 2-2. Financial data for selected manufacturing businesses*.

SIC Number	Type of Business	Cost of Sales	Gross Profit	Operating Expenses	Operating Profit before Taxes
3993	Advertising displays and devices	63.7%	36.3%	31.0%	5.3%
2051	Bread and other bakery products	66.8	33.2	28.6	4.6
3471	Coating, engraving and other allied services	66.6	33.4	28.0	5.4
2751	Commercial printing (letterpress and screen)	64.3	35.7	31.5	4.2
3671	Electronic components and accessories	70.7	29.3	26.2	3.1
3911	Jewelry, precious metals	68.2	31.8	28.5	3.2
3599	Machine shops—jobbing and repair	64.8	35.2	30.9	4.3
3079	Miscellaneous plastic products	69.9	30.1	25.2	4.9
3949	Sporting and athletic goods	69.0	31.0	26.9	4.1
2335	Women's dresses	74.1	25.9	23.3	2.6

*Based on statement studies of firms with fiscal year-ends June 30, 1976 through March 31, 1977. All statistics are expressed in terms of percentages of annual sales volume. (Note: Only data for firms with from $0 to $250,000 in assets have been shown since this would be characteristic of the beginning business.)

Source: Robert Morris Associates, *'77 Annual Statement Studies* (Philadelphia: Robert Morris Associates, 1977). Copyright 1977 by Robert Morris Associates. Used with permission. (See "Interpretation of Statement Sudies Figures" at end of Table 2-8 on page 29.)

Wholesaling

The wholesaling function is to act as an intermediary between manufacturers and retailers—if your business is consumer products—or between manufacturers and industry, commerce, professionals, and other buyers if you're marketing industrial goods. Hence, the term "middleman" is often applied to the wholesale firm.

In 1972, there were approximately 350,000 wholesalers in the United States. More than two-thirds of these firms are merchant wholesalers; the balance are of several types such as manufacturers' sales branches and offices, merchandise agents and brokers, and others. Most merchant wholesalers buy large quantities of merchandise, store them in their warehouses, then break them down into smaller quantities to sell to their customers. Consequently, wholesalers need (1) a warehouse, (2) a large investment in inventory, and (3) a sales staff. In addition, an efficient inventory control system is mandatory.

More information about wholesalers is found in Chapter 14. Meanwhile, Tables 2–3 and 2–4 shed more light on the major types and the more common wholesale enterprises.

TABLE 2–3. Wholesaling in America: Types of businesses (1967)*.

Type of Operation	Approximate Number of Firms	Percent of Total
Merchant wholesalers	213,000	68.4%
Manufacturers' sales offices and branches	30,700	9.8
Petroleum bulk stations and terminals	30,200	9.7
Merchandise agents and brokers	26,500	8.5
Farm products assemblers	11,100	3.6
Total	311,500	100.0%

*Data from the 1972 Census have not been used because of SIC classification changes. Available figures for all wholesale trade categories indicate that 348,200 wholesale firms were in existence during 1972.

Source: Bureau of the Census, U.S. Department of Commerce, *Statistical Abstract of the United States (1976)*, (Washington, D.C.: Department of Commerce, 1977).

TABLE 2–4. More common wholesale businesses (1972)

Kind of Business	Approximate Number of Firms
Machinery, equipment, supplies	64,200
Groceries and related products	39,100
Motor vehicles, automotive equipment	36,500
Petroleum, petroleum products	31,300
Electrical goods	20,600
Hardware, plumbing, heating equipment, supplies	16,200
Lumber, construction materials	15,800
Farm products—raw materials	14,800
Drugs, chemicals, allied products	13,200
Piece goods, notions, apparel	12,400
Paper, paper products (excluding wallpaper)	10,700

Source: Bureau of the Census, U.S. Department of Commerce, *Statistical Abstract of the United States (1976)*, (Washington, D.C.: Department of Commerce, 1977).

Popular wholesale businesses for budding entrepreneurs include chemical cleaning compounds and janitorial supplies, florists, beauty shop supplies, ceramics, confectionery products, stationery, and wall coverings. Table 2–5 contains important financial percentages for fourteen types of wholesale enterprises.

Retailing

In 1972, there were 1.9 million retail businesses in operation in this country. For the most part, these were store retailers; there are other retail firms that engage in direct (house-to-house) retailing, mail order retailing, selling from wagons or roadside stands, and so forth.

By 1977, total retail sales were well in excess of one-half trillion dollars annually. Twelve to thirteen million people are employed in the retail trades.

Store retailers are shopkeepers—merchants who purchase goods from manufacturers or wholesalers for resale to the public. For a new small store operation, you need: a good location, suitable space, fixtures, displays, and an initial stock of merchandise to sell. Depending on the size of the new operation, your investment can either be as low as several thousand dollars or considerably more than $100,000.

Table 2–6 shows nearly three-fifths of all the stores in the country have an annual sales volume of less than $100,000. So, retailing in America is not basically large department stores, discount stores, and chains. Many of our retail businesses are the "mom-and-pop" type. In fact, nearly one-third of our stores do less than $30,000 annually.

TABLE 2-5. Financial data for selected wholesaling businesses*.

SIC Number	Type of Business	Cost of Sales	Gross Profit	Operating Expenses	Operating Profit before Taxes
5013	Automotive equipment	68.0%	32.0%	27.3%	4.7%
5087	Beauty and barber supplies and equipment	65.4	34.6	30.6	3.9
5161	Chemicals and allied products	64.9	35.1	29.1	6.0
5145	Confectionery	76.7	23.3	20.6	2.8
5063	Electrical supplies and apparatus	67.8	32.2	28.1	4.1
5199	Flowers and florists' supplies	67.5	32.5	28.6	4.0
5148	Fresh fruits and vegetables	89.4	10.6	9.3	1.4
5141	General groceries	85.9	14.1	12.1	2.0
5199	General merchandise	76.3	23.7	20.5	3.3
5072 } 5198 }	Hardware and paints	69.2	30.8	26.9	3.9
5087	Janitorial supplies	63.5	36.5	33.8	2.7
5094	Jewelry	76.9	23.1	18.6	4.5
5064	Radios, refrigerators and electrical appliances	77.1	22.9	20.7	2.2
5041	Sporting goods and toys	76.8	23.2	21.5	1.8

*Based on statement studies of firms with fiscal year-ends June 30, 1976 through March 31, 1977. All statistics are expressed in terms of percentages of annual sales volume. (Note: Only data for firms with from $0 to $250,000 in assets have been shown since this would be characteristic of the beginning business.)

Source: Robert Morris Associates, *'77 Annual Statement Studies,* (Philadelphia: Robert Morris Associates, 1977.) Copyright 1977 by Robert Morris Associates. Used with permission. (See "Interpretation of Statement Studies Figures" at end of Table 2–8 on page 29.)

Table 2-6. Retail stores in 1972, by sales volume.*

Annual Sales Volume	Approximate Number of Firms	Percent of Total
Under $30,000	516,000	30.2%
$30,000-$49,999	188,000	11.0
$50,000-$99,999	304,000	17.8
$100,000-$299,999	450,000	26.3
$300,000-$499,999	106,000	6.2
$500,000-$999,999	71,000	4.2
$1,000,000 and over	74,000	4.3

Source: Bureau of the Census, U.S. Department of Commerce, *Statistical Abstract of the United States (1976),* (Washington, D.C.: Department of Commerce, 1977).

*Based on a total of 1,710,000 retail establishments operating for the entire year of 1972.

More numerous types of retail establishments are shown in Table 2–7. Eating places (restaurants, fast-food drive-ins, and the like) lead the pack by far—with grocery stores and bars running close behind. (Deliberately omitted, are gasoline service stations which are retailers too. There were 226,000 of these in 1972.) Table 2–8 contains financial data for the more popular retail businesses that appeal to small operators.

Service Businesses

The services sector of American private enterprise has reflected the sharpest growth in recent years. According to the 1977 Statistical Abstract, during the single decade from 1965 to 1975, the total number of people employed in service businesses jumped by more than one-third—from 11.2 to 15.1 million individuals. Contrast this statistic with the simultaneous increase in wholesaling from 3.4 to 4.2 million, and in the retail trades from 9.7 to 12 million.

TABLE 2–7. Store retailing in America: Selected types (1972).

Kind of Business	Number of Establishments	Estimated Average Annual Sales/Unit*
Eating places	253,136	$120,000
Grocery stores	194,346	480,000
Drinking places (alcoholic beverages)	106,388	60,900
Drug and proprietary stores	51,542	173,700
Women's clothing and specialty stores (and furs)	49,639	393,900
Liquor stores	41,991	235,200
Building materials and supply stores	38,881	393,900
Women's ready-to-wear stores	38,762	218,000
Furniture stores	38,732	269,600
Auto and home supply stores	37,510	201,100
Home furnishing stores	27,973	129,500
Shoe stores	26,850	155,800
Hardware stores	26,374	150,000
Jewelry stores	25,316	123,200
Gift, novelty, and souvenir stores	24,649	49,400
Florists	24,464	65,600
Retail bakeries	19,203	86,600

Source: Bureau of the Census, U.S. Department of Commerce, *Census of Business (1972)*, (Washington, D.C.: Department of Commerce).

*Estimates derived by dividing total sales for each category by the number of firms listed. Actuals should be somewhat higher because some firms were not in operation the entire year.

TABLE 2–8. Financial data for selected retail businesses*.

SIC Number	Type of Business	Cost of Sales	Gross Profit	Operating Expenses	Operating Profit before Taxes
5992	Cut flowers and growing plants	43.5%	56.5%	52.3%	4.3%
5912	Drugs	67.6	32.4	29.4	3.0
5399	Dry goods and general merchandise	64.5	35.5	30.0	5.5
5651	Family clothing	59.2	40.8	36.7	4.0
5713	Floor coverings	66.9	33.1	29.0	4.0
5712	Furniture	62.3	37.7	33.9	3.8
5541	Gasoline service stations	84.2	15.8	13.7	2.1
5411	Groceries and meats	78.4	21.6	19.2	2.4
5251	Hardware	65.7	34.3	28.2	6.1
5722	Household appliances	68.7	31.3	27.1	4.3
5921	Liquor	81.3	18.7	15.5	3.2
5947	Luggage and gifts	56.3	43.7	37.2	6.5
5611	Men's and boy's clothing	60.0	40.0	36.1	3.9
5733	Musical instruments and supplies	64.7	35.3	31.1	4.2
5231	Paint, glass and wallpaper	62.5	37.5	34.1	3.5
5812	Restaurants	46.4	53.6	48.7	4.9
5661	Shoes	58.9	41.1	37.5	3.6
5941	Sporting goods and bicycles	67.2	32.8	27.7	5.1
5621	Women's ready-to-wear	60.0	40.0	36.4	3.6

*Based on statement studies of firms with fiscal year ends June 30, 1976 through March 31, 1977. All statistics are expressed in terms of percentages of annual sales volume. (Note: Only data for firms with from $0 to $250,000 in assets have been shown since this is characteristic of the beginning business.)

Source: Robert Morris Associates, *'77 Annual Statement Studies,* (Philadelphia: Robert Morris Associates, 1977.) Copyright 1977 by Robert Morris Associates. Used with permission. (See "Interpretation of Statement Studies Figures" below.)

Interpretation of Statement Studies Figures

RMA recommends that *Statement Studies* data be regarded only as general guidelines and not as absolute industry norms. There are several reasons why the data may not be fully representative of a given industry:

(1)   The financial statements used in the *Statement Studies* are not selected by any random or statistically reliable method. RMA member banks voluntarily submit the raw data they have available each year, with these being the only constraints: (a) The fiscal year-ends of the companies reported may not be from April 1 through June 29, and (b) their total assets must be less than $50 million.

(2) Many companies have varied product lines; however, the *Statement Studies* categorize them by their primary product Standard Industrial Classification (SIC) number only.

(3) Some of our industry samples are rather small in relation to the total number of firms in a given industry. A relatively small sample can increase the chances that some of our composites do not fully represent an industry.

(4) There is the chance that an extreme statement can be present in a sample, causing a disproportionate influence on the industry composite. This is particularly true in a relatively small sample.

(5) Companies within the same industry may differ in their method of operations which in turn can directly influence their financial statements. Since they are included in our sample, too, these statements can significantly affect our composite calculations.

(6) Other considerations that can result in variations among different companies engaged in the same general line of business are different labor markets; geographical location; different accounting methods; quality of products handled; sources and methods of financing; and terms of sale.

For these reasons, RMA does not recommend the Statement Studies *figures be considered as absolute norms for a given industry. Rather the figures should be used only as general guidelines and in addition to the other methods of financial analysis. RMA makes no claim as to the representativeness of the figures printed in this book.*

Perhaps the most plausible reason for the popularity of service businesses is that there is no need either to carry substantial merchandise inventory for resale—as is the case in retailing or wholesaling—or to make a heavy investment in machinery and other capital goods, as in manufacturing. Often, little more is required than purchasing several relatively inexpensive pieces of equipment, printing up business cards, and placing a few advertisements. Indeed, your own home, garage, or apartment can serve as the place of business until the business grows too big.

Here are just a few of the types of service enterprises that can be launched with little money and some talent/knowledge/skill:

lawn care	tutoring
translation bureau	equipment rental
bartending	upholstering
piano instruction	seminars
consulting	floor waxing
flower decorating	appliance repair

painting   newsletters
home typing   dance instruction
delivery   baby sitting

Many of today's successful service businesses had their beginnings in part-time avocations, hobbies, or home enterprises before growing large enough to require expanded quarters. No doubt, the same will be true for tomorrow's successes. Table 2–9 contains both the more popular kinds of service businesses and representative types in each category.

THE SMALL BUSINESS ADMINISTRATION

This federal agency renders valuable service to small businesses, and to those interested in small business, in close to one hundred branch offices in major cities around the country. The SBA provides an array of services: financial assistance, management aid, technical advice, help in securing government business, procurement advisement, and so forth. In the management assistance area, for example, the SBA arranges for:

- conferences dealing with topics of interest to small business,
- business management courses cosponsored with educational institutions,
- information and counseling,
- small business clinics, and
- hundreds of printed aids, leaflets, and pamphlets free to the public (see "Free Materials" at the end of this chapter).

Moreover, the SBA works closely with the Active Corps of Executives (ACE) and the Service Corps of Retired Executives (SCORE). Both provide consulting advisement to small business free-of-charge.

Financial assistance is provided in the form of loans, mostly in cooperation with banks. Included are many types of special purpose loans, such as those for disadvantaged individuals (Economic Opportunity Loans), for the handicapped, for businesses hit by disasters, and so forth.

Small Business Investment Corporations (SBICs), licensed by the SBA, also make funds available (and provide management assistance) to small enterprises. These were originated as a result of the Small Business Investment Act in 1958. Minority Enterprise Small Business Investment Corporations (MESBICs) provide the same services to minority group members.

TABLE 2–9. Selected service industries, by categories (1972).

Business Classification	Approximate Number of Firms	Representative Types
Personal services	503,378	Laundries, dry cleaners, photographic studios, beauty and barber shops, shoe repair shops, etc.
Business services	326,077	Advertising agencies, cleaning and maintenance services, consulting and public relations services, equipment rental and leasing, etc.
Automotive repair, services, and garages	168,959	Automotive repair shops, automotive rental and leasing, parking lots, car washes, etc.
Miscellaneous repair services	148,925	Electrical and electronic repair shops, reupholstering and furniture repair shops, jewelry repair shops, machinery and equipment repair shops, etc.
Amusement and recreation services	145,983	Motion picture production and distribution services, theaters, orchestras and entertainers, dance studios, bowling alleys, racetracks, golf courses, etc.
Legal services	144,452	(Not broken down)
Hotels and motels	79,685	Hotels, sporting and recreational camps, motels, trailer parks and campsites for transients
Architectural, engineering, and land-surveying services	64,246	(As classification indicates)

Source: Bureau of the Census, U.S. Department of Commerce, *Census of Business (1972)* (Washington, D.C.: Department of Commerce).

In Table 2–10, key profitability ratios are presented for various types of manufacturing, wholesaling, and retail businesses.

TABLE 2–10. Key profitability ratios (1976): Selected business types*.

SIC Number	Type of Business	Net Profits on Net Sales			Net Profits on Tangible Net Worth		
		Median**	Lower Quartile	Upper Quartile	Median	Lower Quartile	Upper Quartile
	Manufacturing Enterprises						
2051–2	Bakery products	1.86%	0.92%	4.13%	9.63%	4.06%	17.01%
2331	Blouses and waists, women's and misses'	2.11	0.77	4.00	11.86	7.77	21.52
2751	Commercial printing except lithographic	2.86	1.21	5.36	9.32	5.28	12.20
3271–5	Concrete, gypsum, and plaster products	2.40	0.86	5.94	8.49	3.35	24.84
2021–4, 2026	Dairy products	1.10	0.23	1.98	10.47	2.08	14.58
3431–3	Heating equipment and plumbing fixtures	5.20	2.06	6.57	13.15	6.00	19.30
3631–6, 3639	Household appliances	3.54	1.13	6.37	11.72	5.43	23.07
	Office and store fixtures	2.32	0.13	4.70	7.29	0.73	14.00
2086	Soft drinks, bottled and canned	5.38	3.03	8.46	19.75	13.73	29.43
2511–12	Wood household furniture and upholstered	2.16	0.71	4.61	6.45	2.71	12.00
2328	Work clothing, men's and boys'	4.27	1.82	5.73	11.19	5.40	15.68
	Wholesaling Enterprises						
5013	Automotive parts and supplies	2.50	1.09	4.37	10.76	4.74	15.33
5161	Chemicals and allied products	3.08	1.93	4.95	14.57	9.52	19.55
5137	Clothing and accessories, women's, children's, and infants'	1.46	0.42	3.08	9.57	2.05	16.46
5145	Confectionery	0.90	0.47	2.35	10.43	4.00	16.79
5139	Footwear	1.05	0.26	3.63	6.17	2.78	16.32
5021, 5023	Furniture and home furnishings	1.41	0.52	2.65	9.94	2.51	17.06
5141	Groceries, general line	0.59	0.24	1.40	7.50	3.00	14.27
5072	Hardware	2.41	1.13	4.39	9.57	4.45	14.70
5198	Paints, varnishes, and supplies	2.03	1.20	3.52	10.00	4.64	18.84
5014	Tires and tubes	1.70	0.98	4.54	10.57	4.40	23.22

5531	Auto and home supply stores	1.41	0.47	4.04	8.21	2.33	15.94
5641	Children's and infants' wear stores	2.45	0.44	4.46	9.06	0.92	17.03
5712	Furniture stores	2.30	0.75	5.35	7.21	1.54	14.06
5541	Gasoline service stations	3.19	1.57	6.96	15.07	8.71	22.68
5411	Grocery stores	0.93	0.53	1.60	11.77	5.60	16.72
5251	Hardware stores	3.23	1.67	6.25	10.83	4.15	16.96
5944	Jewelry stores	4.19	1.79	8.44	7.28	3.55	14.02
5732	Radio and television stores	3.25	2.19	7.03	21.74	8.11	31.32
5661	Shoe stores	1.61	0.00	4.13	6.09	0.00	12.86
5331	Variety stores	2.41	1.15	5.00	9.69	5.00	15.25
5621	Women's ready-to-wear stores	2.37	0.52	5.99	7.83	1.67	16.85

Source: Dun & Bradstreet, Inc., *Key Business Ratios (1976)* (New York: Dun & Bradstreet, Inc., 1978). Used with permission.

*Derived from samples of financial statements from firms surveyed and analyzed by Dun & Bradstreet, Inc. (almost exclusively corporations with a tangible net worth of over $100,000).

**Ratio figures for each individual line of business are arranged in order from best to weakest, and the figure that falls in the middle of each series becomes the median (or "typical") ratio figure. Upper and lower quartile figures typify the experience of firms in the top and bottom halves of the sample, respectively.

FOR FURTHER INFORMATION

Books

Albert, Kenneth J. *How to Pick the Right Small Business Opportunity.* New York: McGraw-Hill, 1978.

Bolen, William H. *Contemporary Retailing.* Englewood Cliffs, N.J.: Prentice-Hall, 1978.

Danenburg, William P., Moncrief, Russel L., and Taylor, William E. *Introduction to Wholesale Distribution.* Englewood Cliffs, N.J.: Prentice-Hall, 1978.

Kuriloff, Arthur H. and Hemphill, John M., Jr. *How to Start Your Own Business and Succeed.* New York: McGraw-Hill, 1978.

Martyn, Sean. *How to Start & Run a Successful Mail Order Business.* New York: Martyn Company, 1969.

Metz, Robert. *Franchising: How to Select a Business of Your Own.* New York: Hawthorn Books, 1969.

Shaffer, Harold and Greenwald, Herbert. *Independent Retailing: A Money-Making Manual.* Englewood Cliffs, N.J.: Prentice-Hall, 1976.

Simon, Julian Lincoln. *How to Start and Operate a Mail-Order Business,* 2nd ed. New York: McGraw-Hill, 1976.

Spohn, Robert F. and Allen, Robert Y. *Retailing.* Reston, Va.: Reston, 1977.

Starr, Martin K. *Production Management: Systems and Synthesis,* 2nd ed. Englewood Cliffs, N.J.: Prentice-Hall, 1972.

Witt, Scott. *How to Make Big Profits in Service Businesses.* West Nyack, N.Y.: Parker Publishing, 1977.

Free Materials from the Small Business Administration
Small Business Bibliographies:
- # 1—"Handicrafts"
- # 2—"Home Businesses"
- # 3—"Selling by Mail Order"
- # 10—"Retailing"
- # 14—"The Nursery Business"
- # 24—"Food Stores"
- # 33—"Drugstores"
- # 42—"Bookstores"
- # 50—"Apparel and Accessories for Women, Misses, and Children"
- # 53—"Hobby Shops"
- # 55—"Wholesaling"
- # 64—"Photographic Dealers and Studios"
- # 66—"Motels"
- # 77—"Tourism and Outdoor Recreation"
- # 88—"Manufacturing Management"

Small Marketers Aids:
- # 150—"Business Plan for Retailers"
- # 153—"Business Plan for Small Service Firms"

Available from the Superintendent of Documents
Starting and Managing Series:
- # 3—"Starting and Managing a Service Station," Stock #045-000-00067-2; 80 pp.; $1.15.
- # 12—"Starting and Managing a Small Dry Cleaning Business," Stock #045-000-00058-3; 80 pp.; 95¢.
- # 14—"Starting and Managing a Carwash," Stock #045-000-00060-5; 76 pp.; $1.10.
- # 18—"Starting and Managing a Retail Flower Shop," Stock #045-000-00064-8; 121 pp.; $1.20.
- # 19—"Starting and Managing a Pet Shop," Stock #045-000-00065-6; 40 pp.; 75¢.
- # 20—"Starting and Managing a Small Retail Music Store," Stock #045-000-00107-5; 81 pp.; $1.30.
- # 21—"Starting and Managing a Small Retail Jewelry Store," Stock #045-000-00099-1; 78 pp.; 90¢.
- # 22—"Starting and Managing an Employment Agency," Stock #045-000-00109-1; 118 pp.; $1.30.
- # 23—"Starting and Managing a Small Drive-in Restaurant," Stock #045-000-00113-0; 65 pp.; 90¢.
- # 24—"Starting and Managing a Small Shoestore," Stock #045-000-00127-0; 104 pp.; $1.35.

3

Customer Targeting: How to Optimize Your Chances for Success

So you've finally selected the one kind of business that you want to go into. Maybe you'lll be fortunate enough to find a top-notch location, clever enough to manufacture or purchase a terrific line of merchandise, shrewd enough to price your goods so that they're profitable yet marketable, and smart enough to institute tight financial controls. Yet, unless you build a steady clientele, you'll find yourself going out of business in a very short time!

Customers are the people who make or break a business.

WHAT CUSTOMERS ARE LIKE

The term "customers" generally applies to the final consumers in this country, like you and me. Yet, millions of firms do not sell directly to the over 220 million consumers that make up our total population. These companies sell everything—raw materials, semi-processed goods, and finished products—to commerce, industry, banks, schools and universities, government agencies, and other establishments.

They sell what is usually categorized "industrial goods and services"; these are generally consumed in the day-to-day business of a company or organization. These products are different from "consumer goods and services" which are sold to the final consumer either directly or through marketing channels (agents, wholesalers, retailers).

Perhaps it's more appropriate to separate all products and services into two basic types: consumer and nonconsumer.

Contrasting These Two Super-Markets

Sharp differences characterize these two markets:

1. While the consumer market consists of several hundred million individuals, the customers that comprise the industrial (or "nonconsumer") market number far fewer. At most, it totals 12 or 13 million—that's the total number of firms in the United States! In addition, this market includes various government agencies at local, state and national levels. Farmers also need supplies and equipment to till the soil.

2. Those who buy for the nonconsumer market are generally trained purchasing agents for the organizations they represent. On the other hand, the average American needs training in the finer, more technical aspects of buying for his or her needs. Moreover, the consumer's buying motives are more confused, often tinged with emotional overtones, and less rational than the motives for purchasing industrial goods and services.

3. While the consumer usually purchases often and in small amounts, the nonconsumer market is characterized by larger, less frequent purchases.

4. Targeting in on the general consumer market is a complex, time-consuming, even frustrating task because of this market's sheer magnitude. By comparison, although selling to industrial customers is difficult, help is available from the government's various reference works, trade associations, and other sources. Consequently, firms that sell products and services to the nonconsumer market get help in customer targeting in the areas of company size, and product usage.

Today's professional industrial marketer thinks in terms of specific submarkets, rather than the total marketplace. He or she has a twofold task: (1) to select groups of customers with similar needs, wants, purchasing power, and the authority to buy what's for sale; and (2) to develop the appropriate mix of products, prices, promotion, and distribution to reach those customers and sell the product effectively. (See Chapter 11.)

The same approach applies to the much broader consumer market. Ways must be explored to select or target in on consumers who are excellent prospects for our goods or services; then we need to learn all we can about these individuals so we can prepare the proper "concoction" (products, prices, promotion, distribution) for wooing and winning them.

CUSTOMER TARGETING HELPS YOU SUCCEED

Aiming at the entire consumer population is a foolish move; it's not much different than shooting off a shotgun indiscriminately into a flock of geese in flight. Here and there, a single pellet might luckily find its mark—but what a waste of good ammunition!

This kind of umbrella targeting is aptly termed the "shotgun" approach (as against the "rifle" approach) and is completely out of the question for the smaller enterprise. Small business has neither the promotional budget, the production capacity, nor the staff to conduct business in this manner.

No one firm should aim at selling to everyone. Locating subgroups within the population—consumers who share similar needs, wants, preferences, and other characteristics—makes more sense. This approach, known as "market segmentation", enables the seller to tailor his or her entire presentation to specific groups, thus "rifling in" on the targets.

The information gathered about the various "submarkets" is of value in helping to set copy and artwork for advertisements or commercials, strengthening sales presentations, and even in product development, pricing, and other facets of the marketing process.

Markets are usually segmented in the following ways:

1. demographically,
2. geographically,
3. psychographically,
4. by benefits, and
5. by usage.

Demographic Segmentation

Demography is the oldest and most popular way to segment the consumer market. This approach analyzes a total group by studying statistical variables such as age, sex, level of income, occupation, nationality, educational level, race, religion, and so forth.

People who fall into one classification may buy quite differently from those in another category. Young women may be the target of one cosmetic line—older women of another. Young married couples without children are more interested in furnishing their homes or apartments with appliances, furniture, and other durable goods than adults at any other stage of the family life cycle.

Geographic Segmentation

Another professional marketing technique is geographic segmentation. Evidently, clothing worn in California, Florida, and other southern states is more informal and lighter in weight than the popular apparel in colder climates. Geography plays an important role when it comes to marketing swimming pools, insect sprays, ski equipment, and many other seasonal products.

One manufacturer-retailer of confectionery products was astounded to encounter massive consumer resistance to the line of dark-covered chocolates offered for sale in newly-opened stores in the Southwestern United States. In this part of the country only light or milk chocolate candies were popular.

Psychographic Segmentation

Under this more recent method, people are grouped according to attitudes, interests, lifestyles, or other personality attributes. There's merit to this approach, especially when used in combination with the more established demographic approaches. For example, all women are logical targets for cosmetic products. Yet, when women are categorized according to lifestyle, a retailer must offer products and advertising with very specific appeal in order to be successful.

Likewise, classifying consumers according to different stages of the family life cycle (demographic) leads to more effective results if they are also cross-categorized according to interests and attitudes.

Remember that consumers often select products—and stores as well—with "personalities" that are very much like their own self-images.

Benefit Segmentation

Grouping people according to the kinds of benefits they seek from a product is still another way of segmenting the consumer population. Automobile manufacturers know that many prospective buyers are primarily interested in economy of operation, while others are more interested in ample interior space and a feeling of luxury. Still others need simply a dependable vehicle that will take them where they want to go.

The technique has been successfully applied to the toothpaste market. Distinct groups have been identified: those who buy toothpaste because they want to prevent cavities, those who want a clean, fresh taste in the mouth in the morning, those who use the product primarily for appearance's sake (they want white teeth) and so forth. Television campaigns have certainly relied on information from benefit segmentation.

Usage Segmentation

This interesting technique first divides the consumer market according to users and non-users of the product, and then further breaks down the users into "heavy," "medium," and "light" according to quantities consumed. Finally, the characteristics of the user subgroups are studied and compared in order to uncover significant differences. Usage segmentation can be an exceptionally valuable tool. In some product categories, the heavy users account for as much as 30, 40, and even 50 percent or more of the total sales.

BUYER PSYCHOLOGY

There have been literally hundreds of articles in the marketing literature in recent years reporting on the results of research into consumer behavior. This subject has been investigated from just about every conceivable angle. At least half a dozen popular college textbooks, identically titled *Consumer Behavior*, are currently available. (See the booklist at the end of this chapter.)

The social sciences (particularly psychology) have furnished the basics for marketing researchers to investigate why people select certain products and services (as opposed to others)—and why they prefer to shop at certain stores. Researchers have probed motives, perceptions, individual needs and wants (innate and learned), attitudes, how people learn and remember or forget, and many other facets of the human personality and psyche. Marketing researchers have devised intricate models of the purchasing process itself to aid the businessperson's understanding of complex consumer behavior.

Researchers have borrowed from studies in sociology and social psychology to understand how social class, culture, subcultures, family influences, reference groups—the entire social environment—affect a consumer's purchasing behavior.

These studies are certainly fascinating! They are also valuable—the information yielded by a single text can provide you with dozens of tips, which you can readily use in your business. Unfortunately, there isn't room in this book for all the details of buyer psychology. The books listed at the end of this chapter contain invaluable information for successful consumer targeting.

Certainly a cardinal requirement for success in business is *know the customer.*

WHAT CONSUMERISM MEANS TO YOU

Consumerism in America is nothing new. The twentieth century witnessed two earlier consumer movements. The first began just before the turn of the century, culminated (in 1906) in two major pro-consumer acts of legislation: the Pure Food and Drug Act and the Meat Inspection Act. The second movement originated in the Great Depression. By 1938, the FDA had been substantially strengthened with the Food, Drug, and Cosmetic Act.

The current movement, spurred during the early 1960s, seems to have resulted from many influences: a more affluent consumer, a higher level of educational attainment, a more relaxed work ethic, a stress on self-assertiveness and other changing values, the unethical practices of business firms, misleading advertising and promotion, inferior products, poor service, and so forth. Among the newer legislation evolving out of the current movement are: the Fair Packaging Act, the Consumer Credit Protection Act, the Truth-in-Lending Act, and the Child Protection and Safety Act. In addition to various consumer associations and cooperatives, and the Better Business Bureaus, the welfare of the consumer is monitored by government consumer protection agencies which have been established in metropolitan areas and in county seats.

This trend means that you, the new small business owner, must thoroughly understand all consumer legislation (federal, state and local) and how such laws affect your particular type of business. You must also realize that today's enlightened customer tolerates no mishandling, mislabeling, misrepresentation, or misunderstanding. You must be fair and above board in your dealings with the public if you want your clientele to remain with you.

YOUR ETHICAL AND SOCIAL RESPONSIBILITIES AS A BUSINESS OWNER

Business today is more than profits and growth—it has a greater obligation to the public good than ever before. The callous disregard for the human element that characterized the first few decades of this century no longer exists. There is an increasing struggle to maintain the quality of modern life as counterpoint to man's deleterious behavior. The new ethos pursues higher and nobler objectives, rather than simply aims at earning profits at any cost.

The small business owner of today must be aware of the needs of the physical environment. Our lakes, streams, and rivers are contaminated with industrial waste. The atmosphere is polluted with dangerous levels of sulphur and carbon compounds from our nation's factories and from millions of vehicles operating daily on our highways. Year after year, our fields and groves are battered—sprayed with pesticides and dusted with chemicals. Poultry, cattle, and other livestock are raised on chemical fatteners. Our giant industrial machine has nearly exhausted many natural resources; shortages are becoming more common. Our ears are assaulted by the din of city traffic, of roaring machinery, and of thundering aircraft overhead.

In recent years, the government has enacted many laws to protect our population from these ravages. Among them: the Clean Air Act (and subsequent amendments), the Solid Waste Disposal Act, the Water Quality Act, the Noise Control Act, and the Pesticide Control Act.

The business owner must be concerned with the social environment as well. Today's corporation is responsible not only to its shareholders and customers but to other groups as well: employees, suppliers, residents of the community where the business is located, and even society-at-large. Inherent in the concept of a democratic society is the belief that those who are more affluent are responsible to the less able and less fortunate. Hence, the Social Security system, anti-discrimination laws, programs for training the hard-core unemployed, the welfare system, and so forth. All such programs aim at aiding the less fortunate, such as the unemployed or poor. The rate of unemployment in the country is disturbingly high, and is not expected to drop in the next few years. Approximately twenty-five million Americans are living today at or below the poverty level.

Small wonder, then, that the public now expects private enterprise, which has taken liberally from the environment and its resources, to return some portion of its profits to the society that nurtured it.

FOR FURTHER INFORMATION

Books

Engel, James F., Blackwell, Roger D., and Kollat, David T. *Consumer Behavior,* 3rd ed. Hinsdale, Ill.: Dryden Press, 1978.

Hanan, Mack. *Life-Styled Marketing.* New York: American Management Associations, 1972.

Reynolds, Fred D. and Wells, William D. *Consumer Behavior.* New York: McGraw-Hill, 1977.

Risley, George. *Modern Industrial Marketing.* New York: McGraw-Hill, 1972.

Schiffman, Leon G. and Kanuk, Leslie Lazar. *Consumer Behavior.* Englewood Cliffs, N.J.: Prentice-Hall, 1978.

Walters, C. Glenn. *Consumer Behavior: Theory and Practice,* 3rd ed. Homewood, Ill.: Irwin, 1978.

Webster, Frederick, Jr. and Wind, Yoram. *Organizational Buying Behavior.* Englewood Cliffs, N.J.: Prentice-Hall, 1972.

II

"Starting-Up" Problems

The five chapters in this next section will give you specific answers to questions you may now have about getting your business off the ground and into operation. Part II contains answers to questions asked over and over by would-be entrepreneurs who have attended my small business institute.

Everybody thinking about starting a business asks:

- *How do I start? Shall I build a brand-new business? If I purchase an existing business, how much I should pay for it? Shall I look into some sort of franchise operation?*
- *What about the location? What are the usual requirements for this type of business? Should I rent the premises or buy? Is it better to build? What's the proper layout for my firm?*
- *How much of an investment will be required? What sources of funds are available to me? How can I estimate how much capital I will need?*

What kinds of expenses should I think about? How much should I expect to do in sales?

- *How do I set up the legal form of the business? What are the pros and cons of taking on a partner? Should I consider forming a corporation? How is this done? What taxes must I pay, and what forms should I file? How do I handle sales tax? What are the withholding regulations?*

- *How can I protect my business? What risks do I face? How do I secure insurance coverage? What types of insurance should I have?*

These and many other questions are answered in the following five chapters.

4

How to Join
the Business Community

Once upon a time, the aspiring entrepreneur had only two alternatives: either to start up a brand new business from scratch or to purchase a thriving business from someone else. (Some lucky people, of course, have a successful enterprise deeded over to them by a parent or wealthy relative!) Both alternatives represented a gamble. Obviously, the new business risked more than one already tested (provided of course that the ongoing business was not already on its way *out*!).

Today people are luckier. A third way to enter the business community has become popular over the last twenty-five years. Now you can go the franchise route. Moreover, a responsible, well-established company behind you improves your chance of making it.

Read the statistics on new ventures—they're grim. Many enterprises fail within the first few years of operation. A good franchised outlet, however, has a very good chance to succeed. According to some reports, nine out of ten franchises are successful.

This chapter is designed to help you avoid becoming another grim statistic. You'll find details on these alternate routes to business. Each has its attractive features and its drawbacks. The differences among them include the amount of investment capital required, the chances of survival, and the profits you can expect.

LAUNCHING THE NEW ENTERPRISE

Most people who try their hand at business select the riskiest approach—they start a brand new business. For many, the motivating factor behind this decision is probably a lack of sufficient capital to purchase an already existing business or a franchise. Other people may want to test their capabilities and ingenuity to the fullest. Still others may covet the challenge of creating their own futures, stone by stone. Some people choose to start a new business because they see a timely opportunity for a new product or service, with no competition.

Whatever the reason for the choice, one thing is certain: This route is by far the most perilous of the three in the long run.

The Positives

Nevertheless, if you choose this route, you'll find all options wide open. You'll have total, unrestricted freedom of choice in all decision-making—the pleasure of choosing when, where, and how you set up shop. You won't be bound to a specific location or facility; you won't be limited to what products or services to manufacture or sell; you won't be tied to any particular suppliers, employees, or customers. All policies and procedures will be up to you—they will be yours alone to establish.

The Negatives

But there is another side to the coin. Here are some troublesome aspects to think about. A new business takes time to get rolling. Weeks—maybe months—may pass before sales reach a high enough level to allow you to draw a small salary. (Compare this to the purchase of a business. Here you also purchase instant sales and instant wages the day you take it over.)

If you need additional funds, you'll probably find it more difficult to borrow money for a brand new business than for an existing business or a franchise unit.

A new business starts off with *zero* customers and *zero* suppliers. Unless you've had prior experience with sources in the same field, you'll have to search out and cultivate a string of suppliers for your new business. This task occupies lots of your time and energy in the beginning. Also, other than a few friends and relatives who may buy from you, you will have to take the initiative to build up, over time, a satisfied and loyal clientele.

With little or nothing charted for you, you should expect to make a good many mistakes along the way. A new business is strictly a "learning-by-doing" experience. You will have to live with, and hopefully learn from, your errors. This may prove costly—in time, money, and perhaps emotions. You should definitely seek the assistance of professionals whenever possible.

How Do You Get Started?

Certainly, it's foolhardy to contemplate setting up a new business without being thoroughly convinced that your business will be special and useful to the network of free enterprise. This means that you must direct your proposed enterprise toward fulfilling unmet needs of specific groups of people.

You need a detailed analysis of possible markets for your particular product. You need an assessment of the strengths and weaknesses of competitors and a study of industry trends. You must pay attention to many other facets of business planning— the type and location of the facility, the amount of financial backing, machinery and equipment needed, and so forth. (If you decide to start a brand new business, Chapters 5 through 7 provide you with the tools for laying a solid foundation.)

TAKING ON A FRANCHISE

Most people regard franchising as something new on the American scene but—it's been around since the turn of the century. At that time the new automobile manufacturers first began to license car dealers, and gas stations opened up across the country.

In the early 1950s most of today's well-known franchises began rapidly expanding their outlets. There are now almost half a million franchised businesses in the United States. In addition, 30 percent of all retail sales are now conducted through franchised outlets.

The more popular franchises are fried chicken, hamburger, pizza, and other fast-food stores, motels and hotels, ice cream parlors, doughnut 'n coffee places, employment agencies, car washes, and convenience superettes. Such names as Stuckeys, Kentucky Fried Chicken, Burger King, Bonanza, Dunkin' Donuts, International House of Pancakes, Carvel, Days Inns, and Howard Johnson's come readily to mind.

The franchise concept is simple to grasp: You (the "franchisee") sign a contract with a successful franchising company (the "franchisor") that spells out the terms and conditions under which you are permitted to operate your business—a unit of a large chain. The contract is a license to operate under the parent firm's trade name, and in accordance with their policies and procedures.

Advantages of the Franchise Form

A franchise offers you the opportunity to jump aboard the bandwagon and become part of a tried-and-proven success story. This is certainly the least risky of the three avenues. Approximately 95 percent of all quality franchises are profitable. You ride with the popularity of the brand name. It's known by hundreds of thousands—if not millions—of people.

When you sign with a franchisor, you purchase a complete package designed to help you succeed. You receive professional assistance in most phases of the business: location-hunting, construction of the facility, the proper equipment to use, inventory control systems, bookkeeping methods, and promotion approaches.

Moreover, the franchising organization has a vital stake in keeping your new branch alive and growing. Consequently, they will continue to give you assistance in such important areas as merchandising, advertising, sales promotion, and even finance. They will literally teach you the business. Most franchisors insist on an initial period of intensive training and continue to render management help through supervision.

Drawbacks

The financial aspects of a franchise merit careful consideration. Depending on the operation, costs can range from as little as several thousand dollars to more than $100,000. These figures involve not only the initial franchise fee but also the entire cost of constructing and equipping the facility. Some of these expenses may be spread out over a period of years under a financing arrangement; in addition, you will probably be required to pay the franchisor a set percentage of your sales for the duration of your franchise.

You'll need a fundamental change in perspective. You will have to relinquish some of your independence. You might feel more like a worker or junior partner than a boss.

The products you carry—as well as the methods that you follow—will be selected for you by the franchisor. You will have little say in these areas and as a result your business may be adversely affected. For example, you may be required to carry one or more items that don't move at all in your particular neighborhood. You might have to sell your products at prices that are either too high or too low for your area.

Furthermore, the franchise is a license granted to you by the franchising firm, and if you want to close up shop someday, you cannot simply sell your business to a third party without involving the franchisor.

The contract is generally written from year to year and most often contains an "escape clause" that favors the franchisor. For instance, if your sales don't meet the expectations spelled out in the agreement, the franchisor may exercise the option not to renew the contract. In this case, you would be forced to remove all identification, signs, products, materials, and so forth that denote your connection with the parent company—and begin operating on your own if you choose. Usually, there's a "buy-back" clause as well. This gives the franchisor the right to re-purchase your franchise at will; this clause could be a serious drawback if you're doing extremely well in the location.

Look Before You Leap—into Franchising

Because of the lucrative opportunities to be found in the franchising of products and services, the franchising field can be lucrative, and so it not only attracts hundreds of responsible, well-managed companies but also a lot of less respectable firms. These fly-by-night companies are more concerned with making a quick buck than in sustaining growth over a long period.

Therefore, you need to proceed with caution and slowly investigate any franchise offer that comes your way.

At the very least, you should resist any pressure exerted by a sales representative trying to sell you a franchise. The rosy picture he may paint for you should be taken with more than a few grains of salt. Even when representing a reliable firm, a salesperson tends to present an overly optimistic assessment of the sales and profit potential of the franchise.

Before you sign anything, consult your accountant, your banker, the local Chamber of Commerce, Dun and Bradstreet's, and the trade organization(s) in your respective field for unbiased information about the company. Make it your business to visit several of the outlets currently operating under contract to the franchisor, and ask their operators how satisfied they are with the situation. Find out whatever additional facts you can. Of course, these units should definitely not be selected for you by the sales representative.

PURCHASING AN ESTABLISHED BUSINESS

Advantages

Much of the tedious planning and downright hard work required to set up a new business is avoided when you buy an ongoing enterprise. There is no need to search for a desirable location, or to construct and lay out a facility. (You can, of course, make changes later on.)

Since the previous owner(s) may have dealt with a number of suppliers before you enter the picture, chances are excellent you'll spend little time initially developing your own sources of supply. With an ongoing business you also acquire experienced employees. They'll help you over the hurdles during the transition period. Likewise, you're rewarded with a bank of customers you can draw on immediately.

This kind of business is often purchased at a good price because the owner wants to sell quickly for some compelling reason (poor health, retirement, or the like.) He or she may even be willing to assist you in the financing. In cases like this, an owner may be satisfied with a partial payment and take notes for the balance; these notes stretch out your obligation for years.

Finally, since the business has had a history, there are internal records available to guide you.

Disadvantages

You may have serious problems with one or two aspects of the business, and you may have to make changes before you move in. You may have to relocate or enlarge the premises. You might have to do extensive repairs or redecoration. The layout may be in sore need of improvement.

Some of the inventory may be unusable, or you may have too many of some things and too few of others. Merchandise may be imperfect, damaged, or outdated. Machinery and equipment may need to be repaired or replaced.

Consider your new employees, suppliers, and customers. In the past, relations between these people and the former owner(s) may not have been good. The "goodwill" you have bought may prove to be "bad will" that will detract from your immediate success. You might inherit several below-average employees whom you'll have to replace in time. If these employees are unionized, this will pose another problem.

What to Look Into Before Buying a Business

No matter how attractive the deal seems to you or how anxious you are to get started, make up your mind to approach buying a new business unemotionally and with caution. Thoroughly check out the following:

1. the business location and premises
2. its past history and estimated future potential, and
3. its assets and liabilities.

Location and Premises.　Visit the location and the surrounding neighborhood. Talk with the manager of the local bank and with other merchants or business owners in the area. Interview neighborhood residents or shoppers. Survey the businesses of competitors in the area. Try to ascertain whether the area is growing, maintaining its status quo, or deteriorating. (See Chapter 5 for more help in evaluating a location.)

Bring in a consultant with experience in the particular kind of business to thoroughly examine the premises. Examine everything closely and make detailed notes. Check: the interior and exterior; the lighting, heating, and plumbing; elevators and staircases; stair wells and basements; shipping and receiving docks; and so forth.

Make certain the facility has ample room not only to conduct the business that you presently enjoy, but also to expand within— or adjacent to—the facility.

Past History and Future Potential.　Ask your accountant and lawyer for help in piecing together a picture of the firm's past. You'll discover problem areas you would be dealing with if you decided to buy as well as trends for projecting into the firm's future. Bear in mind: most businesses for sale are not of "dream quality." There is almost always need for correction or improvement.

Examine company records. In addition to copies of past tax returns and other vital financial reports (annual balance sheets, operating statements, and the like) you'll find important information for future decision-making in records of sales figures, production records, inventory counts, personnel files—even the shipping and receiving room logs. If you properly analyze sales, production, and financial data, you'll possess helpful ratios that can be compared over a succession of years. (See Chapter 17.)

Survey the market potential for your company's products and services vis-à-vis your competitors'. Analyze the demographic characteristics of present customers, as well as their needs and wants. Also survey other market segments from which you could draw additional customers in the future. A worthwhile exercise here is to translate such details into projected dollar-and-cents sales figures, at least for the first two or three years after your takeover.

Assets and Liabilities. "Assets" include not only the cash and securities owned by the company you plan to acquire but also all property, including machinery and equipment, inventories, accounts receivable, contracts, and the like. By extension, it might also include *personnel*! Exercise caution here. This is the primary area to which any purchaser of an existing business must address his or her attention. The major concern here is the *condition* of the assets. "Liabilities" include short- and long-term loans, unpaid taxes, mortgages, monies owed to suppliers (accounts payable), and other business obligations.

These terms are covered in greater detail in Chapter 6.

How to Set the Price

Determining the proper price to pay for a business is a difficult problem. The seller usually tries to get more money for the business than it's worth—and the buyer tries to get it for as little as possible. Somewhere between the two extremes lies a price that is fair to both parties and that is finally agreed upon.

There are two basic methods of approaching this dilemma: (1) the "total-the-assets" method and (2) the "return-through-profits" method.

Total-the-Assets. This method is more frequently used although not, in my judgment, the more desirable of the two. As the name indicates, it calls for a complete audit of the enterprise, usually best conducted by independent auditors. They should appraise the real and other property owned by the firm—including inventories, equipment, machinery, and the like—check into all liabilities, and subtract the liabilities from the property owned. You will then have an estimate of the company's net worth.

Return-through-Profits.   The logic behind this approach runs this way: Buying an established business represents a considerable capital investment; you therefore have every right to expect a good return on your investment. Considering the complexity of investing in a business—including the need for your personal involvement and dedication for years to come (as well as the risk of failure)—your rate of return should certainly exceed by far those rates currently available to investors at banks, in corporate or government bonds, and the like.

There are desirable alternatives to buying a business which require nothing more than plunking down capital. Government bonds, about the safest of all investments, bring you 6 percent annually on your money; the return from a long-term savings certificate pays you an insured 8 percent; good corporate bonds may yield even more. It's illogical to invest in a going business for a return comparable to these other kinds of investments. So, an ideal target to shoot at would be something in the neighborhood of 25 percent—a few percentage points less *only* if you have to!

As an illustration, let's assume that you've found an attractive business somewhere, and the asking price is $40,000. If you placed that amount of money in long-term certificates, you would receive interest totaling about $3,200 annually. These earnings do not require your working hard to protect your money—or leaving your current employment! Suppose, however, that an analysis of the business' operations reveals that its net profits each year would probably be in the $10,000 range. This return would indicate that you could pay back to yourself the cost of your investment within four years; or, simply by dividing $10,000 by $40,000, you could calculate an effective R. O. I. ("return on investment") of 25 percent.

When it comes to setting a fair price for a going business, then, you can use the following rough rule-of-thumb: Multiply the average yearly profit by four (for an R.O.I. of 25 percent) or by five (for a 20 percent R.O.I.).

There is one factor to include in figuring out how much you should pay for a business. If you invest your capital in bonds or certificates, you are able to keep your current job. Once you purchase a business, you of course leave your job—and give up that $10,000, $15,000, or more that you've been earning. The price you eventually pay for a business should take this earnings factor into consideration. Make sure your proposed operations budget covers your current salary (even if you don't choose to draw a salary in the beginning) and the desired annual profit as well.

The current owner(s) may be willing to accept a down payment—maybe $10,000—and take notes for the rest. This arrangement makes it easier for you to buy. Your investment is then only one-quarter of what you originally thought. Don't be tempted to think that an annual profit of only $2,500 is needed to make this a sound investment (because it *seems* you would be earning 25 percent on your money). The fallacy here is that enough additional profit must be generated each year to cover the notes as they mature.

Some Additional Thoughts Before Buying

Never enter into any major transaction such as the purchase of a business without the full knowledge, cooperation, and assistance of both your attorney and your accountant. Your attorney is needed to check on many details: ownership titles; occupancy leases, as well as leases on equipment, machinery, vehicles, and the like; contracts with contractors, services, and employees; zoning restrictions and local permits; compliance with the bulk sales act; and so on. Your accountant must delve into all financial aspects of operations, assist you in preparing pro forma statements, and point out deficiencies and weaknesses.

Don't neglect to obtain from the former owner an agreement to the effect that he or she will not seek to compete with you, for example, by opening a similar business in the area.

Be sure to call in an independent appraiser to determine the value of any property. Don't depend on book inventories; insist on a physical count by you or your representative side by side with the owner.

It's a good idea to investigate all personnel records to ascertain the caliber of the employees and the size of the current payroll. Check union contracts, employee contracts, benefits to be paid, and so forth. Assess the general state of employee morale.

Lastly, check into the owner's real reason for selling. A declaration that he is ready to retire, that she wants to move to Arizona for reasons of health, or that he wants to be near his children may be the truth. On the other hand, such reasons may serve as a "cover" for a poor profit picture, increasing competition, anticipated changes in the neighborhood, or legal problems which threaten the life of the enterprise.

Books

Hagendorf, Stanley. *Tax Guide for Buying and Selling a Business*, 2nd ed. Englewood Cliffs, N.J.: Prentice-Hall, 1971.

Hansen, James M. *Guide to Buying or Selling a Business*. Englewood Cliffs, N.J.: Prentice-Hall, 1975.

Mangold, Maxwell J. *How to Buy a Small Business*. New York: Pilot Books, 1976.

Metz, Robert. *Franchising: How to Select a Business of Your Own*. New York: Hawthorn Books, 1969.

Mendelsohn, M. *The Guide to Franchising*. Elmsford, N.Y.: Pergamon, 1970.

Small, Samuel and Pilot Books Staff. *Directory of Franchising Organizations*, 18th ed. New York: Pilot Books, 1977.

Available from the Superintendent of Documents

Nonseries Publications:

 # B 98—"Buying and Selling a Small Business," Stock #045-000-00003-6; 122 pp.; $2.30.

Small Business Management Series:

 # 35—"Franchise Index/Profile," Stock #045-000-00125-3; 56 pp.; $1.70.

5

Finding the Right Location

Selecting the place to set up your operation is one of the most important decisions you have to make. More often than not, the seeds of business success or demise are sown along with the choice of location.

It's sad but true that many location decisions are based on personal preferences or whim, instead of on an objective, orderly approach to the decision. Often, an entrepreneur chooses to set up shop close to home, or discovers a promising-looking empty store along a busy thoroughfare, or rides past a vacant building that strikes him or her as ideal for a new plant.

This person is relying on intuition. Emotional (nonrational) factors underlie this type of decision. The average new business owner neglects, among other things, to seek out pertinent, helpful materials which are available free from the Small Business Administration, the Government Printing Office, or the local branch of the public library.

If you plan to gamble your life's savings, as many do, you must seize the reins and proceed in a coldly logical, businesslike fashion.

HOW TO ANALYZE YOUR REQUIREMENTS

Obviously, the right choice of location for a retail store can easily mean the difference between success and failure. Many types of retail shops depend almost entirely on passersby for their sales. Your selection of a side street or a deteriorating neighborhood could indeed prove a costly mistake.

Less evident is the importance of the proper site for a service business, wholesale operation, or factory. Yet, even here, you should be concerned about several essential characteristics. Manufacturing plants and wholesale enterprises, for instance, must have access to good transportation facilities, for bringing in raw materials or finished goods and for distributing their products. Similarly, they need a continuous "labor pool" from which to draw office workers, machine operators, supervisory personnel, technicians, and the like.

The requirements for various types of businesses may vary considerably, but there are some common areas to consider when choosing a location, regardless of the kind of business you're setting up. In addition to general considerations such as the character of the community, the local environment, and your personal preferences, study the following:

- accessibility to transportation,
- availability of manpower,
- closeness to the company's markets,
- cost factors, such as land, construction, materials, labor, and the like,
- local ordinances and regulations,
- quality of local services (police and fire protection, and so on),
- sewers, water supply, power, other utilities,
- space for future expansion, and
- tax structure.

THE RETAIL LOCATION

The majority of new enterprises spawned each year are retail stores. These outlets are particularly vulnerable to failure due to the wrong location; consequently, they're treated in more detail here, apart from other types of businesses.

To a large extent, success in a retail store depends on the quantity and the quality of the traffic passing by. Most often, this is pedestrian traffic although in some cases, the number of passing automobiles and available parking facilities can be of vital significance. In addition to the prerequisites of sufficient space not only for the display and sale of merchandise, but also for workroom and storage, consider these factors:

- the extent of the store's "trading area,"
- the demographics of the population in the area (see Chapter 3, "Demographic Segmentation"),
- the nature of the competition,
- the compatibility of neighboring stores,
- parking facilities,
- availability of public transportation,
- the volume of traffic (pedestrian and vehicular),
- the store building itself, and
- the store front.

In cities, consider the benefits of a corner location or a spot within a block, and whether there's a "right" side of the street.

The Trading Area

If you plan to open a retail shop, become familiar with both the concept of a "trading area" and the various types of locations available to you. The trading area is the area surrounding a particular store (or group of stores) from which it draws most of its shoppers. For the average, small "in-city" shop that sells convenience goods and impulse items, the trading area may only extend for a few blocks in one or two directions and for even less in the other directions. The trading area can be far larger for a high-image specialty goods store that caters to an elite clientele. Discount houses and department stores may pull shoppers from many miles away.

The following are various types of locations for retail stores:

Central Business Districts. This is the "downtown" or "center-city" section of a city where a large number of stores are concentrated. This is traditionally a bustling area with office buildings, banks, theaters, restaurants, and many stores. Characteristically, the retail enterprises have large floor space and window frontage. The main branches of department stores and large units of the major chains are usually found here, along with stores offering specialty merchandise. Although the sales picture "downtown" has become bleaker over the years as the population mix in many cities has shifted to a less economically advantaged clientele, many locations in the central business district still enjoy brisk sales. Rents, however, have increased at a prodigious rate. This fact, along with the deteriorating "quality of life" in many of these sections, has tended to induce the typical entrepreneur to react negatively toward such locations.

Secondary Business Districts.   These are found along the major arteries leading out of "center city," and they perhaps present a more attractive situation. Most cities have several secondary districts; metropolitan areas may have many more. Rents here, too, are comparatively high; but these shopping areas are well established and favored by area residents because they can buy just about anything in this concentration of stores. Traffic can be quite heavy, especially during the afternoons and on Saturdays. As a retailer, don't be put off by a high rent—all too often low monthly rent means low monthly sales.

Neighborhood Shopping Streets.   In most cities, there are a good number of neighborhood shopping streets where brisk retail sales are registered. Dependent for the most part on the density of residents in the vicinity, these business sections may extend from one or two city blocks in length to as many as eight or more. The typical neighborhood shopping street presents a well-balanced assortment of store types: small branches of large chain operations (supermarkets, variety stores, fast-food outlets, and so forth); a liberal sprinkling of specialty stores; and a much larger number of shops that sell convenience merchandise. Here you find bakeries, hardware stores, dry cleaners, meat and fish stores, bars and luncheonettes, pharmacies, shoe stores, and the like. Rents in the section are usually moderate, business failures are relatively rare, and empty stores are quickly grabbed up. Woven throughout the residential sections of a city you also find numerous smaller clusters of shops located in less than a city block.

Shopping Centers.   Shopping centers are newer clusters of retail stores found on the outskirts of the city and in the suburbs. These include strip centers, community shopping centers, and the huge, regional centers. The strip center is usually made up of a row of stores, which complement each other, and its main attraction is a large supermarket or variety store. Parking space is available for a limited number of automobiles. When situated in areas that are still building up, strip center locations can be attractive for many types of retail businesses. Their drawing power generally extends for a few miles around.

Community shopping centers have a larger trading area. Often, their cornerstone retailer is a junior department store or discount store of the K mart or Woolco type. There may be twenty or thirty stores in the center—and parking for hundreds of cars.

The regional center is usually a huge complex of chain store units, independent retailers offering both shopping and specialty merchandise, several restaurants, a theater, and one or two major department stores. Most of the successful regional centers around the country today are completely enclosed, all-weather malls. This type of center pulls customers from villages and towns as far as an hour away by car. Parking facilities can handle a thousand or more vehicles.

These locations have their good and bad points. If you rent a store in a shopping center, you are assured of some customers, especially in the evenings and on Saturdays. The majority of shoppers are, of course, attracted by the department store(s); many, however, like to stroll through the rows of other stores in the center. Consumers enjoy the frequent shows, demonstrations, exhibits, and other public relations gestures put on by the shopping center association. The general atmosphere, the security, maintenance, and group sales promotions are all excellent. Yet, as a tenant, you are limited in your display and promotion techniques (many centers, for example, don't permit a store to place a banner on the surface of the store window). You might be compelled to keep your store open in accordance with the shopping center's hours, even on days—or at times— when you do very little business and can't afford to keep on help. You'll also be required to join the mall association and pay your proportion of the dues.

Since the shopping center is a unique type, you should visit a number of them and talk to various store owners. Discuss the pros and cons with real estate people before deciding on this type of location. The position *within* the shopping center is especially important to the success of a retail store.

HOW TO CHOOSE YOUR LOCATION—A PLAN

This section presents an organized, step-by-step procedure designed to widen your horizons and to help you make your location decision. The plan presumes your location hunt will be conducted at a leisurely pace. Above all, avoid the temptation to rush into business. Adopt a leisurely, investigative stance!

1. Convince yourself that you will not limit your choice of location to any one area before taking this entire list into consideration.

2. Tell yourself there are fifty states to choose from. (Trying your hand—and luck—in a foreign country might be more complicated than you would care to attempt at this stage of the game.)

3. Draw on your personal storehouse of information: What have friends, relatives, and co-workers told you about other places? What have you learned about the states from your own travels or through reading?

4. Narrow your thoughts down to two or three states where you'd like to live and, more specifically, where you feel an excellent opportunity exists for the type of business you have in mind.

5. Read everything you can about these states. Write away for information about the climate, the local economy, the per capita income, the characteristics of the population, the industry, and so forth. Try to narrow down your preferences to one state.

6. Next, survey the one state you've targeted in on for half a dozen areas that appear attractive. Preferably, these ought to be growing areas—and places where the quality of life seems to jibe with your own values and attitudes.

For help at this point, you can contact the state development agency and city planning commissions, chambers of commerce, utility companies, local banks, and so forth. The 1972 Census of Business also provides details about the types of businesses in those areas.

7. Now the difficult work begins. You will need to carefully select a set of criteria by which you can evaluate the various locations and make your final decision. Judging each location by this list enables you to rank them in order from "most promising" to "least promising" for your new enterprise.

Read again through the location factors treated in the first few pages of this chapter. Choose the criteria most appropriate for your particular business. Jot them down on a sheet of paper. You may be able to add one or two of your own that has not been listed. For example, you may decide that an important consideration for you is the quality of life in the particular community (in light of your personality, personal goals, and leisure-time preferences). Add the phrase "quality of life" to what you have listed.

8. Prepare a chart like the one shown in Table 5-1, to rate or score the locations you're considering.

9. Use a simple rating scale: for example, a scale of 1 to 5 with 1 signifying a rating of "poor" as follows:

  1 Poor
  2 Fair
  3 Good
  4 Very good
  5 Excellent

Take care to work out the rationale behind your ratings so you understand the numbers you use. For instance in rating "Trading area size," you would assign a 1 to a location with a limited trade area of one or two blocks around, while an extensive area might earn a 4 or 5 rating. Where competition might interfere substantially with your business in a particular location, assign a score of 1; where competition is weak or nonexistent, give a rating of 5.

10. Now rate each of the possible locations, A, B, C, and so on, working on one criterion at a time. After all criteria have been considered, total up the columns. Obviously, the location with the highest score would be the one to select. Or, so it would seem—there's one more step to consider.

11. In any set of criteria, some are always more important than others to you. If you're contemplating opening a retail shop, the

TABLE 5–1. A typical location rating sheet.

Criteria	*Alternative Locations:*					
	A	B	C	D	E	F
Trading area size						
Competition						
Volume of traffic						
Availability of manpower						
Demographics of community						
Space for future expansion						
Parking facilities						
Quality of life for me						
Total Scores:						

volume of pedestrian traffic that passes by is extremely important to business success. Maybe the demographics of the neighborhood (population mix, income characteristics, and so forth) are far more significant than many of the other criteria on your list. If so, some of the criteria ought to be "weighted" in order to take their relative importance into account. To accomplish this, you would assign a weight factor of 2 or 3 to one or more of the characteristics (depending on their value to you) and then multiply your earlier ratings by 2 or 3 across the various locations you're considering. Table 5-2 is a sample score card weighted in this fashion. According to the criteria you have selected and the assigned weightings you have given them, location D in Table 5-2 should be your first choice, locations E and C your second and third choices.

You are still not ready to make your final decision. Once you have ranked the six locations, you must then consider some other factors, such as the comparative rents you will have to pay for the three top locations, the availability of living quarters for yourself in those areas, local living costs, and so on. In other words, any one of the three might be a good choice; now you must narrow it down to the one location best suited to your needs.

BUILD, RENT, OR BUY?

Having set your sights on the best location for your proposed business, you will now have still another major decision area.

TABLE 5–2. A weighted location rating sheet.

| Criteria | Weights | Alternative Locations | | | | | |
		A	B	C	D	E	F
Trading area size	1	3	3	1	2	4	3
Competition	2	6	6	6	10	8	4
Volume of traffic	3	9	3	9	12	6	12
Demographics of community	3	6	3	9	12	3	9
Space for expansion	1	1	3	4	4	3	2
Parking facilities	1	2	5	3	4	3	1
Quality of life for me	3	12	3	9	12	15	6
Total Scores:		39	26	41	56	42	37

Here are just a few of the possibilities:

1. There may not be a location readily available. In this case you might consider buying out someone else's business.

2. Premises—a building or a store—may indeed be available, either for rent or for sale. There's a good chance, however, that the premises may not be suitable for your purposes—a substantial and costly remodeling job might be necessary.

3. If you're thinking about building, you may discover nothing more than a vacant lot (or small piece of land) obtainable in the area. This situation might cause you to have suitable premises erected on the spot. Furthermore, time and cost factors must be weighed carefully.

To Build—or Not to Build?

Ideally, the most positive move is to construct premises of the exact dimensions, type, architectural style, and materials that answer your every purpose down to the most minute specification, with an exacting eye to the future and eventual expansion.

Among the advantages to this move are: a considerable depreciation allowance to help you curtail your tax liability each succeeding year; the benefit of being able to secure a mortgage on your property when you need to improve your cash position; the delight of anticipating a probable, sizable capital gain when you finally dispose of the building, years later.

Of course the big negative here is that you'll need to put out a significant chunk of capital at the very beginning. This is the time when you can least afford such an investment. There are also real problem areas in constructing your own place of business; experts and specialists must be consulted and closely involved in every step along the way.

Why Not Rent?

Renting your business premises is comparatively easy on your wallet. Other than the necessity of putting down a deposit as security and paying rent a month or two in advance, your capital remains relatively untapped. Moreover, with the help of your attorney and a cooperative landlord, you might arrange a favorable lease. So long as you continue to pay your rent regularly and live within the terms of your agreement, you have few problems. You avoid unnecessary headaches. Your landlord worries about paying insurance premiums, meeting property tax liabilities, and repairing, heating, or air conditioning the premises.

Yet, the fact that you remain a tenant does leave you vulnerable to some extent. When your lease finally expires—and if you have not anticipated this situation in the wording of the original lease—your landlord may opt for a sharp rise in your rent. You may even discover that you have lost the location to some other bidder, even though you may have built up the location over years of persistent effort.

Should You Buy?

On the other hand, if you decide to purchase the property, some of the disadvantages of renting are eliminated. You don't have to worry about losing the location or an unexpected rent increase; but you have to take into account increases in real estate taxes as time goes on. History has taught us this lesson. Increasing labor and maintenance costs can also put a dent in profits.

Although buying your premises necessitates a large initial investment, you can reap tax benefits through depreciation. And—as with building your own place—you can always mortgage the premises when you need cash and sell it for a healthy profit.

BUILDINGS—SOME GENERAL CONSIDERATIONS

The style, construction, and overall external appearance of your business building are vital factors in the formulation, over time, of your "company image." A modern, well-maintained building has a far more favorable impact on customers, suppliers and the general public than a seedy-looking facade.

Entrances and exits should be clearly indicated and kept free of litter. Walkways should be kept in excellent repair and hosed down frequently. Lawns, hedges, shrubbery, and the like must be kept neatly trimmed and healthy looking. Steps ought to be avoided if at all possible. Though they may be needed because of different levels between buildings and sidewalks, steps constitute somewhat of a psychological barrier to people. Naturally, an attractive place of business is important to the retail enterprise because it relies heavily on passersby.

THE INTERIOR

Visualize the inside of your business premises as a well-lined box or series of boxes (rooms). Walls, ceilings, and floors all need to be covered by paint or materials of some type.

Walls serve two functions: that of lending some support to the building itself and, more importantly, dividing the inside area into separate compartments for specific business activities. Consequently, their thickness and composition are determined by both support and sound factors. Any columns or pillars necessary to the building structure must remain intact—walls must be built around them, or else they must be incorporated into the walls.

With regard to ceilings, an attentive eye is needed to considerations like good accoustics, space requirements, proper lighting, and the like. Low ceilings convey the impression of tight, confining quarters which, in turn, can psychologically hamper employee productivity; high ceilings, on the other hand, create an open, roomy atmosphere.

Proper lighting for the premises calls for the advice of a specialist. There are basically two types of lighting: flourescent and incandescent. Both have advantages and disadvantages. Flourescent lights provide a high level of light intensity, don't generate much of a heat load in a room, and are relatively inexpensive in their consumption of electricity. Yet, colors often appear different under such lighting—a fact of considerable significance in a ladies' dress shop, for instance. Incandescent bulbs, like those you burn in your table lamps at home, reveal warm, lifelike tones in clothing and other merchandise or when used to highlight special displays.

As to flooring, consider their load-bearing capability (as in the case of a factory containing heavy machinery), their resistance to chemicals, nonskid surfaces to avoid accidents, and so forth. Sometimes, leaving the floor totally uncovered may be more prudent. Or painting might be the solution, with a stone or cement floor in a plant or with a well-made wooden floor in a retail shop. Floor coverings range from linoleums and carpeting of many qualities and shades to an abundant variety of tiles and other materials.

SOME NOTES ON LAYOUT

In addition to these more obvious construction features, premises planning must include: staircases and stair wells, aisles, elevators, conveyors, and the like—all of which facilitate the flow of people, supplies, and merchandise. Moreover, attention must be paid to plumbing, air conditioning, and sanitary facilities as well.

The one overriding factor in setting up a business operation is the understanding that different activities must be performed under one roof. Translated into the proper layout of your premises, this means that internal layout is largely dictated by the functions to be performed. The natural temptation is to fulfill only your immediate requirements because space always seems to be at a premium. Forego that temptation. Even at this early stage, good business administration looks to the future—and to growth. Obviously, you have every reason for hiring, at the outset, the services of an architect experienced in your particular field of business!

Factories and Warehouses

Most manufacturing plants and warehouses share certain activities in common. Special areas are usually needed for receiving incoming deliveries of materials (or merchandise) and supplies, for storage or stockkeeping, for performing office-type activities, and for shipping out completed orders. A factory must also incorporate space for production machinery and equipment, an area for cleaning materials and tools (a maintenance shop), special temperature-controlled rooms for certain types of materials or goods, and so on.

In the ideal factory layout or wholesale warehouse, activities are arranged in as straight a line as possible in order to minimize the flow of materials throughout. The receiving department should be at one end of the building, where the raw materials/finished products are brought in. Here, one or more "bays" are needed for trucks to draw up and unload. There should also be an unloading platform and a checking area where the incoming shipments can be checked off against their bills of lading. At the building's other end, one would expect to find the shipping department where, again, bays and loading platforms are required. In between the two ends, space should be allocated to the warehoused stock (and to machinery in the case of a factory) with special areas sectioned off for office work, machine shop, loading and handling equipment, and other necessary activities.

An alternate layout might be the common U shape, where both shipping and receiving departments are located at the same end of the building, thus enabling the company to avail itself of a single (or double) bay and dock. In this type of layout, stocks and supplies are stored down the center of the U.

In the final analysis, the internal layout of a manufacturing plant depends heavily on the production flow pattern used, on whether the firm employs job, batch, or mass production methods. The type of production set-up determines how the machinery should be arranged.

Retail Stores

In the case of the retail store, layout becomes even more important because of its direct impact upon sales. Again, function determines the internal details. The larger portion of the premises is usually devoted to selling activities—with additional space for workrooms and storage. Important considerations here are an ample entrance, aisles that comfortably permit customer traffic (and merchandise) to flow freely, store fixtures and displays located for maximum customer exposure, good lighting, and an attractive decor.

The entrance usually opens into an unobstructed view of the selling area. Interior layout often follows the grid principle: in-store traffic is compelled to make right-angle turns as it passes deeper into the store (as in the average supermarket or variety store set-up). The free-form layout is another possibility. Here, no attempt is made to direct the traffic. Some stores, of course, combine the basic elements of both approaches to layout.

FOR FURTHER INFORMATION

Books

Francis, Richard L. and White, John A. *Facility Layout and Location: An Analytical Approach.* Englewood Cliffs, N.J.: Prentice-Hall, 1974.

Rams, Edwin M. *Analysis and Valuation of Retail Locations.* Reston, Va.: Reston, 1976.

Free Materials from the Small Business Administration

Management Aids:
  # 201—"Locating or Relocating Your Business"
Small Business Bibliographies:
  # 79—"Small Store Planning and Design"
Small Marketers Aids:
  # 143—"Factors in Considering a Shopping Center Location"
  # 152—"Using a Traffic Study to Select a Retail Site"
  # 154—"Using Census Data to Select a Store Site"
  # 157—"Efficient Lighting in Small Stores"
  # 161—"Signs and Your Business"

Available from the Superintendent of Documents

Small Business Management Series:
  # 21—"Profitable Small Plant Layout," Stock #045-000-00029-0; 48 pp.; 80¢

6

How to Estimate Your Financial Needs

Each year, a surprisingly high percentage of new ventures are launched with insufficient funds behind them. This initial undercapitalization is a major cause of early business failure. Even when an enterprise manages to last for three or four years before going under, its demise is often directly traceable to poor financial planning at the beginning.

Unhappily, there are individuals who scrape together whatever resources they can, perhaps in their eagerness to get started, and go in with an amazingly slim financial commitment. Somehow, they don't realize that money is needed for more than just a month's rent in advance, a few fixtures, and a minimum stock. At the very least, some reserves are needed to cover your personal needs and family responsibilities until the profits start to trickle in.

Of course, we have all heard anecdotes about this or that entrepreneur who in no time at all was able to pyramid an insignificant investment of $300 or $500 to a moderate-sized, going business. Though such stories may contain a few elements of truth, they do represent exceptional cases. In today's environment, the odds are probably a thousand to one (if not higher) *against* your being so fortunate!

Lots of careful thinking and sound planning must characterize your own approach to business, if you want to succeed. Your total capital requirements should be diligently formulated well in advance of taking the plunge.

HOW MUCH CAPITAL DO YOU NEED?

It appears to be fashionable in financial circles to separate the term "capital" into a number of classifications. Terms such as "initial," "operating," "working," and "reserve" are often juxtaposed to the word "capital." Of course, all variations add up to the same theme: Enough money must be available to see the business (and yourself) through to a good start.

You need "initial capital" to cover all your starting-up costs: legal fees, deposits with public utility companies, franchise fees, licenses and permits, machinery and fixtures, advances for the rental of premises, and the like. Included here are funds set aside for your opening promotion; this money is sometimes referred to as "promotional capital."

You need "operating" or "working" capital to purchase raw materials or merchandise for resale and supplies, to pay your employees, and to liquidate obligations—in short, to keep on operating until profits begin to show up.

Finally, you will have need of "reserve capital" not only for unexpected contingencies but also to be able to eat three meals each day, buy clothing, pay your monthly rent bill or mortgage, cover medical expenses, and so on, for yourself and your family.

How to Determine Your Requirements

Now that you know you need three kinds of capital, you must pin down the approximate sales volume you expect your business to attain during its first year. This "sales target" guides you in calculating your overall capital requirements. It should be as accurate as you can make it: neither an optimistic nor a pessimistic estimate, but a fair appraisal of just how much you believe your sales will total.

Using this figure as a base—with the aid of obtainable trade information such as average markups in your kind of business, space productivity, and other ratios—you should be able to deduce other important details. These include the kinds (and numbers) of assets required to reach that level of sales, the size of the facility required, approximate overhead costs, and so on.

As an illustration of this general approach, assume you're planning to open a small gift shop. First you tap the services of your trade association and other sources such as the Accounting Corporation of America's "Barometer of Small Business" (write the Accounting Corporation of America, 1929 First Avenue, San Diego, California 92101). You discover that the average gift shop generally operates on a gross margin (sales, less cost-of-goods sold) of about 40 percent, and overhead expenses total 27 percent of sales. When you think about it, these two little facts alone provide substantial direction for your planning. Say you've set a first year's sales figure of $150,000. From these percentages, you can then calculate that your overhead (for rent, utilities, labor, insurance, advertising, and other expenses) should total around $40,500, and that you ought to realize a gross profit of about $60,000 on some $90,000 worth of merchandise (at cost) to be sold. Subtracting the $40,500 figure from this gross, you would expect to come out with about $19,500 in net profit before taxes.

By the same token, you may learn from available tables that the average rate of turnover of inventory in gift shops is about 2.4 times annually. By dividing your figure of $90,000 cost of merchandise by 2.4 turns of stock, you can then conclude that you will need to keep on hand an average inventory of approximately $37,500. The basic formula to use for this kind of calculation is:

$$\text{Stockturn (at cost)} = \frac{\text{Sales at cost}}{\text{Average stock at cost}}.$$

From trade sources, you can also gain information as to average dollar sales per square foot of selling space in gift shops; this information will help you to decide how many square feet you need in your own store. By checking with other storekeepers, local representatives, and your bank, you are also able to ascertain how much is required for deposits against utility bills—and how much you can expect to be billed each month for utilities, insurance, rent, and other overhead costs.

A Worksheet to Help You Estimate Cash Needs

One of the more popular little pamphlets put out by the Small Business Administration is the "Checklist for Going into Business" Small Marketers Aid No. 71. In addition to a series of questions for the would-be entrepreneur to answer before starting a business, the booklet contains a valuable worksheet designed to help you estimate the amount of capital you need. This form is reproduced as Figure 6-1.

WHERE TO FIND THE MONEY YOU'LL NEED

After you've devoted many hours to planning for your new enterprise and after you have worked and reworked your figures and pared them to the bone, you finally decide you need a minimum of five, ten, or perhaps twenty thousand dollars to assure your business success. Your next hurdle is to locate the required capital.

Many sources of capital are available—and most have strings attached. Perhaps the best type for you to use, if only because it's the least expensive in the long run, is your own personal resources.

Use Your Own Funds Preferably

Knowledgeable business consultants recommend that at least one-half, if not more, of your business investment should come from your own reserves. Consequently, it makes sense for the future entrepreneur to work at a job for several years while trying to accumulate some savings.

Understandably, you'll be somewhat reluctant to gamble your own hard-earned capital. Few individuals escape a confrontation with this dilemma: Why not play with OTHER PEOPLE'S money, instead of with your own?

Face it. Neither individuals nor firms are prone to advance monies to anyone without expecting some sort of gain on their loans. THEIR desired return on investment may be either in the form of "equity" (part ownership) in your business or the payment of an attractive rate of interest. Incidentally, you will also find that banks and other lenders are unwilling to lend you money unless you're prepared to risk your own funds as well.

You need not disturb all your savings; nor do you have to relinquish any part of your business. There are ways to borrow additional funds on favorable terms. A loan on your savings bank passbook, for example, can bring you supplementary capital at low cost. While the bank may charge you 11 or 12 percent, the funds you maintain on deposit in your account continue to earn interest. This interest offsets much of your cost

		WORKSHEET NO. 2		

	ESTIMATED MONTHLY EXPENSES		
Item	Your estimate of monthly expenses based on sales of $ _____ per year	Your estimate of how much cash you need to start your business (See column 3.)	What to put in column 2 (These figures are typical for one kind of business. you will have to decide how many months to allow for in your business.)
	Column 1	Column 2	Column 3
Salary of owner-manager	$	$	2 times column 1
All other salaries and wages			3 times column 1
Rent			3 times column 1
Advertising			3 times column 1
Delivery expense			3 times column 1
Supplies			3 times column 1
Telephone and telegraph			3 times column 1
Other utilities			3 times column 1
Insurance			Payment required by insurance company
Taxes, including Social Security			4 times column 1
Interest			3 times column 1
Maintenance			3 times column 1
Legal and other professional fees			3 times column 1
Miscellaneous			3 times column 1
STARTING COSTS YOU ONLY HAVE TO PAY ONCE			Leave column 2 blank
Fixtures and equipment			Fill in worksheet 3 on page 12 and put the total here
Decorating and remodeling			Talk it over with a contractor
Installation of fixtures and equipment			Talk to suppliers from who you buy these
Starting inventory			Suppliers will probably help you estimate this
Deposits with public utilities			Find out from utilities companies
Legal and other professional fees			Lawyer, accountant, and so on
Licenses and permits			Find out from city offices what you have to have
Advertising and promotion for opening			Estimate what you'll use
Accounts receivable			What you need to buy more stock until credit customers pay
Cash			For unexpected expenses or losses, special purchases, etc.
Other			Make a separate list and enter total
TOTAL ESTIMATED CASH YOU NEED TO START WITH		$	Add up all the numbers in column 2

FIGURE 6–1. SBA checklist

Reproduced from "Checklist for Going into Business" (Small Marketers Aid No. 71) (Washington, D.C.: Small Business Administration, 1975), pp. 6–7.

and results in your paying a differential interest rate of only 6 or 7 percent. Don't forget to deduct from your income the tax you must pay on the interest.

If you own your own home or other real property, there is also the possibility of taking out a mortgage (or refinancing an existing mortgage). The mortgage rates available at the time of the loan or refinancing must be balanced against your rate of return.

Another possibility is the life insurance policy that has accumulated cash value over the years. Loans on such policies generally bear an interest rate of about 5 percent.

Tapping the Resources of Family and Friends

A popular source of additional capital for investment purposes is your family. Needless to say, in most families, it seems to be relatively easy (no pun intended!) to locate family members who might be willing to lend a thousand dollars apiece to the entrepreneur. Good friends might also be eager to help out. Even acquaintances can be sold on investing in a new corporation, if you can persuade them to have faith in you and your ideas.

You have to decide for yourself whether this avenue is for you. It could be sticky. There are some things you ought to think about: How will your relationships with these individuals be affected if your business doesn't succeed? How will you be able to pay them back?

If you decide to borrow from family or friends, you should work out in advance some method of paying them back over time, possibly in installments. Be prepared: They'll have difficulty restraining themselves from getting involved in the operations of your business. You need to be firm from the beginning, to avoid psychological wear and tear on yourself.

Bank Loans

A bank only occasionally gives you a loan to launch a new business—and only when you've accompanied your application with a comprehensive business plan. More often than not, a commercial bank is more interested in loaning monies for operating capital to a business with some history of successful operations behind it. The bank's primary usefulness is for short-term loans for the leasing of equipment, the purchasing of real estate, the buying of additional stocks of goods for resale, and the like.

Finally, many individuals are able to secure personal loans of several thousands of dollars on their signatures alone if they have a preferred credit rating from repaying past loans on time. It helps if you can show personal assets on your loan application in the form of bank accounts, stocks, bonds, and so forth.

Finance Companies

Business executives can often borrow short-term funds from commercial finance companies by offering inventories, receivables, and similar holdings as collateral. Many personal finance companies are more than willing to extend loans to individuals in whom they have confidence. However, the excessively high rates of interest that these firms generally charge should rule out this source for the alert entrepreneur.

Venture Capitalists

You may be able to locate private individuals, small investment groups, and companies in the business of investing in small enterprise. These "venture capitalists" are eager to put their excess financial resources to work. They seldom become involved with a new undertaking, however, unless they are convinced by a well-developed proposal that the new business will indeed be a winner. Yet, these people can be of value to you AFTER your new firm has demonstrated viability and vigor for several years and is in need of additional monies for further growth or expansion. Venture capitalists are usually not interested in granting loans outright; they usually put additional capital into a growing business in exchange for part of the ownership. In short, they are looking for capital gains.

Small Business Investment Corporations (SBICs)

These private companies were authorized by act of Congress nearly two decades ago. SBICs are licensed to provide financial services to small business in the form of equity/venture financing for modernization, expansion, and the like. Especially interested in purchasing stock in the promising small corporation, the SBIC usually seeks to become involved in actual business operation by providing management direction.

The federal government encourages private enterprise by members of minority groups. Minority Enterprise Small Business Investment Corporatons (MESBICs) have been licensed to provide the identical kind of aid to small enterprises owned by minority-group members.

Issuing Stock

If you have organized your new firm into a corporation, your charter specifies the amount of shares the corporation is authorized to issue. You may be able to raise equity funds by selling some of these shares to others, making them shareholders and thereby endowing them with part ownership of your business.

Stocks may be either preferred or common shares. Preferred shares include certain privileges for the shareholder—for example if the business fails, the shareholder is guaranteed a proportionate share of the remaining assets.

Suppliers' Credit

Business makes abundant use of "trade credit." It is a practice of special significance to retailers and wholesalers. If you own a store, your suppliers generally extend credit to you, albeit after some experience. This means they ship goods and supplies to your business, bill you, and give you time to pay the invoice (usually thirty days). This is tantamount to financing of a short-term nature.

Along the same lines, where fixtures, machinery, and other equipment are concerned, suppliers are often more than happy to extend long-term credit. After making a down payment, you pay them back the balance of the debt on an installment basis. Some may even lease the equipment to you instead of insisting on an outright sale.

THE BALANCE SHEET

Every business must properly "balance its books" at the close of its business year, for tax purposes if for nothing else. The culmination of this activity is the issuance of a major accounting statement—the balance sheet.

The balance sheet summarizes the status of the business at that point in time—its assets, liabilities, and net worth. The report is useful, too, for purposes of control, management direction, and decision-making. Through interpreting the balance sheet, management is able to glean insights that are of value in planning. For example, the "current ratio" (one of the so-called "liquidity ratios") is calculated by simply dividing the business' current assets by its current liabilities—to assess the business' ability to pay off its debts promptly. As a general rule, this ratio ought to be at least two to one.

In Table 6-1, a sample balance sheet for a small manufacturing company shows that the current ratio is well in excess of the usual figure. A brief explanaton of the major items on the balance sheet follows:

TABLE 6–1. A sample year-end statement.

ADG-Tenafly Manufacturing Company
Balance Sheet
December 31, 1978

Assets		
Current Assets		
Cash on hand	$ 250	
Cash in bank	3,950	
Accounts receivable, less allowance for bad debts	5,400	
Merchandise inventory	6,600	
Total current assets		$16,200
Fixed Assets		
Land	4,200	
Building, less depreciation	17,400	
Equipment, less depreciation	6,700	
Furniture and fixtures, less depreciation	3,300	
Total fixed assets		31,600
Total Assets		$47,800
Liabilities		
Current Liabilities		
Accounts payable	$ 2,600	
Notes payable within one year	800	
Accrued payroll taxes	1,100	
Total current liabilities		$ 4,500
Long-term Liabilities		
Note payable, due 1984	2,000	
Note payable, due 1987	3,500	
Total long-term liabilities		5,500
Capital (Net Worth)		
Capital, December 31, 1978		37,800
Total Liabilities and Capital		$47,800

- *Assets*—cash, property, and other items owned by the company
- *Current assets*—cash and property temporarily in your possession that can be quickly liquidated
- *Cash*—in addition to currency and coin, this includes checks and money orders
- *Accounts receivable*—a collective term for monies owed you on credit
- *Fixed assets*—tangible property of a long-term or permanent nature
- *Liabilities*—the debts your business must pay back
- *Current liabilities*—debts which must be met within a relatively short time, such as your "accounts payable" (monies owed out to suppliers), short-term loans, accrued taxes, and the like
- *Long-term liabilities*—Debts of a long-term nature

- *Capital*—Also referred to as "owner's equity" or "net worth," this is the excess of your assets over your liabilities. It is equivalent to what you originally invested in the business plus subsequent additions or subtractions. In the case of a corporation, the outstanding capital stock (at its original issue price) is listed here, as well as any accumulated profit.

THE PROFIT AND LOSS STATEMENT

Also called an "income statement" or "operating statement," the profit and loss statement is another major accounting device. Prepared at the very minimum on an annual basis, it depicts the results of business operations for the period covered. An abbreviated Profit and Loss Statement for a small retail shop is shown in Table 6-2. A major element of the "P&L" is the "bottom-line" figure—the one that reveals how much net profit the company earned during the particular period or, perhaps, the magnitude of the loss it may have suffered.

Management that allows a full year to go by without seeing a P&L statement shows signs of shortsightedness. Any attempts to correct an unfavorable picture are negated once months have rolled past. The smart business owner insists on having an income statement prepared by the accountant or bookkeeping staff on at least a quarterly basis—or, even better, each month. This way he or she can keep current with what is happening and take immediate steps to rectify any problems. Moreover, he or she can take advantage of any opportunities that crop up unexpectedly.

PREPARE YOUR STATEMENTS IN ADVANCE

One of the healthiest steps you can take before starting up your business is to work out, well ahead of time, both an estimated balance sheet and an estimated profit and loss statement for the first year of operations. This suggestion is not simply an exercise in thinking things through. It provides you with marvelous foresight: You are able to see what is going to happen, to be prepared for it, and to rule out the unexpected.

Several small booklets are offered, free of charge, by the Small Business Administration (see the end of this chapter for a book list). These carry such titles as "Business Plan for Retailers" and are available for small manufacturers, wholesalers, and service businesses as well. A feature of the booklets is the two-page "Expenses Worksheet" (reproduced in Figure 6-2), which you can use to compute your (expected!) profit or loss on a month by month basis.

TABLE 6–2. A sample "P & L".

The Two Sisters' Dress Shoppe
Profit and Loss Statement
March, 1978

Gross sales for March	$11,600	
Less returns and allowances	250	
Net Sales		$11,350
Cost of goods:		
Merchandise inventory, March 1	3,000	
Purchases during month	6,800	
Freight charges	60	
Total merchandise handled	9,860	
Less inventory, March 31	3,120	
Cost of goods sold		6,740
Gross profit		4,610
Operating expenses:		
Salaries	1,830	
Utilities	280	
Rent	530	
Stationery and printing	90	
Insurance	160	
Advertising and promotion	150	
Telephone	110	
Travel and entertainment	50	
Dues and subscriptions	30	
Bad debts	130	
Depreciation	390	
Total operating expenses		3,750
Operating profit		$ 860
Other income:		
Dividends		70
Interest on bank account		20
Total income before taxes		$ 950
Less provision for income taxes		400
Net Income (or Loss)		$ 550

HOW TO AVOID CASH-FLOW PROBLEMS

At one time or another during the year, an acute shortage of cash seems to plague many businesses. At times the business is extremely "tight" for operating capital; it may temporarily lack the funds to purchase merchandise, to buy supplies, or to pay various bills.

	Sample Figures for Hardware Stores _Percent of sales_	% of Your Sales	Your Annual Sales Dollar	Your Dollars JAN	Your Dollars FEB	Your Dollars MAR
Net sales	100.00	—	—	—	—	—
Cost of goods sold	66.05	—	—	—	—	—
		—	—	—	—	—
Margin	33.95	—	—	—	—	—
Salary Expense:		═	═	═		
Owners and managers. . .	7.15	—	—	—		
Salespeople, office, and other	9.60	—	—	—	—	—
Total Salaries	16.75	—	—	—	—	—
Other Expense:						
Office supplies and postage ...	0.40	—	—	—	—	—
Advertising	1.55	—	—	—	—	—
Donations	0.05	—	—	—	—	—
Telephone and telegraph	0.30	—	—	—	—	—
Losses on notes and accounts receivable	0.15	—	—	—	—	—
Delivery expense (exclusive of wages)	0.50	—	—	—	—	—
Depreciation of delivery equipment	0.25	—	—	—	—	—
Depreciation of furniture, fixtures, and tools	0.35	—	—	—	—	—
Rent	2.70	—	—	—	—	—
Repairs to building	0.10	—	—	—	—	—
Heat, light, water, and power ..	0.80	—	—	—	—	—
Insurance	0.80	—	—	—	—	—
Taxes (not including Federal income tax)	1.10	—	—	—	—	—
Interest on borrowed money ..	0.05*	—	—	—	—	—
Unclassified (including store supplies)	1.20	—	—	—	—	—
Total Expense (not including interest on investment)	27.05	—	—	—	—	—
Net Profit	6.90	—	—	—	—	—

*The interest on funds used for start-up costs if yours is a new store.

FIGURE 6–2. SBA Expenses Worksheet
Reproduced from "Business Plan for Retailers" (Small Marketers Aid No. 150)
(Washington, D.C.: Small Business Administration, 1970), pp. 18–19.

WORKSHEET

Your Dollars APR	Your Dollars MAY	Your Dollars JUN	Your Dollars JUL	Your Dollars AUG	Your Dollars SEP	Your Dollars OCT	Your Dollars NOV	Your Dollars DEC
—	—	—	—	—	—	—	—	—
—	—	—	—	—	—	—	—	—
—	—	—	—	—	—	—	—	—
—	—	—	—	—	—	—	—	—
—	—	—	—	—	—	—	—	—
—	—	—	—	—	—	—	—	—
—	—	—	—	—	—	—	—	—
—	—	—	—	—	—	—	—	—
—	—	—	—	—	—	—	—	—
—	—	—	—	—	—	—	—	—
—	—	—	—	—	—	—	—	—
—	—	—	—	—	—	—	—	—
—	—	—	—	—	—	—	—	—
—	—	—	—	—	—	—	—	—
—	—	—	—	—	—	—	—	—
—	—	—	—	—	—	—	—	—
—	—	—	—	—	—	—	—	—
—	—	—	—	—	—	—	—	—
—	—	—	—	—	—	—	—	—
—	—	—	—	—	—	—	—	—

ESTIMATED CASH FORECAST

	Jan.	Feb.	Mar.	April	May	June	July	Aug.	Sept.	Oct.	Nov.	Dec.
(1) Cash in Bank (Start of Month)												
(2) Petty Cash (Start of Month)												
(3) Total Cash (add 1) and (2)												
(4) Expected Cash Sales												
(5) Expected Collections												
(6) Other Money Expected												
(7) Total Receipts (add 4, 5 and 6)												
(8) Total Cash and Receipts (add 3 and 7)												
(9) All Disbursements (for month)												
(10) Cash Balance at End of Month. in Bank Account and Petty Cash (subtract (9) from (8)*												

*This balance is your starting cash balance for the next month.

FIGURE 6–3. A funds flow statement
Reproduced from "Business Plan for Retailers" (Small Marketers Aid No. 150) (Washington, D.C.: Small Business Administration, 1970), p. 17.

To maintain good financial control of your business, managing the cash flow is imperative. The "ebb and flow" of ready cash within the year can actually be plotted out in advance with a simplified "funds flow" form, such as the one in Figure 6-3. Details are, of course, filled in from the monthly profit and loss statements you have developed.

FOR FURTHER INFORMATION

Free Materials from the Small Business Administration

Management Aids:

#218—"Business Plan for Small Manufacturers"

#221—"Business Plan for Small Construction Firms"

Small Marketers Aids:

71—"Checklist for Going Into Business"

#150—"Business Plan for Retailers"

#153—"Business Plan for Small Service Firms"

Available from the Superintendent of Documents

15—"Handbook of Small Business Finance," Stock #045-000-00139-3; 63 pp.; 75¢.

7

Legal and Tax Pointers for the Small Business

YOUR NEED FOR PROFESSIONAL ASSISTANCE

If you are like other entrepreneurs, you are undoubtedly highly motivated and convinced that you will be able to manage all aspects of your new business masterfully and by yourself. You also plan to run your affairs in a professional, open, and aboveboard manner. You want to treat your customers and your suppliers equally, conform to all legal requirements and restrictions, maintain accurate records, pay your taxes on time (lest you suffer penalties!), and so on.

Despite your high level of self-confidence, however, you must realize that the complexities of today's total environment call for reliance on the assistance of specialists. Minimally, you need an accountant, a banker, an insurance agent or broker, possibly one or two business consultants, and, of course, an attorney.

The accountant helps you set up your books according to approved accounting procedures. This enables you to make vital merchandising and other decisions in the future. He can also help you keep tabs on your business growth, point out minor problems before they become serious, and complete your tax returns.

Your banker can furnish you with information about the kind of business you're considering and about the community where it will be situated. Furthermore, he'll be happy to recommend other professionals if you need them, assist your operation with loans and lines of credit, and advise you generally on economic trends.

Your insurance representative takes care of your special business needs in this field.

Consultants are usually tapped for a variety of one-shot problems: designing a plant or store layout, appraising a going business in which you're interested, making a feasibility study for a new store location or for EDP equipment under consideration, setting up an initial advertising campaign, and so on.

If at all feasible, it is worth your while to engage an attorney for your business on a retainer basis. His or her services are valuable at the very beginning, in assisting you with all the legal aspects of starting a business—setting up the legal form of the business, negotiating leases and contracts, securing necessary licenses and permits, preparing partnership or stockholder agreements, and so forth. Subsequently, he'll see to it that you're thoroughly familiar with the details of various legislative acts and local ordinances. These run the gamut from the minimum wage and labor laws, through health and safety regulations, to tax responsibilities. You will call on your attorney later for assistance in a variety of situations too numerous to mention.

PROPRIETORSHIP, PARTNERSHIP, OR CORPORATION?

Early in the game, you have to decide on the legal form of ownership for your business: the sole proprietorship, the partnership, or the corporation. Each form has drawbacks as well as advantages. Consider carefully the pros and cons of each. The key is to select the one that will best meet your specific needs. This is the customary procedure followed by many people who launch a new enterprise:

1. Start out as a sole proprietor *if* you have enough funds for the required investment and *if* you have enough self-confidence.

2. Select the partnership form if you don't have the funds or the confidence, or when the expected workload will be too much for one person to handle.

3. Form a corporation for the long pull and for growth. (This need not be done at the outset; a corporation can be formed after the business has demonstrated its viability.)

THE SOLE PROPRIETORSHIP

This is the simplest of the three legal forms of ownership and the way the majority of new businesses start off. You cannot beat this form for its simplicity of organization and its absolute obedience to your every wish and command (right or wrong!).

What's Good About a Proprietorship?

It's the easiest and quickest form to initiate. At least three-quarters of all thirteen million businesses in the country reflect this ownership type. If you believe in the old "safety in numbers" approach and know that so many choose this particular route, how can you go wrong? Barring the need for special licenses or permits, all you have to do to get a business off the ground is to start working at it.

There is no cost involved in setting up, as long as you plan on doing business under your own name. You might decide (as many people do) that you prefer to operate under a trade name instead. In this case you have to file the details with the local authorities at the offices of the town/city/county clerk. The form used for this purpose is available at business stationery stores and is called a "Certificate of Doing Business Under an Assumed Name." The fee for filing is minimal—a few dollars at most.

You also save on legal fees with a proprietorship, since no special contracts or agreements need to be drawn up, as is the case with a partnership or corporation.

A sole proprietorship offers you the greatest psychic rewards because you can run the business as you see fit. There are no bosses to issue orders to you, supervise your comings and goings, challenge your decisions, or take you to task for errors. This means you must pit all your resources—mental, physical, and emotional as well as financial—against the environment. Quite a challenge! It's somewhat like playing football without team-mates: You not only get to carry the ball, but if you make it through the goalposts, you get to keep all the profits—after taxes, of course!

If you run your business honorably and in an aboveboard

fashion (and keep accurate records), no one will interfere with how you conduct your business. Furthermore, you avoid unnecessary pressure from the Better Business Bureau, consumer groups, the Internal Revenue Service or any other government agency. Of the three forms of ownership, this is the one that gets the least attention from the federal bureaucracy. (The corporate form receives the most!)

Tax-wise, you and your sole proprietorship are treated as inseparable companions. This identity can be helpful to you. Typically, the new venture ends up its first six months (and often longer) in the red. This initial lack of success can be disheartening, especially if you have left a good-paying job to try your hand at business. If your business incurs a loss for the year, you are entitled to deduct those lost dollars on your tax return against any other income you may have earned that year. Moreover, this holds true for all succeeding years.

As a last point, terminating your proprietorship is also simple. To close down the operation, all you need to do is liquidate your assets, pay off your debts, lock the door, and walk away from it all. (Of course, it is much better all around to simply sell it—providing that it's a successful business.)

Now for the Minuses . . .

Perhaps the most serious drawback to the sole proprietorship is the problem of unlimited personal liability. Legally, you and the business are one and the same; therefore, all the liabilities of the enterprise are yours.

Of course, no one expects to fail when he or she first starts up a venture. Despite all your thorough preparation and planning (let alone your financial commitment!), you must have a healthy outlook and plan for a possible failure. (Indeed, some business advisors claim that it's more probable than possible!) If your business fails and the business assets you're able to muster at that point are not sufficient to cover your obligations, your creditors can move in and take away your home, your automobile, your bank accounts, and any other personal assets you hold until the debts are fully satisfied. (The type of items that can be taken from you depends on different state bankruptcy rules and regulations and on different civil procedure laws.) Consequently, if your personal holdings are considerable, you might be better off opting for the corporate mode.

As a one-person operation, your business is limited to your own skills and capabilities. Under the right circumstances, you should hire additional talent, specialists who can provide the expertise you lack. The tendency is to avoid hiring high-priced experts until a business has expanded enough to absorb this additional cost (and only if the business is certain to profit).

The success of your business will be in jeopardy if you become seriously ill or disabled through accidental injury. You can and should anticipate this and take steps early in the game to prevent it. You ought to train one or two of your key people to shoulder the responsibility at the helm, in the event that you are incapacitated for any considerable length of time.

Furthermore, because the business *is* the proprietor, you will probably find it difficult to attract more capital into your enterprise, say for growth or expansion. Understandably banks and other financial sources might be reluctant to advance funds to you. After all, the debt would have to be paid back over time by a single, fragile human being. What if something were to happen and render you incapable of managing the business?

This point leads us to the last consideration: If you die while owning the business, your sole proprietorship automatically terminates.

THE PARTNERSHIP

You should consider forming a partnership if you cannot generate enough capital to make your new business a success, or if the workload is too heavy for you alone, or if you simply need moral support and are afraid of going it alone.

In many respects, this form of ownership is not very different from the sole proprietorship, except that you can count on one or more associates to help you share the responsibilities, the work, and the decision-making. Of course, you must expect to share the profits as well.

This sharing aspect is based on the assumption that two or more ordinary, or "general," partners are involved in the business. Another type of partner is the "limited partner"; this kind of arrangement permits a quasi-corporate entity to exist. It is recognized in many states while not permitted in others. In this situation, one or more individuals makes an investment in the business and is given part ownership in return. However, they don't participate in the operation of the business; the enterprise is run by the general partner(s). Limited partners earn their share of company profits but avoid the danger of being held personally liable for business debts.

Two clarion notes of caution should be trumpeted at this point.

First, take care that your emotions don't interfere with sound logic and common sense; a clear head at this early stage can save you lots of grief later. Second, avoid the all-too-common temptation to back up your partnership with nothing more than a verbal understanding and an amicable handshake. Not only for the sake of good business practice but also for your own peace of mind thereafter, you should draw up a partnership agreement with the help of your attorney. This legal instrument not only spells out the duties and responsibilities of the partners, but also should include a "buy-sell" clause to forestall future headaches.

As a concluding comment, don't go into a partnership (if at all possible!) unless you hold 51 percent of the ownership.

Advantages of the Partnership Form

Like the sole proprietorship, a partnership is relatively easy and inexpensive to establish. You most likely want to operate under an assumed name, requiring you to file a Certificate of Conducting Business as Partners. Having the partnership contract prepared is an additional cost.

Naturally, you can count on more initial capital than if you go it alone; the pooled investments of two or more individuals are involved. You also have more leverage when seeking trade credit, loans, or additional equity capital in the future; this is simply because several people are involved.

Rarely does one individual possess all the skills and experience required to make a new enterprise a success. If you are not that rare person, taking on a partner or two can provide the missing elements. A broader array of talent can be brought to bear on your business operations. (Of course, you must be astute enough to select partners who complement you, who make up for your shortcomings.)

Finally, the partnership form is relatively free of government red tape. Little is required in the way of paperwork (as is the case with a corporation). Each year, however, you must complete an information return, Form 1065 (U.S. Partnership Return of Income). This form is described later on in this chapter under "Taxes."

Drawbacks to the Partnership

If you elect this form of ownership, be prepared to relinquish a good deal of your freedom. You have to work along with one or more co-bosses; you must share the authority and the responsibilities. The need to cooperate can provide a continuing assault on your entrepreneurial spirit; no longer do you enjoy the thrill and the challenge of running the entire show.

There can also be formidable adjustment problems. Arguments with partners can develop over not only important business problems, but over such insignificant trivia as who will open up (or close) on Wednesdays or Saturdays, when to take vacations (and for how long), who will run the machines, do the buying, supervise the office clerks, and so forth. It's difficult enough at times for spouses to get along with each other. Imagine the tensions inherent in a situation where two or more individuals, often unrelated, must act, work, plan, and operate in tandem for years and years! It's wise to make certain that your new partner(s) are as highly motivated and cooperative as you are and that your personalities don't clash. Be especially wary of close friends and relatives. Your affection, loyalty, or friendship can easily blind you to their deficiencies and lead you to make allowances for their mistakes.

In any event, you and the others have to learn to live together if your business is to be successful. If you do become unhappy with the situation, only three courses are open to you: (1) sell out your share of the business to the others, (2) buy them out, or (3) stay put and learn to live with it.

Be aware that any business decisions or actions taken by your partner(s) legally bind you as well under the general rules of agency, even in a case where you knew nothing about the move. This obligation is something to think about: It applies to any contracts that may be signed as well as to other acts.

Again, as with the sole proprietorship, there is the considerable risk of incurring personal liability. As a general partner, your personal assets (as well as those of other general partners) are subject to seizure for the payment of business debts.

Finally, this form of ownership is also subject to the frailties of human nature. The death of any one partner, unless provided for in the partnership contract, automatically terminates the partnership.

THE CORPORATION

The third major legal form of business ownership is the corporation. To set up a corporation, usually three or more individuals must apply for a charter within the state where they want to transact business and where the principal office of the business is located. (Note: The number of individuals involved depends on state regulations; most states require only one director in order to create a corporate entity.) Application is accomplished by preparing a Certificate of Incorporation in detail (names and addresses of both the proposed corporation and of the incorporators, purpose and type of business activities contemplated, amount of stock authorized, and so on), filing the certificate with the Secretary of State, and paying the required fee.

While it's not absolutely necessary, I strongly recommend that your attorney handle all the details. Corporation law is complicated; a lawyer saves you needless headaches in the future. At the very least, the lawyer may widen the horizons of your business by broadening the purposes of your activities listed in the application. State law limits the activities of your corporation to those spelled out in the charter. Moreover, your attorney can help you prepare a Preincorporation Agreement with the other principals.

Why Incorporate?

Of the three legal forms, this is the only one with a built-in capacity for permanence in that the death of one or more of its founders or stockholders doesn't affect the business' legal status. The corporation is recognized as a legal entity in and of itself. It exists apart from its stockholders, who can come and go.

Consequently, you avoid the problem of unlimited liability that characterizes the two other forms of ownership. Your liability is limited to the amount of your investment. Your personal holdings do not come up for grabs, if the corporation becomes insolvent and its assets are insufficient to satisfy the creditors. This single fact alone explains the attraction of the corporate form for many who start their own businesses.

Banks and other lenders are generally more willing to advance loans to a corporation that has been operating successfully for some time or to a new corporation with sufficient equity and promise. (The lender sometimes insists on collateral or requires personal signatures from stockholders as a precautionary measure.) Individuals with money to invest might purchase some of the new corporation's stock.

You're not locked into the corporation forever. If you some day decide you want to embark on an entirely different enterprise, relocate, or retire, all you have to do is sell your stock in the company. Ownership of stock is readily transferred.

As a final point, there can be certain advantages to the corporate form in the area of fringe benefits, such as pension and stock plans, insurance, and the like.

Disadvantages of Incorporation

A major limitation to the corporate form is the problem of double taxation. In other words, corporate profits are taxed once per se since a corporation is a distinct taxable entity; and they're taxed again as income, when distributed to the stockholders. Although you serve as corporation president and chairman of the board, you are legally an employee of the business, and liable for income tax not only on your salary but also on your share of the distributed profits. The total tax bite can be substantial.

Unfortunately, any losses sustained by a corporation are not available to stockholders as deductions from other earned income!

It takes time and effort as well as money to set up a corporation. Your costs can run from as little as several hundred dollars to well over a thousand dollars.

Corporations are closely regulated by the state in which they are franchised. In your home state, yours is known as a "domestic" corporation. "Foreign" corporation is the term applied to your firm when you operate in another state. In reality, you are not supposed to conduct business in a second or third state without making formal application to the respective secretaries of state for permission to conduct operations there. Generally, this regulation comes up in matters of a corporation's right to sue for non-payments, etc. A company doing business in another state is not stopped merely because of failure to file.

A corporation is also required to promulgate by-laws, hold stockholders' meetings, keep records, ad infinitum. (Most states use preprinted forms which alleviate much of the initial preparations.) Of all three forms of ownership, the corporation comes under the most scrutiny by the federal government.

TAXES AND YOUR BUSINESS

It's been said that nothing is as certain as death and taxes. This is unfortunately a truism, and your new business is no exception to the rule.

Your enterprise is subject to taxes at all three levels of government: federal, state, and local. This alone ought to convince you that you are in dire need of as much professionalism in the tax management area as in all segments of your business—production, sales, personnel, and so on. Because of the complexities of tax law, frequent new rulings, changing regulations, and difficulties of interpretation, it's nearly impossible to adopt a do-it-yourself stance in this field.

The Internal Revenue Service offers assistance in the form of a comprehensive *Tax Guide for Small Business*. Its scope ranges from a treatment of the different forms of ownership, to a description of accounting periods, procedures, and recordkeeping, as well as instructions for completing the proper tax forms and information returns. Contact your local IRS office for a copy of their publication 334. Nevertheless, consultation with a capable tax advisor is strongly recommended!

What taxes do you face? Let's first consider those imposed by the federal government.

FEDERAL TAXES

The major tax bite taken by Uncle Sam is in the form of income and social security taxes. Incidentally, new responsibilities accompany your transition from worker to business owner. Not only are you taxed on your earnings but you are automatically conscripted into service as a deputy tax collector.

Federal Income Taxes

The legal form of ownership you select has a major impact on the way tax regulations apply to your new enterprise.

Sole Proprietorship. You will recall that, for legal purposes (which of course include taxation), the individual owner and the business activity are inseparable. Consequently, if you choose this form, you are required to file your annual federal tax return on the familiar Form 1040 (Individual Income Tax Return). This is the same form you completed as an employee.

In addition, you need to complete and submit, attached to your Form 1040, a separate Schedule C (Profit or Loss from Business or Profession–Sole Proprietorship). A sample of the schedule is shown in Figure 7–1.

On this schedule, you must furnish details about your business activity for the year just ended: your sales, the cost of goods sold (and how you arrived at the figures), the resulting gross profit, your business expenses and other deductions, explanations of such items as depreciation, and your net profit. This last figure is added to other income you earned during the year and put on your Form 1040.

SCHEDULE C (Form 1040)

Department of the Treasury
Internal Revenue Service

Profit or (Loss) From Business or Profession
(Sole Proprietorship)
Partnerships, Joint Ventures, etc., Must File Form 1065.
▶ Attach to Form 1040 or Form 1041.   ▶ See Instructions for Schedule C (Form 1040).

1979
09

Name of proprietor	Social security number of proprietor
Susan J. Brown	481 44 6957

A Main business activity (see Instructions) ▶ Retail   ; product ▶ ladies apparel

B Business name ▶ Milady Fashions

C Employer identification number

D Business address (number and street) ▶ 725 Big Sur Drive
City, State and Zip Code ▶ Franklin, New York 18725   111 481 1 1838

E Accounting method: (1) ☐ Cash   (2) ☒ Accrual   (3) ☐ Other (specify) ▶ _____

F Method(s) used to value closing inventory:
(1) ☐ Cost   (2) ☒ Lower of cost or market   (3) ☐ Other (if other, attach explanation)

	Yes	No
G Was there any major change in determining quantities, costs, or valuations between opening and closing inventory? . . If "Yes," attach explanation.		☒
H Did you deduct expenses for an office in your home?		☒
I Did you elect to claim amortization (under section 191) or depreciation (under section 167(o)) for a rehabilitated certified historic structure (see Instructions)? . . . . (Amortizable basis (see Instructions) ▶ _____)		☒

C

Part I   Income

[1]	1 a Gross receipts or sales	1a	$ 372,742 73			
	b Returns and allowances	1b	1,442 10			
[2]	c Balance (subtract line 1b from line 1a)			1c	$ 371,300	63
	2 Cost of goods sold and/or operations (Schedule C–1, line 8) .			2	239,349	49
[3]	3 Gross profit (subtract line 2 from line 1c)			3	$ 131,951	14
[4]	4 Other income (attach schedule)			4		
[5]	5 Total income (add lines 3 and 4) . . . . ▶			5	$ 131,951	14

Part II   Deductions

[6]

[16]	6 Advertising	3,500 00	31 a Wages . .	43,450 00	
[13]	7 Amortization		b Jobs credit	4,500 00	
[11]	8 Bad debts from sales or services .	279 00	c WIN credit		
	9 Bank charges		d Total credits	4,500 00	
	10 Car and truck expenses . . .		e Subtract line 31d from 31a .	38,950 00	
	11 Commissions		32 Other expenses (specify): ◀[16]		
[12]	12 Depletion		a Chamber of Commerce	25 00	
	13 Depreciation (explain in Schedule C–2) .	3,052 50	b Credit reports	475 00	
	14 Dues and publications		c Trash removal	300 00	
	15 Employee benefit programs . .		d Window dressing	298 10	
[16]	16 Freight (not included on Schedule C–1) .		e Gasoline and Oil	1,250 14	
[16]	17 Insurance	950 00	f		
[10]	18 Interest on business indebtedness .	633 19	g		
	19 Laundry and cleaning		h		
	20 Legal and professional services .		i		
[14]	21 Office supplies		j		
[16]	22 Pension and profit-sharing plans .	6,517 50	k		
[16]	23 Postage	516 12	l		
[7]	24 Rent on business property . . .	4,800 00	m		
[8]	25 Repairs	1,774 15	n		
[16]	26 Supplies (not included on Schedule C–1) .	1,203 80	o		
[9]	27 Taxes	4,802 75	p		
	28 Telephone	298 08	q		
[16]	29 Travel and entertainment . . .		r		
	30 Utilities	1,872 16	s		

33 Total deductions (add amounts in columns for lines 6 through 32s) . . . . ▶	33	$ 71,497	49
34 Net profit or (loss) (subtract line 33 from line 5). If a profit, enter on Form 1040, line 13, and on Schedule SE, Part II, line 5a (or Form 1041, line 6). If a loss, go on to line 35	34	$ 60,453	65

35 If you have a loss, do you have amounts for which you are not "at risk" in this business (see Instructions)? . . ☐ Yes ☐ No

FIGURE 7–1(A)*

Source: Internal Revenue Service, "Tax Guide for Small Business, 1980 Edition," Publication No. 334 (Washington, D.C.: Internal Revenue Service, 1979).

SCHEDULE C-1.—Cost of Goods Sold and/or Operations (See Schedule C Instructions for Part I, line 2)

1 Inventory at beginning of year (if different from last year's closing inventory, attach explanation) .	1	$ 32,843 66
2 a Purchases . . . . 2a $ 241,026 51		
b Cost of items withdrawn for personal use 2b 774 42		
c Balance (subtract line 2b from line 2a)	2c	240,252 09
3 Cost of labor (do not include salary paid to yourself)	3	
4 Materials and supplies	4	
5 Other costs (attach schedule)	5	
6 Add lines 1, 2c, and 3 through 5	6	$ 273,095 75
7 Inventory at end of year	7	33,746 26
8 Cost of goods sold and/or operations (subtract line 7 from line 6). Enter here and on Part I, line 2. ▶	8	$ 239,349 49

SCHEDULE C-2.—Depreciation (See Schedule C Instructions for line 13)
If you need more space, please use Form 4562.

Description of property (a)	Date acquired (b)	Cost or other basis (c)	Depreciation allowed or allowable in prior years (d)	Method of computing depreciation (e)	Life or rate (f)	Depreciation for this year (g)
1 Total additional first-year depreciation (do not include in items below)——————————▶						
2 Other depreciation:						
Buildings						
Furniture and fixtures . . .						
Transportation equipment . .						
Machinery and other equipment .						
Other (specify)						
Delivery truck #1	1-12-77	$ 4,500	$ 2,250	S.L.	4 yrs	$ 1,125 00
Delivery truck #2	1-5-78	5,000	1,250	S.L.	4	1,250 00
Store counters and fixtures	1-3-75	5,250	2,100	S.L.	10	525 00
Office equipment	1-11-75	1,525	610	S.L.	10	152 50
3 Totals		$ 16,275	. . . . .		3	$ 3,052 50
4 Depreciation claimed in Schedule C-1					4	
5 Balance (subtract line 4 from line 3). Enter here and on Part II, line 13 . . . . ▶					5	$ 3,052 50

SCHEDULE C-3.—Expense Account Information (See Schedule C Instructions for Schedule C-3)

Enter information for yourself and your five highest paid employees. In determining the five highest paid employees, add expense account allowances to the salaries and wages. However, you don't have to provide the information for any employee for whom the combined amount is less than $25,000, or for yourself if your expense account allowance plus line 34, page 1, is less than $25,000.

Name (a)	Expense account (b)	Salaries and wages (c)
Owner		
1		
2		
3		
4		
5		

Did you claim a deduction for expenses connected with:	Yes	No
A Entertainment facility (boat, resort, ranch, etc.)?		X
B Living accommodations (except employees on business)?		X
C Conventions or meetings you or your employees attended outside the U.S. or its possessions? (See Instructions) . .		X
D Employees' families at conventions or meetings?		X
If "Yes," were any of these conventions or meetings outside the U.S. or its possessions?		
E Vacations for employees or their families not reported on Form W-2?		X

FIGURE 7–1(B)   *Numbers in brackets and arrows refer to explanations furnished in the IRS publication.

As sole proprietor, you are also required to calculate what your *expected* income tax will be for the coming year. Submit Form 1040ES (Declaration of Estimated Tax for Individuals) along with your Form 1040. The I.R.S. provides you with instructions, a worksheet on which you can work out your estimated tax, and four declaration vouchers. Each of these vouchers must be mailed, in turn, before the fifteenth of April, June, September, and January. Part payment of your estimated tax must accompany each voucher.

Partnership As with the sole proprietorship, tax liability is assessed only for the earned incomes of the individual partners involved and not against the business directly. Each partner files his return on Form 1040, where his or her distributive share of the business profits is noted.

In addition, you are required to submit a report of your business operation on Form 1065 (U.S. Partnership Return of Income). This is only an information report; no tax payment accompanies its submission. A sample of Form 1065 is included in Figure 7–2.

As with the sole proprietor, each partner also files an estimated tax.

Corporation If you have elected this form of ownership, your tax reporting problems are more complicated. As an employee of the corporation, you report your earnings (and other income) during the taxable year—as well as dividends from the corporation—on the individual Form 1040. As a separate entity, the corporation must file its own return as well; for this purpose, use Form 1120 (U.S. Corporation Income Tax Return). If the firm operates on the calendar year basis, the return is due on or before March 15th. Many corporations, however, prefer the fiscal year basis; in such cases, the corporation tax return is due by the 15th of the third month following the close of its fiscal year. A sample Form 1120 is shown in Figure 7–3.

If you need more time for any valid reason, the corporation may file Form 7004 (Application for Automatic Extension of Time to File Corporate Income Tax Return). Still another extension may be sought by submitting Form 7005.

Estimated tax payments must be made by every corporation whose tax liability is expected to be $40 or more. Payments are made to an authorized commercial bank depositary or to your regional Federal Reserve Bank and accompanied by a completed Form 503 (Federal Tax Deposit, Corporation Income Taxes).

At present, corporations are required to pay federal income tax on profits for the year according to the following schedule:

Form **1065**	**U.S. Partnership Return of Income** For calendar year 1979,				**1979**	

Form 1065
Department of the Treasury
Internal Revenue Service

U.S. Partnership Return of Income For calendar year 1979,
or fiscal year beginning ...., 1979, and ending ...., 19......

1979

A Principal business activity (see page 12 of Instructions) *Wholesale*	Use IRS label. Otherwise please print or type.	Name *A & B Distributing Company*	D Employer identification no. *71-9367974*
B Principal product or service (see page 12 of Instructions) *Sundries*		Number and street *334 West Main Street*	E Date business started *10-1-75*
C Business code number (see page 12 of Instructions) *5195*		City or town, State, and ZIP code *Anytown, California 98603*	F Enter total assets from Schedule L, line 13, column (D). $

G Check method of accounting:
(1) ☐ Cash (2) ☒ Accrual (3) ☐ Other (attach explanation)

H Is this a final return?
☐ Yes ☒ No

IMPORTANT—You must fill in all lines and schedules. If more space is needed, see page 2 of Instructions. Enter any items specially allocated to the partners on Schedule K, line 16, and not on the numbered lines on this page or in Schedules A through J.

<1>	1a Gross receipts or sales $ *109,920* 1b Less returns and allowances $ *3,365* Balance ▶	1c	$ *106,555*
<2>	2 Cost of goods sold and/or operations (Schedule A, line 34)	2	*67,641*
<3>	3 Gross profit (subtract line 2 from line 1c)	3	*38,914*
	4 Ordinary income (loss) from other partnerships and fiduciaries (attach statement) . .	4	
	5 Nonqualifying dividends	5	
	6 Interest	6	*104*
<4>	7 Net income (loss) from rents (Schedule H, line 2)	7	
	8 Net income (loss) from royalties (attach schedule)	8	
	9 Net farm profit (loss) (attach Schedule F (Form 1040))	9	
	10 Net gain (loss) (Form 4797, line 11)	10	*400*
	11 Other income (attach schedule)	11	
<5>	12 **TOTAL** income (loss) (combine lines 3 through 11)	12	$ *39,418*
<6>	13a Salaries and wages (other than to partners) $ *14,350* 13b Less Jobs Credit $ .... Balance ▶	13c	$ *14,350*
	14 Guaranteed payments to partners (see page 4 of Instructions)	14	*5,000*
<7>	15 Rent	15	*1,500*
<10>	16 Interest	16	*871*
<9>	17 Taxes	17	*4,988*
<11>	18 Bad debts (see page 5 of Instructions)	18	*250*
<8>	19 Repairs	19	*235*
<12>	20 Depreciation (Schedule J, line 5)	20	*2,083*
	21 Amortization (attach schedule)	21	
<13>	22 Depletion (other than oil and gas, attach schedule—see page 5 of Instructions) . .	22	
	23a Retirement plans, etc. (see page 5 of Instructions). (Enter number of plans ▶ ....). . .	23a	
<14>	23b Employee benefit programs (see page 5 of Instructions)	23b	
<16>	24 Other deductions (attach schedule)	24	*3,947*
<17>	25 **TOTAL** deductions (add lines 13c through 24)	25	$ *30,224*
<18>	26 Ordinary income (loss) (subtract line 25 from line 12)	26	$ *9,194*

Schedule A—COST OF GOODS SOLD AND/OR OPERATIONS (See Page 3 of Instructions)

27	Inventory at beginning of year (if different from last year's closing inventory, attach explanation) . .	27	$ *18,125*
28a	Purchases $ *69,275* 28b Less cost of items withdrawn for personal use $ *534* Balance ▶	28c	*68,741*
29	Cost of labor	29	
30	Materials and supplies	30	
31	Other costs (attach schedule)	31	
32	Total of lines 27 through 31	32	$ *86,866*
33	Inventory at end of year	33	*19,225*
34	Cost of goods sold (subtract line 33 from line 32). Enter here and on line 2, above	34	$ *67,641*

Under penalties of perjury, I declare that I have examined this return, including accompanying schedules and statements, and to the best of my knowledge and belief, it is true, correct, and complete. Declaration of preparer (other than taxpayer) is based on all information of which preparer has any knowledge.

Please Sign Here

Signature of general partner *Frank W. Able* Date ▶ *4-3-80*

Paid Preparer's Information

Preparer's signature and date ▶	Check if self-employed ▶ ☐	Preparer's social security no.
Firm's name (or yours, if self-employed) and address ▶	E.I. No. ▶	
	ZIP code ▶	

FIGURE 7-2(A)* *Numbers in brackets and arrows refer to explanations furnished in the IRS publication.

Source: Internal Revenue Service, "Tax Guide for Small Business, 1980 Edition," Publication No. 334 (Washington, D.C.: Internal Revenue Service, 1979).

35 a Check all methods used for valuing closing inventory: *(i)* ☐ Cost *(ii)* ☑ Lower of cost or market as described in regulations section 1.471–4 (see page 6 of Instructions) *(iii)* ☐ Writedown of "subnormal" goods as described in regulations section 1.471–2(c) (see page 6 of Instructions)

	Yes	No
b Did you use any other method of inventory valuation not described in line 35a? . . . . If "Yes," specify methods used and attach explanation.		✔
c Is Form 970 or other statement attached for adoption of LIFO inventory methods?		✔
d Are you engaged in manufacturing? . . . . If "Yes," did you value your inventory using the full absorption method (regulations section 1.471–11)?		✔
e Was there any substantial change in determining quantities, cost, or valuations between opening and closing inventory? . If "Yes," attach explanation.		✔

Schedule D—CAPITAL GAINS AND LOSSES (See Page 6 of Instructions)

Part I Short-term Capital Gains and Losses—Assets Held One Year or Less

a. Kind of property and description (Example, 100 shares of "Z" Co.)	b. Date acquired (mo., day, yr.)	c. Date sold (mo., day, yr.)	d. Gross sales price less expense of sale	e. Cost or other basis	f. Gain (loss) for the year (d less e)
1 XYZ Chemical Co. Inc. 20 Shares Common	1-6-79	3-13-79	$ 2,300	$ 2,200	$ 100

2 Partnership's share of net short-term gain (loss), including specially allocated items, from other partnerships and from fiduciaries . . . .

3 Net short-term gain (loss) from lines 1 and 2. Enter here and on Schedule K (Form 1065), line 5 . . . . . $ 100

Part II Long-term Capital Gains and Losses—Assets Held More Than One Year

4 ABC Motors Inc. 100 Shares Common	2-7-78	11-27-79	$ 1,200	$ 1,000	$ 200

5 Partnership's share of net long-term gain (loss), including specially allocated items, from other partnerships and from fiduciaries . . . .

6 Capital gain distributions . . . .

7 Net long-term gain (loss) from lines 4, 5, and 6. Enter here and on Schedule K (Form 1065), line 6 . . . . . $ 200

Schedule H—INCOME FROM RENTS (See Page 4 of Instructions) If more space is needed, attach schedule.

a. Kind and location of property	b. Amount of rent	c. Depreciation (explain in Schedule J)	d. Repairs (attach schedule)	e. Other expenses (attach schedule)

1 Totals . . . .

2 Net income (loss) (subtract total of columns c, d, and e from column b). Enter here and on page 1, line 7 . . .

Schedule I—BAD DEBTS (See Page 5 of Instructions)

a. Year	b. Trade notes and accounts receivable outstanding at end of year	c. Sales on account	d. Current year's provision	e. Recoveries	f. Amount charged against reserve	g. Reserve for bad debts at end of year
1974						
1975						
1976						
1977						
1978						
1979						

Schedule J—DEPRECIATION (See Page 6 of Instructions) If more space is needed, use Form 4562.

a. Description of property	b. Date acquired	c. Cost or other basis	d. Depreciation allowed or allowable in prior years	e. Method of computing depreciation	f. Life or rate	g. Depreciation for this year
1 Total additional first-year depreciation (**NOT** to exceed $2,000). (Do not include in items below. Enter here and on Schedule K, line 2.)				$ 600		
2 Other depreciation:						
Buildings	12-23-78	$ 6,000		150% DB	60 yrs	$ 150
Furniture and fixtures . . .	Various	6,500	$ 3,913	S.L.	Var.	4,550
Transportation equipment . .						
Machinery and other equipment . .	7-1-79	2,400	—	S.L.	10	120
Other (specify): Warehouse equipment	10-5-78	3,500	87	S.L.	10	263
3 Totals		$ 18,400				$ 2,083

4 Amount of depreciation claimed in Schedules A and H . . . .

5 Balance (subtract line 4 from line 3). Enter here and on page 1, line 20 . . . . $ 2,083

FIGURE 7–2(B)

Schedule K—PARTNERS' SHARES OF INCOME, CREDITS, DEDUCTIONS, ETC. (See Pages 7–10 of Instructions)

Enter the total distributive amount for each applicable item listed below.
Note: *Enter each partner's distributive share on Schedule K–1. Prepare a separate Schedule K–1 for each partner.*

Enter the number of partners in the partnership ▶ **2**

Are any partners in this partnership also partnerships? . . ☐ Yes ☒ No

a. Distributive share items	b. Total amount
<6> ➤ **1 a** Guaranteed payments to partners: (1) Deductible by the partnership (page 1, line 14)	$ 5,000
(2) Capitalized by the partnership (see page 4 of Instructions)	
<18> ➤ **b** Ordinary income (loss) (page 1, line 26)	$ 9,194
2 Additional first-year depreciation (Schedule J, line 1)	$ 600
3 Gross farming or fishing income	
4 Dividends qualifying for exclusion (attach list)	$ 150
5 Net short-term capital gain (loss) } **a** After 10/31/78	$ 100
from transactions entered into: } **b** Before 11/1/78	
6 Net long-term capital gain (loss) } **a** After 10/31/78	$ 200
from transactions entered into: } **b** Before 11/1/78	
7 Net gain (loss) from involuntary } **a** After 10/31/78	
conversions due to casualty or theft: } **b** Before 11/1/78	
8 Other net gain (loss) under section } **a** After 10/31/78	$ 750
1231 from transactions entered into: } **b** Before 11/1/78	
9 Net earnings (loss) from self-employment (Schedule N, line 12)	$ 13,794
<15> ➤ **10 a** Charitable contributions (attach list): 50% $ 50 , 30% , 20%	$ 50
b Other itemized deductions (attach list)	
11 Expense account allowance	
12 Jobs credit	
13 Taxes paid by regulated investment companies on undistributed capital gains (attach schedule)	
14 a Payments for partners to a Keogh Plan. (Type of plan ▶................................)	
b Payments for partners to an IRA or Simplified Employee Pension (SEP)	
15 a Foreign taxes paid (see page 9 of Instructions)	
b Other income, deductions, etc. (attach schedule)	
c Oil and gas depletion. (Enter amount (not for partner's use) ▶................................)	//////////
16 Specially allocated items (attach schedule): **a** Short-term capital gain (loss)	
b Long-term capital gain (loss)	
c Ordinary gain (loss)	
d Other	
17 Tax preference items (see page 10 of Instructions): **a** Accelerated depreciation on real property:	
(1) Certified historic structure rehabilitation (167(o) or amortization under 191)	
(2) Low-income rental housing (167(k))	
(3) Other government assisted low-income housing	
(4) Other real property	
b Accelerated depreciation on personal property subject to a lease	
Amortization: **c** ...., **d** ...., **e** ...., **f**	
g Reserves for losses on bad debts of financial institutions	
h Depletion (other than oil and gas)	
i (1) Excess intangible drilling costs from oil, gas or geothermal wells	
(2) Net income from oil, gas or geothermal wells	
18 Interest on investment indebtedness: **a** Investment interest expense: **(1)** Indebtedness incurred before 12/17/69 .	
(2) Indebtedness incurred before 9/11/75, but after 12/16/69	
(3) Indebtedness incurred after 9/10/75	
b Net investment income (loss)	
c Excess expenses from "net lease property"	
d Excess of net long-term capital gain over net short-term capital loss from investment property	

19 Investment in property that qualifies for investment credit:	Basis of new investment property	a 3 or more but less than 5 years	
		b 5 or more but less than 7 years	
		c 7 or more years	$ 3,000
	New commuter highway vehicle	d 3 or more years	
	Qualified progress expenditures	e 7 or more years 1974 through 1978	
		f 7 or more years 1979	
	Cost of used investment property	g 3 or more but less than 5 years	
		h 5 or more but less than 7 years	
		i 7 or more years	
	Used commuter highway vehicle	i 3 or more years	

FIGURE 7–2(C)

Partner's Share of Income, Credits, Deductions, etc.—1979
For calendar year 1979 or fiscal year
beginning ...., 1979, and ending ...., 19........
(Complete for each partner—See instructions on back of Copy C)

Copy A
(File with Form
1065)

Partner's identifying number ▶ **480-16-2080**

Partnership's identifying number ▶ **71-9367974**

Partner's name, address, and ZIP code

Frank W. Able
10 Green Street
Anytown, California 98603

Partnership's name, address, and ZIP code

A & B Distributing Company
334 West Main Street
Anytown, California 98603

		Yes	No
A (i) Date(s) partner acquired any partnership interest during the year ▶			
(ii) Did partner have any partnership interest before 1/1/77? .		✔	
B Is partner a nonresident alien?			✔
C (i) Is partner a limited partner (see page 2 of Instructions)? .			✔
(ii) If "Yes," is partner also a general partner?			
D (i) Did partner ever contribute property other than money to the partnership (if "Yes," complete line 21)? . .		✔	
(ii) Did partner ever receive a distribution other than money from the partnership (if "Yes," complete line 22)? . .			✔
(iii) Was any part of the partner's interest ever acquired from another partner?		✔	
E (i) Did partnership interest terminate during the year? . .			✔
(ii) Did partnership interest decrease during the year? . . .			✔

Time devoted to business .... **100** %

G IRS Center where partnership return filed ▶ .... **Fresno, Ca.**

H What type of entity is this partner? ▶

I Partner's share of liabilities (see page 8 of Instructions):

	(i) Incurred before 1/1/77	(ii) Incurred after 12/31/76
Nonrecourse . . .	$	$
Other	$	$ **14,681**

J Enter total amount of liabilities other than nonrecourse for which the partner is protected against loss through guarantees, stop loss agreements, or similar arrangements of which the partnership has knowledge:

Incurred before 1/1/77 . . . . $

Incurred after 12/31/76 . . . . . . $

K Partner's share of any pre-1976 loss(es) from a section 465(c)(1) activity (i.e. film or video tape, section 1245 property leasing, farm, or oil and gas property) for which there existed a corresponding amount of nonrecourse liability at the end of the year in which loss(es) occurred . . . . $

F Enter partner's percentage of:

	(i) Before decrease or termination	(ii) End of year
Profit sharing	..............%	**50** %
Loss sharing	..............%	**50** %
Ownership of capital . . .		**48.3** %

M Reconciliation of partner's capital account:

a. Capital account at beginning of year	b. Capital contributed during year	c. Ordinary income (loss) from line 1b	d. Income not included in column c, plus non-taxable income	e. Losses not included in column c, plus unallowable deductions	f. Withdrawals and distributions	g. Capital account at end of year
$ **6,500**	$ **4,597**	$ **625**	$ **325**	$ **4,252**	$ **7,145**	

	a. Distributive share item	b. Amount	c. 1040 filers enter col. b amount as shown
<6> ▶	1 a Guaranteed payments to partner: (1) Deductible by the partnership . . .	$ **5,000**	Sch. E, Part III
	(2) Capitalized by the partnership		Sch. E, Part III
<18> ▶	b Ordinary income (loss)	$ **4,597**	Sch. E, Part III
	2 Additional first-year depreciation	$ **300**	Sch. E, Part III
	3 Gross farming or fishing income		Sch. E, Part IV
	4 Dividends qualifying for exclusion	$ **75**	Sch. B, Part II, line 3
	5 Net short-term capital gain (loss) ⎰ a After 10/31/78	$ **50**	Sch. D, line 2
	from transactions entered into: ⎱ b Before 11/1/78		Sch. D, line 7
	6 Net long-term capital gain (loss) ⎰ a After 10/31/78	$ **100**	Sch. D, line 10
	from transactions entered into: ⎱ b Before 11/1/78		Sch. D, line 19
	7 Net gain (loss) from involuntary ⎰ a After 10/31/78		Form 4797, line 1
	conversions due to casualty or theft: ⎱ b Before 11/1/78		Form 4797, line 1
	8 Other net gain (loss) under section ⎰ a After 10/31/78	$ **375**	Form 4797, line 4
	1231 from transactions entered into: ⎱ b Before 11/1/78		Form 4797, line 4
	9 Net earnings (loss) from self-employment	$ **9,397**	Sch. SE, Part I or Part II
<15> ▶	10 a Charitable contributions: 50% $ **25** ......, 30% ...., 20%	$ **25**	Sch. A, line 21 or 22

19 Property qualified for investment credit:				
Basis of new investment property	a 3 or more but less than 5 years			Form 3468, line 1(a)
	b 5 or more but less than 7 years			Form 3468, line 1(b)
	c 7 or more years	$ **1,500**		Form 3468, line 1(c)
New commuter highway vehicle	d 3 or more years			Form 3468, line 1(d)
Qualified progress expenditures	e 7 or more years	1974 through 1978 . . .		Form 3468, line 1(e)
	f 7 or more years	1979		Form 3468, line 1(f)
Cost of used investment property	g 3 or more but less than 5 years			Form 3468, line 1(g)
	h 5 or more but less than 7 years			Form 3468, line 1(h)
	i 7 or more years			Form 3468, line 1(i)
Used commuter highway vehicle	j 3 or more years			Form 3468, line 1(j)

23 Partnership information on international boycotting. For partner's reporting requirements see Form 5713.	Yes	No		Yes	No
a Did partnership have operations in a boycotting country? .		✔	b Did partnership participate in or cooperate with an international boycott?		✔
			c Did partnership file Form 5713?		✔

FIGURE 7–2(D)

Schedule L—BALANCE SHEETS (See Page 10 of Instructions)

ASSETS	Beginning of taxable year		End of taxable year	
	(A) Amount	(B) Total	(C) Amount	(D) Total
1 Cash		$ 405		$ 8,620
2 Trade notes and accounts receivable	$ 7,150		$ 10,990	
a Less allowance for bad debts		7,150		10,990
3 Inventories		18,175		19,225
4 Government obligations: a U.S. and instrumentalities		1,000		4,000
b State, subdivisions thereof, etc.				
5 Other current assets (attach schedule)				
6 Mortgage and real estate loans				
7 Other investments (attach schedule)		1,000		
8 Buildings and other fixed depreciable assets	$ 16,000		$ 8,900	
a Less accumulated depreciation	4,000	12,000	5,583	3,317
9 Depletable assets				
a Less accumulated depletion				
10 Land (net of any amortization)		500		4,000
11 Intangible assets (amortizable only)				
a Less accumulated amortization				
12 Other assets (attach schedule)				
13 Total assets		$ 40,180		$ 44,152
LIABILITIES AND CAPITAL				
14 Accounts payable		$ 9,180		$ 10,462
15 Mortgages, notes, and bonds payable in less than 1 year		3,600		4,000
16 Other current liabilities (attach schedule)				
17 All nonrecourse loans (attach schedule)				
18 Mortgages, notes, and bonds payable in 1 year or more		14,900		14,900
19 Other liabilities (attach schedule)				
20 Partners' capital accounts		12,500		14,790
21 Total liabilities and capital		$ 40,180		$ 44,152

Schedule M—RECONCILIATION OF PARTNERS' CAPITAL ACCOUNTS (See Page 11 of Instructions)
(Show reconciliation of each partner's capital account on Schedule K-1, block M)

a. Capital account at beginning of year	b. Capital contributed during year	c. Ordinary income (loss) from page 1, line 26	d. Income not included in column c, plus non-taxable income	e. Losses not included in column c, plus unallowable deductions	f. Withdrawals and distributions	g. Capital account at end of year
$ 12,500	$ 1,000	$ 9,194	$ 1,250	$ 650	$ 8,504	$ 14,790

Schedule N—COMPUTATION OF NET EARNINGS FROM SELF-EMPLOYMENT (See Page 11 of Instructions)

1 Ordinary income (loss) (Form 1065, page 1, line 26)		1	$ 9,194
2 Guaranteed payments to partners included on Schedule K, lines 1a(1) and 1a(2)	2 $ 5,000		
3 Net loss from rental of real estate	3		
4 Net loss from Form 4797 (Form 1065, page 1, line 10)	4		
5 Total (add lines 2, 3, and 4)		5	5,000
6 Add lines 1 and 5. (If line 1 is a loss, reduce line 1 by the amount on line 5)		6	$ 14,194
7 Nonqualifying dividends (Form 1065, page 1, line 5)	7		
8 Interest	8		
9 Net income from rental of real estate	9		
10 Net gain from Form 4797 (Form 1065, page 1, line 10)	10 $ 400		
11 Total (add lines 7, 8, 9, and 10)		11	400
12 Net earnings (loss) from self-employment (subtract line 11 from line 6). Enter on Schedule K, line 9		12	$ 13,794

Additional Information Required

	Yes	No
I Is the partnership a limited partnership (see page 2 of Instructions)?		✓
J Is this partnership a partner in another partnership?		✓
K (1) Did you elect to claim amortization (under section 191) or depreciation (under section 167(o)) for a rehabilitated certified historic structure (see page 11 of Instructions)?		✓
(2) Amortizable basis (see page 11 of Instructions) ▶		

	Yes	No
L Will the character of any liabilities in Schedule L (Balance Sheets), other than line 17, change to nonrecourse or become covered by a guarantee or similar arrangement in the future? If "Yes," enter the year(s) and amount(s) of the anticipated changes ▶		✓

	Yes	No
M Has any material regarding the offering of a partnership interest or other security ever been registered or filed with a Federal or State agency or authority? If "Yes," attach a statement giving the name and address of the agency(s)		✓
N At any time during the tax year, did the partnership have an interest in or a signature or other authority over a bank account, securities account, or other financial account in a foreign country (see page 11 of Instructions)?		✓
O Was the partnership the grantor of, or transferor to, a foreign trust which existed during the current tax year, whether or not the partnership or any partner has any beneficial interest in it? If "Yes," you may have to file Forms 3520, 3520-A, or 926. (See page 11 of Instructions.)		✓

FIGURE 7-2(E)

Form 1120 — U.S. Corporation Income Tax Return

Form 1120
Department of the Treasury
Internal Revenue Service

U.S. Corporation Income Tax Return
For calendar year 1979 or other taxable year beginning
.............................., 1979, ending ...., 19......

1979

Check if a—
A Consolidated return ☐
B Personal Holding Co. ☐
C Business Code No. (See Page 8 of instructions) **3070**

Use IRS label. Otherwise please print or type.

Name **Tentex Novelties, Inc.**
Number and street **36 Division Street**
City or town, State, and ZIP code **Anytown, Illinois 60930**

D Employer identification number (see instruction W) **71-0395674**
E Date incorporated **3-1-68**
F Enter total assets (see instruction X) $ **873,178**

/1/	1 (a) Gross receipts or sales $ 1,940,000 (b) Less returns and allowances $ 20,000 Balance ▶	1(c) **1,920,000**
/2/	2 Less: Cost of goods sold (Schedule A) and/or operations (attach schedule)	2 **1,520,000**
/3/	3 Gross profit	3 **400,000**
	4 Dividends (Schedule C)	4 **10,000**
	5 Interest on obligations of the United States and U.S. instrumentalities	5
	6 Other interest	6 **5,500**
/4/	7 Gross rents	7
	8 Gross royalties	8
	9 (a) Capital gain net income (attach separate Schedule D)	9(a)
	(b) Net gain or (loss) from Form 4797, line 11, Part II (attach Form 4797)	9(b)
	10 Other income (see instructions—attach schedule)	10
/5/	11 TOTAL income—Add lines 3 through 10	11 **415,500**
	12 Compensation of officers (Schedule E)	12 **40,000**
/6/	13 (a) Salaries and wages 34,000 13(b) Less WIN and jobs credit(s) 6,000 Balance ▶	13(c) **28,000**
/8/	14 Repairs (see instructions)	14 **800**
/11/	15 Bad debts (Schedule F if reserve method is used)	15 **1,600**
/7/	16 Rents	16 **4,200**
/9/	17 Taxes	17 **10,000**
/10/	18 Interest	18 **7,200**
/15/	19 Contributions (not over 5% of line 30 adjusted per instructions—attach schedule)	19 **11,575**
/13/	20 Amortization (attach schedule)	20
/12/	21 Depreciation from Form 4562 (attach Form 4562) 17,600 , less depreciation claimed in Schedule A and elsewhere on return 12,400 , Balance ▶	21 **5,200**
/13/	22 Depletion	22
/16/	23 Advertising	23 **8,700**
/14/	24 Pension, profit-sharing, etc. plans (see instructions) (enter number of plans ▶ ....)	24
	25 Employee benefit programs (see instructions)	25
/16/	26 Other deductions (attach schedule)	26 **78,300**
/17/	27 TOTAL deductions—Add lines 12 through 26	27 **195,575**
	28 Taxable income before net operating loss deduction and special deductions (subtract line 27 from line 11)	28 **219,925**
/18/	29 Less: (a) Net operating loss deduction (see instructions—attach schedule) 29(a)	
	(b) Special deductions (Schedule I) 29(b) 8,500	29 **8,500**
	30 Taxable income (subtract line 29 from line 28)	30 **211,425**
	31 TOTAL TAX (Schedule J)	31 **71,806**
	32 Credits: (a) Overpayment from 1978 allowed as a credit	
	(b) 1979 estimated tax payments 77,372	
	(c) Less refund of 1979 estimated tax applied for on Form 4466 ( ) 77,372	
	(d) Tax deposited: Form 7004 .... Form 7005 (attach) .... Total ▶	
	(e) Credit from regulated investment companies (attach Form 2439)	
	(f) Federal tax on special fuels and oils (attach Form 4136 or 4136-T)	32 **77,372**
	33 TAX DUE (subtract line 32 from line 31). See instruction G for depositary method of payment.	33
	(Check ▶ ☐ if Form 2220 is attached. See page 3 of instructions.) ▶ $	
	34 OVERPAYMENT (subtract line 31 from line 32)	34 **5,566**
	35 Enter amount of line 34 you want: Credited to 1980 estimated tax ▶ 5,566 Refunded ▶	35

Under penalties of perjury, I declare that I have examined this return, including accompanying schedules and statements, and to the best of my knowledge and belief, it is true, correct, and complete. Declaration of preparer (other than taxpayer) is based on all information of which preparer has any knowledge.

Please Sign Here
▶ *James Q. Adams* Signature of officer Date **3-6-80** Title ▶ *President*

Paid Preparer's Information
Preparer's signature and date ▶
Firm's name (or yours, if self-employed) and address ▶
Check if self-employed ▶ ☐
Preparer's social security no.
E.I. No. ▶
ZIP code ▶

FIGURE 7–3(A)*

*Numbers in brackets and arrows refer to explanations furnished in the IRS publication.

1 Inventory at beginning of year . . . . | 126,000
2 Merchandise bought for manufacture or sale . . . . | 1,127,100
3 Salaries and wages . . . . | 402,000
4 Other costs (attach schedule) . . . . | 163,300
5 Total . . . . | 1,818,400
6 Less: Inventory at end of year . . . . | 298,400
7 Cost of goods sold—Enter here and on line 2, page 1 . . . . | 1,520,000
8 (a) Check all methods used for valuing closing inventory: *(i)* ☐ Cost　*(ii)* ☒ Lower of cost or market as described in Regulations section 1.471–4 (see instructions)　*(iii)* ☐ Writedown of "subnormal" goods as described in Regulations section 1.471–2(c) (see instructions)

(b) Did you use any other method of inventory valuation not described above? . . . . ☐ Yes ☒ No
If "Yes," specify method used and attach explanation ▶ ....

(c) Check if this is the first year LIFO inventory method was adopted and used. (If checked, attach Form 970.) . . . . . . ☐

(d) If the LIFO inventory method was used for this taxable year, enter percentage (or amounts) of closing inventory computed under LIFO . . . . |

(e) Is the corporation engaged in manufacturing activities? . . . . ☒ Yes ☐ No
If "Yes," are inventories valued under Regulations section 1.471–11 (full absorption accounting method)? . ☒ Yes ☐ No

(f) Was there any substantial change in determining quantities, cost, or valuations between opening and closing inventory? . . . ☐ Yes ☒ No
If "Yes," attach explanation.

Schedule C　Dividends (See instruction 4)

1 Domestic corporations subject to 85% deduction . . . . | 10,000
2 Certain preferred stock of public utilities . . . . |
3 Foreign corporations subject to 85% deduction . . . . |
4 Dividends from wholly-owned foreign subsidiaries subject to 100% deduction (section 245(b)) . . . . . |
5 Other dividends from foreign corporations . . . . |
6 Includible income from controlled foreign corporations under subpart F (attach Forms 3646) . . . . . |
7 Foreign dividend gross-up (section 78) . . . . |
8 Qualifying dividends received from affiliated groups and subject to the 100% deduction (section 243(a)(3)) . |
9 Taxable dividends from a DISC or former DISC not included in line 1 (section 246(d)) . . . . |
10 Other dividends . . . . |
11 Total—Enter here and on line 4, page 1 . . . . | 10,000

Schedule E　Compensation of Officers (See instruction 12)

1. Name of officer	2. Social security number	3. Time devoted to business	Percent of corporation stock owned		6. Amount of compensation	7. Expense account allowances
			4. Common	5. Preferred		
James Q. Adams	581-93-0936	100%	45%		23,000	
George M. Barclay	477-55-2604	100%	15%		12,000	
Samuel Collins	401-33-2611	50%	2%		5,000	
Total compensation of officers—Enter here and on line 12, page 1					40,000	

Schedule F　Bad Debts—Reserve Method (See instruction 15)

1. Year	2. Trade notes and accounts receivable outstanding at end of year	3. Sales on account	Amount added to reserve		6. Amount charged against reserve	7. Reserve for bad debts at end of year
			4. Current year's provision	5. Recoveries		
1974						
1975						
1976						
1977						
1978						
1979						

Schedule I　Special Deductions (See instructions for Schedule I)

1 (a) 85% of Schedule C, line 1 . . . . | 8,500
　(b) 59.13% of Schedule C, line 2 . . . . |
　(c) 85% of Schedule C, line 3 . . . . |
　(d) 100% of Schedule C, line 4 . . . . |
2 Total—See instructions for limitation . . . . | 8,500
3 100% of Schedule C, line 8 . . . . |
4 Deduction for dividends paid on certain preferred stock of public utilities (see instructions) . . . . . . |
5 Deduction for Western Hemisphere trade corporations (see instructions) . . . . |
6 Total special deductions—Add lines 2 through 5. Enter here and on line 29(b), page 1 . . . . | 8,500

FIGURE 7–3(B)

Source: Internal Revenue Service, "Tax Guide for Small Business, 1980 Edition," Publication No. 334 (Washington, D.C.: Internal Revenue Service, 1979).

Schedule J Tax Computation

1 Taxable income (line 30, page 1) **211,425**

2 (a) Are you a member of a controlled group? . . . . □ Yes ☒ No

   (b) If "Yes," see instructions and enter your portion of the $25,000 amount in each taxable income bracket:

   (i) $............................ *(ii)* $............................ *(iii)* $............................ *(iv)* $............................

3 Income tax (see instructions to figure the tax; enter this tax or alternative tax from Schedule D, whichever is less). Check if from Schedule D ▶ □ **78,006**

4 (a) Foreign tax credit (attach Form 1118) . . . .

   (b) Investment credit (attach Form 3468) **200**

   (c) Work incentive (WIN) credit (attach Form 4874) . . . . .

   (d) Jobs credit (attach Form 5884) **6,000**

5 Total of lines 4(a), (b), (c), and (d) **6,200**

6 Subtract line 5 from line 3 . . . . **71,806**

7 Personal holding company tax (attach Schedule PH (Form 1120)) . . . . .

8 Tax from recomputing prior-year investment credit (attach Form 4255) . . .

9 Tax from recomputing prior-year WIN credit (attach computation) . . . .

10 Minimum tax on tax preference items (see instructions—attach Form 4626) . .

11 Total tax—Add lines 6 through 10. Enter here and on line 31, page 1 . . . . **71,806**

Schedule K Record of Federal Tax Deposit Forms 503
(List deposits in order of date made—See instruction G)

Date of deposit	Amount	Date of deposit	Amount	Date of deposit	Amount
4-12-79	19,343	12-13-79	19,343		
6-13-79	19,343				
9-13-79	19,343				

		Yes	No
G (1)	Did you claim a deduction for expenses connected with:		
	(a) Entertainment facility (boat, resort, ranch, etc.)? . . .		X
	(b) Living accommodations (except employees on business)? .		X
	(c) Employees attending conventions or meetings outside the U.S. or its possessions?		X
	(d) Employee's families at conventions or meetings? . . .		X
	If "Yes," were any of these conventions or meetings outside the United States or its possessions? . . .		
	(e) Employee or family vacations not reported on Form W–2? .		X

(2) Enter total amount claimed on Form 1120 for entertainment, entertainment facilities, gifts, travel, and conventions of the type for which substantiation is required under section 274(d). (See instruction Y.) ▶ **3,365**

H (1) Did you at the end of the taxable year own, directly or indirectly, 50% or more of the voting stock of a domestic corporation? (For rules of attribution, see section 267(c).) . . . | | X

If "Yes," attach a schedule showing: (a) name, address, and identifying number; (b) percentage owned; (c) taxable income or (loss) (e.g., if a Form 1120: from Form 1120, line 28, page 1) of such corporation for the taxable year ending with or within your taxable year; (d) highest amount owed by you to such corporation during the year; and (e) highest amount owed to you by such corporation during the year.

(2) Did any individual, partnership, corporation, estate or trust at the end of the taxable year own, directly or indirectly, 50% or more of your voting stock? (For rules of attribution, see section 267(c).) If "Yes," complete (a) through (e) . . . | | X

(a) Attach a schedule showing name, address, and identifying number; (b) Enter percentage owned ▶..........................

(c) Was the owner of such voting stock a person other than a U.S. person? (See instruction S.) . . . . . .

If "Yes," enter owner's country ▶..........................

(d) Enter highest amount owed by you to such owner during the year ▶..........................

(e) Enter highest amount owed to you by such owner during the year ▶..........................

(Note: For purposes of H(1) and H(2), "highest amount owed" includes loans and accounts receivable/payable.)

		Yes	No
I	Did you ever declare a stock dividend?		X

J Taxable income or (loss) from Form 1120, line 28, page 1, for your taxable year beginning in:

1976 **107,000** , 1977 **120,000** , 1978 **115,000**

K If you were a member of a controlled group subject to the provisions of section 1561, check the type of relationship:

(1) □ parent-subsidiary   (2) □ brother-sister

(3) □ combination of (1) and (2) (See section 1563.)

L Refer to page 8 of instructions and state the principal:

Business activity **Manufacturing**

Product or service **Misc. Plastic Products**

		Yes	No
M	Did you file all required Forms 1087, 1096 and 1099?		X
N	Were you a U.S. shareholder of any controlled foreign corporation? (See sections 951 and 957.) If "Yes," attach Form 3646 for each such corporation		X
O	At any time during the tax year, did you have an interest in or a signature or other authority over a bank account, securities account, or other financial account in a foreign country (see instruction V)?		X
P	Were you the grantor of, or transferor to, a foreign trust which existed during the current tax year, whether or not you have any beneficial interest in it?		X

If "Yes" you may have to file Forms 3520, 3520–A or 926.

Q During this taxable year, did you pay dividends (other than stock dividends and distributions in exchange for stock) in excess of your current and accumulated earnings and profits? (See sections 301 and 316.) . . . . | | X

If "Yes," file Form 5452. If this is a consolidated return, answer here for parent corporation and on Form 851, Affiliations Schedule, for each subsidiary.

R During this tax year was any part of your tax accounting records maintained on a computerized system? . . . . . . | X |

S (1) Did you elect to claim amortization (under section 191) or depreciation (under section 167(o)) for a rehabilitated certified historic structure (see instructions for line 20)? . . | | X

(2) Amortizable basis (see instructions for line 20):

FIGURE 7–3(C)

Schedule L   Balance Sheets

ASSETS	(A) Amount	(B) Total	(C) Amount	(D) Total
		Beginning of taxable year		End of taxable year
1 Cash		14,700		23,712
2 Trade notes and accounts receivable	98,400		103,700	
(a) Less allowance for bad debts		98,400		103,700
3 Inventories		126,000		298,400
4 Gov't obligations: (a) U.S. and instrumentalities				
(b) State, subdivisions thereof, etc.		100,000		120,000
5 Other current assets (attach schedule)		26,300		17,266
6 Loans to stockholders				
7 Mortgage and real estate loans				
8 Other investments (attach schedule)		100,000		80,000
9 Buildings and other fixed depreciable assets	272,400		296,700	
(a) Less accumulated depreciation	88,300	184,100	105,900	190,800
10 Depletable assets				
(a) Less accumulated depletion				
11 Land (net of any amortization)		20,000		20,000
12 Intangible assets (amortizable only)				
(a) Less accumulated amortization				
13 Other assets (attach schedule)		14,800		19,300
14 Total assets		684,300		873,178
LIABILITIES AND STOCKHOLDERS' EQUITY				
15 Accounts payable		28,500		34,834
16 Mtges., notes, bonds payable in less than 1 yr.		4,300		4,300
17 Other current liabilities (attach schedule)		6,800		7,200
18 Loans from stockholders				
19 Mtges., notes, bonds payable in 1 yr. or more		176,700		264,100
20 Other liabilities (attach schedule)				
21 Capital stock: (a) Preferred stock				
(b) Common stock	200,000	200,000	200,000	200,000
22 Paid-in or capital surplus				
23 Retained earnings—Appropriated (attach sch.)		30,000		40,000
24 Retained earnings—Unappropriated		238,000		322,744
25 Less cost of treasury stock		( )		( )
26 Total liabilities and stockholders' equity		684,300		873,178

Schedule M-1   Reconciliation of Income Per Books With Income Per Return

1 Net income per books	141,744	7 Income recorded on books this year not included in this return (itemize)		
2 Federal income tax	71,806			
3 Excess of capital losses over capital gains	3,600	(a) Tax-exempt interest $ 5,000		
4 Income subject to tax not recorded on books this year (itemize)		(b) Insurance Proceeds 9,500		
				14,500
5 Expenses recorded on books this year not deducted in this return (itemize)		8 Deductions in this tax return not charged against book income this year (itemize)		
(a) Depreciation . . . . $		(a) Depreciation . . $		
(b) Depletion . . . . $		(b) Depletion . . $		
See Itemized Statement Attached	17,275	9 Total of lines 7 and 8		14,500
6 Total of lines 1 through 5	234,425	10 Income (line 28, page 1)—line 6 less 9		219,925

Schedule M-2   Analysis of Unappropriated Retained Earnings Per Books (line 24 above)

1 Balance at beginning of year	238,000	5 Distributions: (a) Cash	65,000
2 Net income per books	141,744	(b) Stock	
3 Other increases (itemize)		(c) Property	
Refund of 1978 Income Tax	18,000	6 Other decreases (itemize) Reserve for Contingencies	10,000
		7 Total of lines 5 and 6	75,000
4 Total of lines 1, 2, and 3	397,744	8 Balance at end of year (line 4 less 7)	322,744

FIGURE 7–3(D)

17% of the first $25,000,
20% of the second $25,000,
30% of the third $25,000,
40% of the fourth $25,000, and
46% of any excess over $100,000.

This new schedule went into effect following the passage of the Revenue Act of 1978. Prior corporate tax rates were 20% on the first $25,000 plus 22% on the next $25,000, and 48% on all over $50,000.

Let's assume, for the sake of illustration, that your year's profit before taxes totals $60,000. Here's the tax picture under old and new rates:

Amount of Profit	Taxable Year 1978 Tax Due	Taxable Year 1979 Tax Due
First $25,000	$ 5,000	$ 4,250
Second $25,000	5,500	5,000
Additional $10,000	4,800	3,000
Total Tax Due	$15,300	$12,250

That's a tax savings of $3,050. And–the spread between old and new rates becomes greater, should you be lucky enough to come up with more of a profit.

Nevertheless, you'll still need to pay Uncle Sam one-fifth of your $60,000 profit. (And this figure does not include the "bites" taken out by state and local governments in many areas!)

Isn't this sufficient reason to involve a top-notch accountant to watch over that bottom-line figure on your Profit and Loss Statement?

Small Business Corporation. You may elect to be taxed as an S-type corporation and thereby avoid being taxed as the usual corporation. In this case, you report your income and taxable dividends in much the same fashion as do the partners of a partnership. Certain restrictions obtain in this situation: Yours must be a domestic corporation with only one classification of stock issued; this stock must be held by no more than ten shareholders; and the shareholders may not be nonresident aliens. (Consult your tax advisor for further information.)

An information form is required by the federal government. This is Form 1120S Small Business Corporation Income Tax Return. A sample of this form is shown in Figure 7–4.

FIGURE 7–4(A)   ⟶

*Numbers in brackets and arrows refer to explanations furnished in the IRS publication mentioned below.

Form **1120S**
Department of the Treasury
Internal Revenue Service

U.S. Small Business Corporation
Income Tax Return for calendar year 1979 or

other tax year beginning ...., 1979, ending ...., 19......

1979

A Date of election as small business corporation

1-10-79

B Business code no. (see page 8 of instructions)

3070

Use IRS label. Otherwise, please print or type.

Name
Estex Fabricators, Inc.
Number and street
482 Winston Street
City or town, State, and ZIP code
Metro City, Ohio 43704

C Employer identification no. (see instruction S)
74-4487964

D Date incorporated
3-1-68

E Enter total assets from Schedule L, line 14, column (D) (see instruction T)
$ 945,184

IMPORTANT—All applicable lines and schedules must be filled in. If the space on the schedules is not sufficient, see instruction N.
Note: If section 465 (deductions limited to amount at risk) applies, see instruction for line 28.

>1<	1 (a) Gross receipts or sales $1,940,000 1(b) Less returns and allowances $ 20,000 Balance ▶	1(c)	1,920,000
>2<	2 Cost of goods sold (Schedule A) or operations (attach schedule)	2	1,520,000
>3<	3 Gross profit (subtract line 2 from line 1(c))	3	400,000
	4 (a) Domestic dividends	4(a)	10,000
	(b) Foreign dividends	4(b)	
	5 Interest on obligations of the U.S. and U.S. instrumentalities	5	
	6 Other interest	6	5,500
>4<	7 Gross rents	7	
	8 Gross royalties	8	
	9 Gains and losses (attach separate Schedule D (Form 1120S)):		
	(a) Net short-term capital gain reduced by any net long-term capital loss	9(a)	
	(b) Net capital gain (if more than $25,000, see instructions for Part IV of Schedule D (Form 1120S))	9(b)	
	(c) Ordinary gain or (loss) from Form 4797, Part II, line 11 (attach Form 4797)	9(c)	
	10 Other income (see instructions—attach schedule)	10	
>5<	11 TOTAL income—Add lines 3 through 10	11	415,500

>6<	12 Compensation of officers (Schedule E)	12	40,000
	13 (a) Salaries and wages 34,000 13(b) Less jobs credit 6,000 Balance ▶	13c	28,000
>8<	14 Repairs (see instructions)	14	800
>11<	15 Bad debts (Schedule F if reserve method is used)	15	1,600
>7<	16 Rents	16	4,200
>9<	17 Taxes	17	10,000
>10<	18 Interest	18	7,200
>15<	19 Contributions (not over 5% of line 28 adjusted per instructions—attach schedule)	19	11,575
>13<	20 Amortization (attach schedule)	20	
>12<	21 Depreciation from Form 4562 (attach Form 4562) 17,600, less depreciation claimed in Schedule A and elsewhere on return 12,400, Balance ▶	21	5,200
>13<	22 Depletion (attach schedule)	22	
>16<	23 Advertising	23	8,700
>14<	24 Pension, profit-sharing, etc. plans (see instructions) (enter number of plans ▶..............)	24	
	25 Employee benefit programs (see instructions)	25	
>16<	26 Other deductions (attach schedule)	26	78,300
>17<	27 ▶ TOTAL deductions—Add lines 12 through 26	27	195,575
>18<	28 Taxable income (loss) (subtract line 27 from line 11) (see instructions)	28	219,925

	29 Income tax on capital gains (Schedule D (Form 1120S), Part IV)	29	
	30 Minimum tax (see instructions—attach Form 4626)	30	
	31 Total tax (add lines 29 and 30)	31	
	32 Payments: (a) Tax deposited with Form 7004	32(a)	
	(b) Tax deposited with Form 7005 (attach copy)	32(b)	
	(c) Federal tax on special fuels and oils (attach Form 4136 or 4136-T)	32(c)	
	33 TAX DUE (subtract line 32 from line 31). See instruction G for depositary method of payment ▶	33	
	34 OVERPAYMENT (subtract line 31 from line 32) ▶	34	

Under penalties of perjury, I declare that I have examined this return, including accompanying schedules and statements, and to the best of my knowledge and belief, it is true, correct, and complete. Declaration of preparer (other than taxpayer) is based on all information of which preparer has any knowledge.

Please Sign Here

John H. Anderson   3-10-80   ▶ President
Signature of officer   Date   Title

Paid Preparer's Information

Preparer's signature and date ▶

Check if self-employed ▶ ☐

Preparer's social security no.

Firm's name (or yours, if self-employed) and address ▶

E.I. No. ▶

ZIP code ▶

Schedule A Cost of Goods Sold (See instructions for Line 2)

1 Inventory at beginning of year	126,000
2 Merchandise bought for manufacture or sale	1,127,100
3 Salaries and wages	402,000
4 Other costs (attach schedule)	163,300
5 Total of lines 1 through 4	1,818,400
6 Less: Inventory at end of year	298,400
7 Cost of goods sold—Enter here and on line 2, page 1	1,520,000

8 (a) Check all methods used for valuing closing inventory:

    (i) ☐ Cost (ii) ☒ Lower of cost or market as described in regulations section 1.471–4 (see instructions)

    (iii) ☐ Writedown of "subnormal" goods as described in regulations section 1.471–2(c) (see instructions)

  (b) Did you use any other method of inventory valuation not described above?   ☐ Yes ☒ No

    If "Yes," specify method used and attach explanation ▶

  (c) Check if this is the first year LIFO inventory method was adopted and used (if checked, attach Form 970)   ☐

  (d) If the LIFO inventory method was used for this taxable year, enter percentage (or amounts) of closing inventory computed under LIFO

  (e) Is the corporation engaged in manufacturing activities?   ☒ Yes ☐ No

    If "Yes," are inventories valued under regulations section 1.471–11 (full absorption accounting method)?   ☒ Yes ☐ No

  (f) Was there any substantial change in determining quantities, cost, or valuations between opening and closing inventory?   ☐ Yes ☒ No

    If "Yes," attach explanation.

Schedule E Compensation of Officers (See instruction 12)

1. Name of officer	2. Social security number	3. Time devoted to business	4. Percentage of corporation stock owned	5. Amount of compensation	6. Expense account allowances
John H. Anderson	458-74-0327	100%	45%	23,000	
Donald Briggs	560-89-5801	100%	15%	12,000	
Howard Carson	411-01-1416	50%	2%	5,000	
Total compensation of officers—Enter here and on line 12, page 1				40,000	

Schedule F Bad Debts—Reserve Method (See instruction 15)

1. Year	2. Trade notes and accounts receivable outstanding at end of year	3. Sales on account	4. Current year's provision	5. Recoveries	6. Amount charged against reserve	7. Reserve for bad debts at end of year
1974						
1975						
1976						
1977						
1978						
1979						

Additional Information Required

	Yes	No
F Did you at the end of the tax year own, directly or indirectly, 50% or more of the voting stock of a domestic corporation? (For rules of attribution, see section 267(c).)		X

If "Yes," attach a schedule showing: (1) name, address, and employer identification number; (2) percentage owned; (3) highest amount owed by you to such corporation during the year; and (4) highest amount owed to you by such corporation during the year. (**Note:** For purposes of F(3) and F(4), "highest amount owed" includes loans and accounts receivable/payable.)

G Taxable income or (loss) from line 28, page 1, Form 1120S for your tax year beginning in:

1976 ▶ _____ ; 1977 ▶ _____ ; 1978 ▶ _____

H Refer to page 8 of instructions and state the principal:

Business activity ▶ Manufacturing ; Product or service ▶ Paper Products   X

I Were you a member of a controlled group subject to the provisions of section 1561?

J If the corporation has a loss in an activity for the year, does the corporation have amounts for which it is not "at risk" in the activity (see instruction for line 28)?

K Answer only if (1) this is the first 1120S return filed since your election to be treated as a small business corporation and (2) the corporation was in existence for the tax year prior to the election and had investment credit property: Was an agreement filed under section 1.47–4(b) of the regulations?   X

FIGURE 7–4(B)

		Yes	No
L (1) Did you claim a deduction for expenses connected with:			
(a) Entertainment facility (boat, resort, ranch, etc.)?			X
(b) Living accommodations (except for employees on business)?			X
(c) Employees attending conventions or meetings outside the U.S. or its possessions?			X
(d) Employee's families at conventions or meetings?			X
If "Yes," were any of these conventions or meetings outside the United States or its possessions?			
(e) Employee or family vacations not reported on Form W–2?			X
(2) Enter total amount claimed on Form 1120S for entertainment, entertainment facilities, gifts, travel, and conventions of the type for which substantiation is required under section 274(d). (See instruction U.) ▶ **3,365**			
M Did you file all required Forms 1087, 1096, and 1099?		X	
N At any time during the tax year, did you have an interest in or a signature or other authority over a bank account, securities account, or other financial account in a foreign country (see instruction R)?			X
O Were you the grantor of, or transferor to, a foreign trust which existed during the current tax year, whether or not you have any beneficial interest in it? If "Yes," you may have to file Forms 3520, 3520–A or 926			X
P During this tax year was any part of your tax accounting records maintained on a computerized system?			X
Q (1) Did you elect to claim amortization (under section 191) or depreciation (under section 167(o)) for a rehabilitated certified historic structure (see instruction for line 20)?			X
(2) Amortizable basis (see instruction for line 20) ▶			

Schedule K Computation of Undistributed Taxable Income and Summary of Distributions and Other Items

Computation of Corporation's Undistributed Taxable Income

1 Taxable income (line 28, page 1)		219,925
2 Less: (a) Money distributed as dividends out of earnings and profits of the tax year .	65,000	
(b) Tax imposed on certain capital gains (line 31, page 1)		65,000
3 Corporation's undistributed taxable income		154,925
4 Actual dividend distributions taxable as ordinary income. (Do not include amounts shown on line 6) .		65,000
5 Actual dividend distributions taxable as long-term capital gains (after tax)		
6 Actual dividend distributions taxable as ordinary income and qualifying for dividend exclusion . . .		
7 Nondividend distributions		
8 Undistributed taxable income—taxable as ordinary income or (loss)		154,925
9 (a) Undistributed taxable income—taxable as long-term capital gain (after tax) (see instructions) .		
(b) Portion of line 9(a) attributable to transactions after 10–31–78 (after tax) (if a loss, enter zero) .		
(c) Portion of line 9(a) attributable to transactions before 11–1–78—Subtract line 9(b) from 9(a) .		

			Cost or basis
10 Investment credit property			
Basis of new investment property	(a) 3 or more but less than 5 years		
	(b) 5 or more but less than 7 years		
	(c) 7 or more years		
New commuter highway vehicle	(d) 3 or more		2,000
Qualified progress expenditures	(e) 7 or more years	1974 through 1978	
	(f) 7 or more years	1979	
Cost of used investment property	(g) 3 or more but less than 5 years		
	(h) 5 or more but less than 7 years		
	(i) 7 or more years		
Used commuter highway vehicle	(j) 3 or more		

11 Interest on investment indebtedness:		
(a) (1) Interest on investment indebtedness incurred before 12–17–69		
(2) Interest on investment indebtedness incurred before 9–11–75, but after 12–16–69		
(3) Interest on investment indebtedness incurred after 9–10–75		3,000
(b) Net investment income or (loss)		15,000
(c) Excess expenses from "net lease property"		
(d) Net capital gain attributable to investment property		
12 Items of tax preference (see instructions): (a) Accelerated depreciation on—(1) Low income rental housing . .		
(2) Other real property		
(3) Personal property subject to a lease		
(b) Amortization: (1) ...., (2) ...., (3) ...., (4)		
(c) Reserve for losses on bad debts of financial institutions		
(d) Depletion		
(e) Intangible drilling costs		
(f) Net capital gain (after tax)		
13 Jobs credit		6,000

FIGURE 7–4(C)

Form 1120S (1979)

Schedule L Balance Sheets

Assets	Beginning of tax year		End of tax year	
	(A) Amount	(B) Total	(C) Amount	(D) Total
1 Cash		14,700		101,084
2 Trade notes and accounts receivable	98,400		103,700	
(a) Less allowances for bad debts		98,400		103,700
3 Inventories		126,000		298,400
4 Gov't obligations: (a) U.S. and instrumentalities				
(b) State, subdivisions thereof, etc.		100,000		120,000
5 Other current assets (attach schedule)		26,300		11,900
6 Loans to shareholders				
7 Mortgage and real estate loans				
8 Other investments (attach schedule)		100,000		80,000
9 Buildings and other fixed depreciable assets	272,400		296,700	
(a) Less accumulated depreciation	88,300	184,100	105,900	190,800
10 Depletable assets				
(a) Less accumulated depletion				
11 Land (net of any amortization)		20,000		20,000
12 Intangible assets (amortizable only)				
(a) Less accumulated amortization				
13 Other assets (attach schedule)		14,800		19,300
14 Total assets		684,300		945,184
Liabilities and Shareholders' Equity				
15 Accounts payable		28,500		34,834
16 Mtges., notes, bonds payable in less than 1 year		4,300		4,300
17 Other current liabilities (attach schedule)		6,800		7,400
18 Loans from shareholders				
19 Mtges., notes, bonds payable in 1 year or more		176,700		264,100
20 Other liabilities (attach schedule)				
21 Capital stock		200,000		200,000
22 Paid-in or capital surplus				
23 Retained earnings—appropriated (attach schedule)		30,000		40,000
24 Retained earnings—unappropriated		238,000		239,625
25 Shareholders' undistributed taxable income previously taxed				154,925
26 Less cost of treasury stock		( )		( )
27 Total liabilities and shareholders' equity		684,300		945,184

Schedule M-1 Reconciliation of Income Per Books With Income Per Return

1 Net income per books	213,550	7 Income recorded on books this year not included in this return (itemize)	
2 Federal income tax		(a) Tax-exempt interest $ 5,000	
3 Excess of capital losses over capital gains	3,600	(b) Insurance proceeds 9,500	14,500
4 Income subject to tax not recorded on books this year (itemize)		8 Deductions in this tax return not charged against book income this year (itemize)	
5 Expenses recorded on books this year not deducted in this return (itemize)		(a) Depreciation . . . $	
(a) Depreciation . . . $			
See itemized schedule attached	17,275	9 Total of lines 7 and 8	14,500
6 Total of lines 1 through 5	234,425	10 Income (line 28, page 1)—line 6 less line 9	219,925

Schedule M-2 Analysis of Unappropriated Retained Earnings Per Books (line 24 above)

1 Balance at beginning of year	238,000	5 Distributions out of current or accumulated earnings and profits: (a) Cash	65,000
2 Net income per books	213,550	(b) Stock	
3 Other increases (itemize) Refund of 1978 income tax	18,000	(c) Property	
		6 Current year's undistributed taxable income or net operating loss (total of lines 8 and 9(a), Schedule K)	154,925
		7 Other decreases (itemize) Reserve for contingencies	10,000
		8 Total of lines 5, 6, and 7	229,925
4 Total of lines 1, 2, and 3	469,550	9 Balance at end of year (line 4 less line 8)	239,625

FIGURE 7–4(D)

Social Security Taxes

According to the provisions of the Federal Insurance Contributions Act, your employees are covered by old age, survivors, disability, and hospital insurance. To pay for such coverage, social security (FICA) taxes are levied on both employee and employer. The employer is responsible for collecting this tax from employees by withholding it the same way the employees' income tax is withheld.

Currently, this deduction is fixed at the rate of 6.05 percent of each employee's annual earnings, up to the first $17,700 of wages. This limit, or wage base is due to be gradually increased over the next few years. In addition, the firm is required to match the total amount collected from its employees, at the same rate of 6.05 percent.

Unemployment Tax

The employer is also subject to federal unemployment tax if he or she has paid wages of $1,500 or more during any quarter of the calendar year, or if one or more employees were working at least once each week (not necessarily for a full day) during each of twenty calendar weeks. The rate of taxation is 3.2 percent on the first $4,200 of wages paid to each employee during the year. However, partial credit is granted for contributions made to state unemployment taxes.

Deposits are required if the firm's tax liability exceeds $100 for any calendar quarter. Such deposits are made to a Federal Reserve bank or to an authorized commercial bank, and they are accompanied by Form 508 (Federal Unemployment Tax Deposit). The employer must file an annual return on Form 940 (Employer's Annual Federal Unemployment Tax Return) on or before January 31.

Excise Taxes

Excise taxes are levied on the sale of certain articles, on certain types of transactions and occupations, and on the use of certain products. Such taxes are not to be included in the selling price of such items but are to be charged separately by the manufacturer or the retailer.

Among the more common excise taxes are: retailers' excise taxes on diesel and aviation fuels; manufacturers' excise taxes on truck and bus bodies, tires and inner tubes, gasoline and lubricating oils, fishing equipment, and firearms; and taxes on transportation and communications services.

Businesses liable for such taxes must file Form 720 (Quarterly

Federal Excise Tax Return) even if no tax is due within any one quarter. If the tax liability exceeds $100 for any one month, deposits must be made monthly in a Federal Reserve bank or other authorized depositary. Should the tax due exceed $2,000 in any single month, deposits are made semi-monthly. All deposits are accompanied by a completed Form 504 (Federal Tax Deposit, Excise Taxes).

How to Handle Withholding Taxes

The federal government insists that business managers withhold from the regular paychecks of all employees a percentage of their earnings for income and social security taxes. Further, you are required to turn over such monies to the government on a regular basis.

Consequently, you should ask all new employees to complete a W-4 form (Employee's Withholding Allowance Certificate). Based on the information contained therein, you withhold the required percentage of each employee's gross earnings according to tables available from the Internal Revenue Service. These tables are available for different payroll periods—weekly, semi-monthly, monthly, etc. Thereafter, each succeeding year (before December 1) you should check every employee for changes in status. If there has been a change, the employee should complete a new W-4 form.

Each year, before the end of January, you must also furnish each of your employees with a completed W-2 form (Wage and Tax Statement) for the year just ended.

Withholding monies must be deposited regularly in your district's Federal Reserve bank or authorized commercial bank. Frequency of deposits will depend on the amount of your tax liability. Deposits are accompanied by Form 501 (Federal Tax Deposit—Withheld Income and F.I.C.A. Taxes). In addition, you are required to file Form 941 (Employer's Quarterly Federal Tax Return) every three months, reporting monies collected by withholding for both income and social security taxes. When you file this form for the last quarter of the year, you must provide Form W-3 (Transmittal of Income and Tax Statements) along with copies of each withholding statement issued during the year.

STATE AND LOCAL TAXES

Tax rates and other specifics vary from locale to locale across the country. Prominent among such taxes are the state (and sometimes the city) tax on gross income, real estate taxes, and sales taxes. Income taxes are tied in most ways to the details you provide on your federal income tax return; real estate taxes furnish most of the revenue required for the operation of local governments and the services they provide; sales taxes are levied on the retail prices of products or services (and collected for the taxing agencies by the retailer).

You might be responsible for other lesser taxes including unemployment and disability taxes, the corporation (or the unincorporated business) tax, and taxes on licenses and permits, among others.

FOR FURTHER INFORMATION

Books

Beckman, Gail McKnight, Berdal, Walter F., and Brainard, David G. *Law for Business and Management*. New York: McGraw-Hill, 1975.

Bower, James B. and Langenderfer, Harold Q. *Income Tax Procedure*. Cincinnati: South-Western, 1978.

Corley, Robert N. et al. *The Legal Environment of Business*. 4th ed. New York: McGraw-Hill, 1977.

Getz, G. *Business Law*, 5th ed. Englewood Cliffs, N.J.: Prentice-Hall, 1977.

J.K. Lasser Tax Institute. *How to Run a Small Business*, 4th ed. New York: McGraw-Hill, 1974.

Lane, Marc J. *Legal Handbook for Small Business*. New York: American Management Associations, 1978.

Litka, Michael P. *Business Law*, 2nd ed. Columbus: Grid Publishing, 1977.

Rosenberg, R. Robert and Ott, William G. *Business & the Law*. New York: McGraw-Hill, 1975.

Zelermeyer, William. *Introduction to Business Law*, 2nd ed. New York: Macmillan, 1971

Free Materials from the Small Business Administration

Management Aids
> #223—"Incorporating a Small Business"
>
> #231—"Selecting the Legal Structure for Your Business"

Small Marketers Aids
> #118—"Legal Services for Small Retail and Service Firms"
>
> #132—"The Federal Wage-Hour Law in Small Firms"
>
> #135—"Arbitration: Peace-Maker in Small Business"
>
> #139—"Understanding Truth-in-Lending"
>
> #142—"Steps in Meeting Your Tax Obligations"
>
> #144—"Getting the Facts for Income Tax Reporting"

8

How to Protect
Your Business

Every new business venture represents a gamble, for the future is difficult to predict. Even with a well-conceived business plan, adequate financing, and managerial experience in the same field, the entrepreneur still finds the chances for success hovering around the fifty-fifty mark at best. The odds are no different from those you face in flipping a dime and calling "Heads!" or "Tails!" The risk present in this situation is two-directional; either you win or you lose.

Many of us willingly embrace speculative risk where, although we might lose, it's also possible to win—at times a substantial sum. Indeed, the psychic excitement of the gambling situation is a well-known phenomenon. Witness the thousands who participate daily in such popular pastimes as going to the race track, buying lottery tickets (or common stocks), betting at jai-alai, or playing poker.

In some situations, the risk might run in only one direction, that of loss. Should a fire, for example, suddenly envelop your home or apartment the expected outcome can only involve loss, not gain. This kind of risk is called "pure" risk. Insurance exists primarily to protect individuals and businesses against loss caused by damage to property, life, or limb in such situations.

Yes, accidents can happen. Disaster can strike without warning. Furthermore, there is no way any business, much less any individual, can be exempted from such calamities. A serious fire can put you out of business overnight—or in an hour. A lesser blaze could cause considerable property damage, forcing you to close down your operation for weeks. A lawsuit seeking to hold you accountable for negligence that resulted in injury can threaten not only your business but also your personal assets (if your business is not incorporated).

To protect your business, it's imperative that you not only accept the existence of pure risk but also learn how to live with, and manage, it.

HOW TO APPROACH THE RISK MANAGEMENT PROBLEM

Managements adopt a variety of positions on this problem of handling risk. These range from doing nothing at all, thereby consigning their chances to fate, to attempting to cover just about every possible calamity with some kind of insurance policy.

If you don't want to join the thoroughly illogical do-nothing school, here are some common ways to approach risk management:

1. *Set up risk-reduction programs* to reduce the possibility of property damage or loss and accidental injuries within your place of business (see the list under "Protection Means More than Insurance" later in this chapter).

2. *Transfer your risk to insurance companies*, especially the major perils such as fire and casualty.

3. *Assign risk to third parties*, where possible, as in the case of the retailer who requests product liability coverage from the manufacturer in order to protect himself from possible litigation.

4. *Set aside as large a contingency fund* as you can manage, to cover potential losses, thus adopting a self-insurance posture.

5. *List your risk priorities.* Write down the various perils that could affect your business, consult with the professional, and then arrange them in order from most to least serious in their potential for damaging your business. Obviously, insurance protection against a catastrophe should find itself toward the top of your list. Included in this category are property insurance, casualty insurance, and workers compensation insurance. At the tail end of the list should be less probable risks involving the loss of smaller amounts of money. These risks you can cover with rent insurance, credit insurance, plate glass insurance, and so on.

Basic Pointers

1. *Think in terms of a well-planned program* which you need to set up initially and then maintain throughout the life of your business. Risk management consists of more than a set of insurance policies, even though such coverage will play a substantial role in the program.

2. *Seek professional help at the outset.* You are certainly not an expert in this field. Your most valuable asset here is a knowledgeable and capable insurance representative. This agent (or broker) can tailor a program to your needs, place your insurance with responsible companies, help you in negotiating claims, and advise you when in doubt.

3. *Hold down excessive costs* in several ways: set up the internal risk-reduction programs, talk frankly with your representative over policy terms and conditions, compare insurance coverages and companies where premiums might be exhorbitant or where the loss value incurred would be small, and use deductibles. Finally, it's a wise move to investigate the advantages of package policies.

4. *Keep accurate records* not only of your various coverages but also of all insured property. In the event of a claim, say, for property destroyed by fire, the insurance company requires a complete listing, down to description, age, cost or replacement value, and so forth. In this respect, "a picture is worth a thousand words!" Put these detailed descriptions in your vault or give them to your insurance agent. You must update your property lists annually.

5. *Adapt your insurance policies to changing conditions.* Keep your eye on both internal (within the firm) and external conditions and be sure you have sufficient coverage. It's wise to review your

risk management program annually and make necessary changes to ensure the vitality of your business.

PROTECTING YOUR PROPERTY: FIRE INSURANCE

No business should be initiated without insuring against the fire hazard. Although chances are good that your store or plant will never burn down, the fact that it *could* happen—that your fixtures, machinery, equipment, or inventory can be damaged, if not destroyed, by fire—should convey the urgency of such coverage.

A fire insurance policy will put you back where you were prior to the loss. It is also important for credit reasons. Unless your place is insured against this hazard, you will find it just about impossible to obtain a mortgage on it.

While the basic fire policy insures only against damage from fire or lightning, most business owners extend the scope of coverage to include additional perils, such as smoke, windstorm, hail, explosion, and riot. Protection against possible damage from vandalism and malicious mischief can also be included in your fire policy. The cost of adding these various coverages to the fire premium itself is relatively small.

A fire policy will exclude coverage for other types of items, such as cash, stock certificates, bonds, property deeds, and so forth. To cover these, additional "floater" policies might be required.

The premium you pay will be based on several factors including the location of your business (the town it is in, the neighborhood, the surrounding buildings, etc.), the condition and maintenance of your premises, and the structure and type of your building.

When you first apply for this type of coverage, it's wise to set the overall amount based on what is referred to as the actual cash value. This is the replacement cost of the property at current market prices less depreciation. The alternative is to use the purchase cost. Bear in mind, however, that when your insured amount has been based on initial cost, an allowance for depreciation over several years could bring down the covered sum considerably. A piece of equipment that originally cost you $3,000 might now be valued at less than $2,000.

Coinsurance

The concept of coinsurance, often misunderstood by the small business owner, merits some explanation. Coinsurance is designed to spread the cost of fire insurance more equitably among users. In effect, it grants lower premium rates to those who insure their property more fully. The insured firm agrees to maintain coverage on its property at a stipulated percentage of its current value (the most commonly used percentage is 80 percent). Should this agreed-upon figure not be continued and a loss occur, then the firm suffers a penalty in proportion to the deficiency.

For example, firms X and Y have each taken out a policy on their respective property (valued in each case at $200,000). Firm X has arranged for 80 percent coinsurance; its policy carries a face amount (for total loss) of $160,000. It pays about $3,000 annually in premiums. Firm Y's management feels that the chances of a total loss due to fire are rather remote and wants to "save" on its premium payments. Firm Y secures a policy in the amount of $100,000, and finds that its annual cost is about $1,900—or $1,100 less than the cost to firm X. Assume, now, that both firms have fires—and the damage in both instances totals $20,000. Firm X can then expect to receive the full $20,000 that it claims; however, firm Y is penalized because it was "underinsured." Because it had been insured for only one-half of the actual value ($100,000, instead of $200,000), only one-half of the claim value is paid—$10,000.

LIABILITY INSURANCE AND OTHER COVERAGES

There is always the possibility that you may become embroiled in legal actions brought by individuals who suffer injuries and then seek to attribute them to negligence on your part. This is an ever-present threat, one that can have serious (even fatal) consequences to a small business. Unfortunately, courts and jurists in recent years have more often favored the claimant than the defendant in such cases. Moreover, the amounts of judgments awarded in these lawsuits have skyrocketed. These actions not only cover medical, surgical, disability, and funeral expenses but also include compensation for "loss of future earnings" to dependents, the costs of defending the action, and the like.

In this context, you may be sued by anyone: customers or passersby, messengers and deliverymen, employees and, peculiarly enough, trespassers. Court action can follow such common situations as these: someone breaking a capped tooth on a piece of shell in a bowl of soup or on a chocolate covered filbert; a person tripping over a broken tile or slipping on an overly waxed floor, an individual being knocked down by another as he enters through the doorway of your store or plant, and so on.

Moreover, the accident does not have to take place on your business premises. One of your employees, on the way to the bank to make a deposit, may accidentally hurt another person—who may promptly initiate a suit against your employee and you. According to both common and statutory law, you can be held accountable for negligence that causes personal injury. Consequently, you need liability coverage for protection in this area. These policies generally cover such things as the costs of defending suits, the medical and surgical expenses involved, judgments awarded, and so on. They also contain specified limits.

It's important to realize that the amount of liability coverage can usually be increased substantially with a small increase in premium. Based upon the actual, unfortunate experiences of a good many small companies, it's prudent to seek greater coverage in this area, rather than lesser.

Automobile Insurance

Generally, a business firm insures its automobiles, trucks, and other vehicles against the possibility of physical damage and theft, as well as against bodily injury to others. To this end, they purchase commercial vehicle coverage, including collision. Rates vary considerably from one locale to another. The rates depend not only on the particular area but also on the type and age of the vehicles involved, the distances traveled by the vehicles, the ages of the drivers, and so forth.

Other Types of Insurance for Your Business

A good many other kinds of business situations which involve risk can be covered by insurance. Some of the more common risks are listed in this section. Of course, not every one is necessarily applicable to your business, nor would they all be advisable. You should discuss your particular needs in depth with your insurance agent or broker.

Business Interruption Insurance. In the event that your premises suffer a serious fire, the insurance policy you carry covers your direct losses in merchandise, equipment, the plant itself, and so forth. However, you may sustain other, indirect losses. You might not be able to get back into operation for weeks or months after extensive fire damage. This setback means that little or no income will be forthcoming for some time. Yet, you may want to continue paying salaries to your key people in the interim. At the same time, you may have to pay your monthly utility bills, meet payments on loans, send in insurance premiums that fall due, and so on.

Business interruption insurance will compensate you for the

fixed expenses that ordinarily have to be paid out while your business is interrupted.

Fidelity and Surety Bonds. Fidelity bonds are obtained from insurance or bonding companies. They are designed to protect your business against loss due to dishonesty on the part of your employees. Such bonds are available on an individual or group basis. They are especially useful where employees have access to large sums of money or inventory.

Surety bonds are of a similar nature, except that they are generally issued to guarantee performance by contractors.

Glass Insurance. Through a comprehensive glass policy, your business can be insured against damage to glass panes, doors, showcases, counter tops, signs, and the like.

Crime Insurance. The small business owner seldom links the possibility of loss through robbery, burglary, or theft to the concept of insurance coverage. Yet, it has been estimated that the total amount of business property damaged each year by fire might be, in fact, *less* than losses due to criminal acts.

Robbery insurance covers you against property loss by force or threat of violence; burglary insurance covers property stolen by someone who leaves visible signs of forced entry. The Storekeeper's Burglary and Robbery Policy is a special form of insurance available to retailers.

Comprehensive crime policies will cover both of these perils as well as other types of property theft, disappearance, or destruction. Crime insurance may not be readily available in high-risk areas. In such cases, the entrepreneur can seek coverage under the Federal Crime Program. (Your agent or broker can provide you with details.)

Water Damage Insurance. Property may be insured against accidental damage caused by water in various forms: escaping steam, overflows from refrigeration and air conditioning equipment, melting snow that leaks through roofs or basement walls, and the like.

Boiler and Machinery Insurance. Small business owners find this type of insurance of considerable interest. It is also called "power plant insurance." It protects a firm against loss due to the explosion of boilers, furnaces, engines, and similar equipment.

Group Health Insurance. This popular type of insurance policy covers you and your employees for sickness, injury, or accidental death. Three classes of coverage are usually afforded: a basic medical plan, including hospitalization and surgery; a major medical plan that provides for the high cost of physician and nurse expense both in and out of the hospital; and a disability income plan that compensates for lost earnings due to accidental injury or an illness.

WORKERS COMPENSATION INSURANCE

Under common law, you must to the best of your ability provide for your employees an environment free from the possibility of accidental injury (or occupational and radiation diseases). Responsibilities include: safe working conditions; adequate servicing and maintenance of machinery, tools, and equipment; and work procedures that prevent accidents on the job. You are even required to exercise care in hiring, selecting, and assigning workers in your business.

One of the most important features of workers compensation laws is that employees are made eligible for benefits regardless of whether you, as an employer, are guilty of negligence or not. Compliance with the laws of the various states is usually accomplished by acquiring a standard form of insurance policy. This insurance provides benefits to injured employees in the form of medical expense reimbursement and replacement of lost wages.

Your premium is based on the size of your payroll and on the kinds of jobs within your organization. The extent of the hazards faced in your type of business is also a factor. Your premium could range from as little as 1 percent of your payroll to as high as 20 percent or more. You can lower your premium, over time, through internal safety measures that reduce the accident rate in your place below the average for that particular type of business.

LIFE INSURANCE

Why Business Life Insurance?

Few mature individuals need to be convinced of the benefits offered by personal life insurance. As responsible people, they are prone to seek protection from life's uncertainties by purchasing one or more life insurance policies in addition to their homeowners' and automobile policies. Yet, many business owners are reluctant to think in terms of *business* life insurance, feeling this is a luxury they cannot afford.

This is a shortsighted attitude which I hope you do not share. Indeed, business life coverage may be something you can't afford to be without! I'm referring to long-range possibilities. When you die, or if you become disabled, what will happen to that successful business you have built? How will your family manage? If the business must be liquidated, who will take care of this? Or, if yours is a partnership, and a partner passes away, how can you protect your share of ownership?

With the help of your life insurance representative (and your attorney and accountant), you can tailor your business life insurance to your specific needs.

Business life policies can be written to protect owners and their families against financial loss due to death or serious injury. Prearrangements can be made to assure the business continues in this event. With life insurance to provide necessary cash and a properly-prepared "buy-and-sell" agreement, the deceased's share of ownership may be returned quickly and fully to the heirs, and the surviving owners are enabled to carry on the business without interruption.

"Key man" insurance provides a similar kind of protection. The untimely death of a valuable employee (for example, a top salesman, the manager of a meat department, a chief designer, or someone important) can seriously affect the performance of a firm. The insurance proceeds from "key man" coverage can be used by your business to offset a loss in profits or to pay for the cost of hiring and training a replacement.

Incidentally, an important benefit of business life insurance lies in the fact that the cash accumulation in the permanent-type policy is available as a reserve fund for contingencies, or even for retirement.

Types of Life Insurance

Four basic types of life insurance are described in this section.

Whole Life. This is also known as "ordinary" or "straight" life. You are covered for the face amount of the policy throughout your lifetime. The premium, too, is calculated to be paid over the course of your lifetime. This type of policy carries a limited cash surrender value as well as loan privileges and other nonforfeiture values.

Limited Payment Life. A variation of whole life insurance, the limited policy requires the payment of premiums for a set number of years (fifteen, twenty, or more). At the end of this period, no more premiums are paid—the policy is then fully paid up. Thereafter, the insured remains covered for the rest of his or her life. Since the premiums are higher than those paid for a whole life policy, this type has a substantial cash surrender and loan value.

Endowment Life. This form of insurance has many provisions similar to the limited payment life policy in that the policy owner continues to pay premiums for a designated number of years until the policy is fully paid up. At this point, the accumulated cash value equals the face amount and is paid out in a lump sum (endowment) to the policy owner. Other provisions for payment are also available.

Term Life. Generally, this requires the lowest dollar outlay for life insurance because the premiums paid are completely used up for the sole purpose of insurance protection. Because of this, the policy does not accumulate a cash reserve for the insured and, consequently, has no cash surrender value or loan possibilities.

Term policies, as the name implies, provide protection for a given period of time. However, many types are renewable for a similar period of time. Some common types are the annual renewable, five-year renewable, and mortgage decreasing-term policies.

PROTECTION MEANS MORE THAN INSURANCE

Even though insurance coverage is available to protect your business against nearly every kind of threat, relying only on insurance is foolhardy. You can take many steps to help reduce risk. Consider carefully the various kinds of risk and how to guard against them, and you will keep your losses down.

Some Ways to Avoid Casualty Losses

You can also take many preventive measures to safeguard your business against fire or accidental injury:

1. Place approved fire extinguishers in selected spots around the facility. Check them on a regular basis. See to it that your personnel know of their locations.

2. Hold fire drills periodically until everyone in your place knows exactly what to do and where to go in case of fire.

3. Store inflammable materials in proper, closed containers and keep these containers in a cool area.

4. Install a sprinkler system. Use smoke alarms in storage rooms.

5. Make certain that fire doors and exits are clearly marked.

6. Keep aisles, passageways, and stairwells free from all encumbrances.

7. Maintain all equipment and machines in good condition. Place guard rails and other protective devices around machinery with moving parts. Train employees thoroughly in the proper handling of all equipment.

8. Practice good housekeeping. Don't permit trash to accumulate on the premises.

Burglary, Robbery, and Theft

Every business is vulnerable to loss through criminal activity. Theft is a blanket term: It includes shoplifting, embezzlement, and employee pilferage as well as the more "professional" crimes of burglary and robbery.

Shoplifting. Retail enterprises are particularly susceptible to larceny by shoplifters, amateurs as well as professionals. Unfortunately, assaults upon the retailer's profit picture are so prevalent these days that department stores, discount houses, and other mass merchandisers maintain their own private security forces, in addition to employing every imaginable type of security device.

Small-scale retailing can't afford this kind of expense.

Employee Theft. Employees can steal small, inexpensive articles (pencils, typewriter ribbons, rubber bands, and the like), and they can take home larger merchandise, too. Occasionally an employee who is in a position of substantial trust steals money from the cash drawer or juggles the books to conceal theft.

Ways to Reduce Losses from Theft

The business owner can take many steps to hold down losses from criminal acts.

Your Employees Can Help

1. Train your employees to be alert: to watch people who enter your store with coats over their arms or carrying shopping bags or bulky packages; to keep an eye on those who look or act suspicious; to wait promptly on customers.

2. In hiring new people, make certain your selection and screening procedures are good. Make it known from the begin-

ning that you expect honesty in all your employees, and set a personal example with your own behavior at all times.

3. Train your personnel to be calm and cooperative in the event of a holdup. A life is a priceless thing that no amount of money can replace.

4. If possible, always schedule at least two individuals to open up in the morning and close at night, and to make bank deposits.

5. Try to maintain adequate floor coverage by adding extra clerks during busy hours.

Tighten Up on Procedures and Policies
6. Keep good records in accordance with good accounting procedures.

7. If possible, sign all checks yourself. Never sign blank checks to leave behind when traveling or on vacation.

8. Make certain all cash disbursements have your personal approval.

9. Try to reconcile all bank statements throughout the year. Review all canceled checks and their endorsements.

10. Keep close watch over the shipping and receiving functions. This includes setting up tight recordkeeping systems within both departments, supervising the loading and unloading of trucks, and even fencing off the two areas from other departments.

11. Always remove excess cash from the cash register and place in the safe. Bank frequently, and at different times from day to day. Leave the cash drawer empty and open at night (to avoid possible forced entry that might damage the equipment).

12. Keep all keys locked up when not in use, and issue as few as you have to, in order to avoid unnecessary duplication.

13. Prosecute any shoplifter who is apprehended and any employee caught stealing. (If there is any doubt whatsoever in a particular incident, it might be wiser to avoid prosecution because of the possibility of a lawsuit for false arrest.)

14. To prevent sales clerks pocketing change or bills from the register, insist on issuing register receipts to all customers. An even better arrangement is making out sales slips for each and every sale.

What to Do With the Premises

15. Use anti-shoplifting signs around the premises to discourage petty larceny.

16. Equip your store with convex wall mirrors, two-way mirrors, and closed-circuit television cameras that move to encompass a view of a wide area (even if these are only dummies!).

17. In retail stores, place small, expensive items in locked showcases. Tie down merchandise on display wherever practical.

18. Locate your check-out stand or cash register near the store's exit. If you can afford to, station a guard at the exit as well.

19. Your business premises should be adequately illuminated at night. This applies to the area around the building or store (front/sides/back) as well as inside.

20. Install a good alarm system, preferably a central system, on the premises. In high-risk areas, consider additional safeguards, such as gratings, a private patrol service, and so on.

21. Protect all doors and entrances with properly installed, pin-tumbler type cylinder locks.

22. Safes should be of high quality, fire resistant, and fastened to the building itself.

FOR FURTHER INFORMATION

Books

Greene, Mark R. *Risk and Insurance*, 4th ed. Cincinnati: South-Western, 1977.

Mehr, Robert I. and Cammack, Emerson. *Principles of Insurance*, 6th ed. Homewood, Ill.: Irwin, 1976.

Mehr, Robert I. and Hedges, Bole A. *Risk Management: Concepts and Applications*. Homewood, Ill.: Irwin, 1974.

Mehr, Robert I. *Life Insurance: Theory and Practice*, rev. ed. Dallas: Business Publications, 1977.

Riegel, Robert, Miller, Jerome S., and Williams, C. Arthur, Jr. *Insurance Principles and Practices: Property and Liability*, 6th ed. Englewood Cliffs, N.J.: Prentice-Hall, 1976.

White, Edwin H. and Chasman, Herbert. *Business Insurance*, 4th ed. Englewood Cliffs, N.J.: Prentice-Hall, 1974.

Williams, C. Arthur, Jr. and Heins, Richard M. *Risk Management and Insurance*, 3rd ed. New York: McGraw-Hill, 1976.

Free Materials from the Small Business Administration

Management Aids

#209—"Preventing Employee Pilferage"

#222—"Business Life Insurance"

Small Marketers Aids

#119—"Preventing Retail Theft"

#129—"Reducing Shoplifting Losses"

#134—"Preventing Burglary and Robbery Loss"

#137—"Outwitting Bad Check Passers"

#148—"Insurance Checklist for Small Business"

#151—"Preventing Embezzlement"

Available from the Superintendent of Documents

Small Business Management Series:

#30—"Insurance and Risk Management for Small Business," Stock
#045-000-00037-1; 72 pp.; $1.90.

III

Business Foundations

Now that the preliminaries are well behind you, it's time to get down to business!

Remember: A lack of managerial experience is one of the prime reasons for failure in small business. Clearly, the majority of new entrepreneurs are not capable, trained managers. Worse yet, they lack the benefit of a formal education in business administration.

Although it's no replacement for actual high-level experience, a thorough knowledge of business management essentials will definitely help your chances for success.

Included in this next section (the largest section of the book) are all the major facets of running a business. You will find chapters on business administration and on leadership, five solid chapters on the various components of the marketing process, and other chapters that deal with production management, finances, and personnel.

The material in Part III of this book represents a condensed college curiculum in business administration.

9

An Introduction to Business Administration

A vital component of human rationality, which distinguishes humankind from the beast, is the faculty for making order out of chaos. Human beings must organize innumerable pieces of knowledge into usable wholes in order to function effectively in their environment. Organizing involves arranging, classifying, and systematizing, as well as thinking and planning. These processes are characteristic of individuals and of groups. Every organization or institution reflects those processes because they are established and administered by human beings. Moreover, since people are so incredibly diverse, we find that all their groupings and institutions reflect a myriad of variations in both form and substance.

On a purely philosophical plane, it appears to me that all living things are motivated toward two basic goals: the programmed will to maintain their existence (to continue to live, to protect, to defend and when necessary, to repair themselves) and the instinct to grow, to perpetuate their kind.

Plants, animals, the tiniest of microscopic organisms, and we humans as well, all possess these essential twin motivations. Furthermore, all human groups display these same drives, whether they be families or social groups, religious denominations or political associations, small villages or sprawling nations.

Your new business is just such a grouping, engaged in a purposeful activity and endowed with a spirit and vitality that stem from those built-in goals. Your group is a curious mixture of people, things, and activities which ideally is so ordered, so arranged and woven into an intricate network, so purposeful and coordinated that it is able to strive towards those two overriding objectives like a single, though complex, organism. Operating like a complicated piece of machinery, your firm is a system of individual pieces, parts, cogs, and wheels all working together in common endeavor—to continue its existence and to grow.

Every business is a society in miniature with its own body of rules and regulations, its uses, ways, and customs. As in our larger society, its "citizens" play out their assigned roles. A business is also a stratified—that is, a grouped and subgrouped—society that designates expected behavior for each person according to status, class and other criteria.

To demonstrate this, think about the traditional department store organization with its hundreds of employees distributed throughout a hierarchy of power and authority. Top management includes the board of directors, its chairman, and the corporation's president. Next is the operating management, generally a committee of assorted vice presidents heading up specialized functions of store operations, merchandising, personnel management and others. Then there are various levels of middle and lower management including the merchandise managers, the floor and department managers, the buyers, the salesclerks and cashiers.

Within this society in miniature, there are two kinds of people: the leaders who use their power and authority, skills and techniques to influence the others, and the rest, the larger number of helpers who collectively push the organization toward its objectives.

Yes, the structure and organization in your company is integrated into a total master plan which you design to accomplish your goals. This network places people into niches, and each niche becomes a vital link in the overall effective operation of this dynamic system.

WHAT ADMINISTRATION IS

To administer any activity (or, for that matter, any business or institution) is to run it, to direct it, or, more simply, to manage it. From giant multinational corporations to tiny one-person operations, *every* enterprise needs an astute administration to direct and integrate all the components—the people, the equipment, the practices and techniques applied in daily functioning, the financial aspects, and so forth.

The words "administrator, " "executive," "leader," and "manager" all connote the same basic work, illustrated in the following example: A seasoned army general is preparing for a major battle. Together with his staff officers, he first sets his objectives and then prepares a comprehensive battle plan designed to garner victory. Subsequently, he gathers, arranges, and coordinates, all his *matériel de guerre:* his intelligence reports; his troops and their officers; the tanks, guns, and ammunition; gasoline, food, and medical supplies; his air cover and other support systems. (Here we see the military leader exercise two of the four basic management functions: *planning* and *organizing.*)

Once the master plan has been fully devised and all elements coordinated, the general then puts the plan into action. He directs the activities as the plan unfolds, supervising the details and evaluating the results as events occur. He does this carefully, so that any deviations from the planned outcome can be confronted as they happen, and contingency actions can be taken to bring things back into line and on target. (Here are the other two management functions in action: *directing* and *controlling.*)

With relation to your business, you are the general, the directing force. To administer your business successfully, you will find that you must be continually exercising one or more of those four functions.

You need to operate on a two-dimensional front. In the impersonal dimension you are engaged in activities such as setting priorities, allocating resources, scheduling, decision-making, and the like. On the personal side of things you must lead and motivate people, train and develop their skills, counsel them, and so forth.

Both dimensions involve particular *skills* and specific *functions*. All of Chapter 10 is devoted to the skills of "Leadership in Management." Here follows a discussion of the four functions of a good administrator—planning, organizing, directing, and controlling.

PLANNING

No doubt about it. Planning is hard work; it involves thinking and thinking is always hard work. In essence, planning is problem-solving and decision-making: considering alternatives; speculating on the future (near and far); and setting objectives (long- and short-range).

Future planning necessitates flexibility to cope with the unexpected, setting timetables, fixing priorities, and deciding methods to be used and the people who'll be involved. As administrator you must analyze the existing situation, formulate targets, and apply both logic and creativity to all the details in between.

Small business owners are generally busy running their operations and often shunt planning to the sidelines. Yet, I cannot overemphasize its importance! As the owner of a small business, you *must* plan for it even more intensively than the chairman of the board of a large company because you don't have the large financial reserves to cover a serious mistake. Poor planning can put you out of business.

Planning: An Overview   Here is a list of preliminary planning activities for small business managers.

1. Explore diligently your firm's *raison d'être* and clarify the purposes for which you've established it.
2. After careful discussion of these purposes, formulate your overall, long-term company goals.
3. Examine these goals, one by one, and then make a list of specific objectives to be accomplished over, say, the next five years.
4. Designate specific objectives for each subdivision within your firm (such as marketing, finance, and personnel).

5. Decide on policies for each department, making sure they conform with those objectives.

6. Finally, outline strategies for accomplishing the objectives, using the available company resources.

Planning Isn't Easy

Talk to any business executive: Chances are that he or she is usually far too busy trying to surmount day-to-day problems to spend much time at all at planning. If you follow an administrator throughout the day, you will see that person spending time and effort doing things like visiting his people at their daily chores, chatting with them, making suggestions, and providing assistance. That's probably because it is far easier to move about, to do something of a physical nature, than to think. Thinking requires lots of concentration, plenty of mental effort.

Some people are a bit suspicious about planning because they realize it has to do with the future, not the present, and the future is really unpredictable. So (they think) why bother? Furthermore, many people have never been taught how to plan and haven't the foggiest idea as to how to proceed. Maybe they resist the need for imposing self-discipline or don't have enough confidence in themselves. Perhaps they are reluctant to think on a conceptual plane. Perhaps they have never mastered the art of establishing priorities.

Whatever the reasons, planning is often deferred to the future. Yet, planning gives purpose and direction to daily business activities. Without it, such activities are aimless and uncoordinated.

Types of Plans   Long- and short-term plans and "master plans" are set up by top management to give overall direction to company efforts. Plans of a strategic nature cope with the changing environment. "Operational plans" design day-to-day work details. "Single-use" plans are formulated for specific situations. "Standing" plans, on the other hand, are set up for repeated use over a longer period of time.

Company policies are examples of standing plans. They serve as guidelines for management and employees, imparting a solidarity and dependability to company operations. These policies exist in all areas of a well-administered business—in production, pricing, distribution, personnel, finance, and the like. A few examples of production policies: (1) to manufacture only those products that enjoy a brisk sales volume (that is, over 10,000 units a month); (2) to add to the product line up to three new items each year; (3) to produce only items requiring raw materials that can be purchased domestically and from several sources.

Budgets are plans that have been translated into dollars-and-cents projections and that are the culmination of a lot of careful analysis. In effect, they are both guides to follow and targets to shoot for. Materials budgets and sales budgets, budgets for labor, and budgets for capital expenditures—all become standards for management action. Good budgeting is needed to direct internal activity and to assign responsibility.

Planning: A Step-By-Step Approach   Using the outline below, plan for two or three separate events; this exercise will help you internalize the method rapidly. Practice, after all, makes perfect! It's helpful to plan for something concrete for the first go-round, such as a major promotion for the Spring.

1. Assess the present state of affairs, external (the economy, your competition, and the like) as well as internal.
2. Set the target date for the activation of the plan.
3. Make a forecast of the future state of affairs (at the target date and, thereafter, for the duration of the plan-to-be).
4. List specific objectives that are both reasonable and attainable.
5. Develop methods for reaching the objectives.
6. Work out the details by using the Five Ws (Who? What? Where? When? Why?)—and How? Determine your resources and structure your plan with a time schedule.
7. Set up a control system to monitor the plan's operation and to make adjustments for deviations from planned outcomes.
8. As the plan unfolds, make the necessary adjustments to compensate for such deviations.

Some Comments on Forecasting   Planning is disciplined thinking, which is based on the present and oriented to the future. Plans begin with an analysis of the way things are and with a forecast of the way things will (or should) be. Of course, predicting future events based on an extrapolation of current—and incomplete—information can never be entirely accurate.

Begin any major forecasting effort with a full consideration of the general state of the economy. Then move down to the next level and appraise conditions within the industry of which your firm is a member. After that evaluate the state of the firm itself.

Among the variables affecting your forecast are such uncontrollable factors as the Gross National Product (present and future), unemployment levels, productivity indexes, population trends, government policies, and the like. When you make predictions, watch the various business indicators and project accordingly: stock prices, corporate profits, wholesale price levels, and others.

Not only should you use such indexes and study trends, but also gather opinions and interpretations from other people. You must also exercise a personal judgment; for example, when you make projections for next year's sales, not only use the available statistics but also evaluate the capabilities of your sales force and sales manager.

ORGANIZING AND ORGANIZATION

As your business grows, you will discover that along with increasing volume there are increasing duties and responsibilities. Eventually, you'll reach the point where you have to seek assistance so you can allocate your energies and time more beneficially to your business.

At that point, the seeds of your new organization have sprouted. Now you must pay heed to management principles like specialization and the division of work.

As each new employee is hired, he or she must be placed in an appropriate niche and assigned a specific set of duties. As the business administrator, your task is to define those niches and then locate the right poeple to fill them. Briefly, you must match people with jobs.

Figure 9–1, for example, describes some of the activities you need to perform in a small retail business in its pre-organization or one-man-operation stage. According to this chart, the owner must allocate time to three activity areas: buying, selling, and controlling finances. In addition, however, each work cluster or category involves a number of specific tasks. Purchasing merchandise for resale, for example, would include seeking out and visiting sources of supply, viewing potential merchandise to carry in the store, negotiating prices and terms, arranging for delivery, and so forth.

At first, all these necessary functions are performed by one individual. Then, as sales increase, there's more work to be done. When an owner hires the first employee, or helper, there's an inclination to delegate very few tasks. An owner does not permit the newcomer to do the buying simply because experience is needed before a person can do the purchasing job well. Moreover, purchasing the right goods at the right prices is a major factor in the profit picture and an owner is certainly reluctant to relinquish control over this important area.

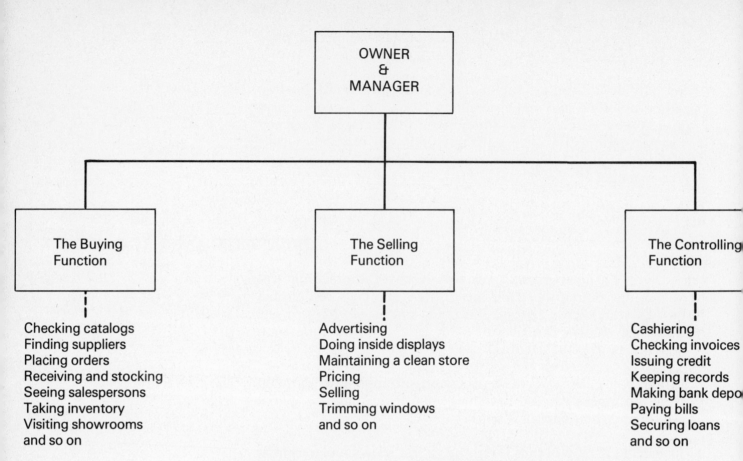

FIGURE 9–1. A typical one-man retail "organization" chart.

For similar reasons, an owner resists turning over any of the major financial aspects of the business to the new employee. So, in most cases the employee in the typical small store is assigned to the selling function, thus affording the owner more time to do a better job at both purchasing and controlling finances.

The simple chart in Figure 9–2 depicts the work responsibilities of a small retail company with four employees. Over time, a company's management is increasingly challenged by the task of coordinating the burgeoning activities of daily operations. Each business depends on the people within who, interlocked and strategically deployed in some structural arrangement, perform all the functions necessary for the total system to accomplish its objectives. This framework or structure called "organization" represents, in actuality, the overall strategic design for operation. A positive, forward-looking structure, it is a unified plan of action.

Some Basics from Organization Theory

Organization is not and cannot be an exact science; theories of organization cannot specify wholly right answers. Nevertheless,

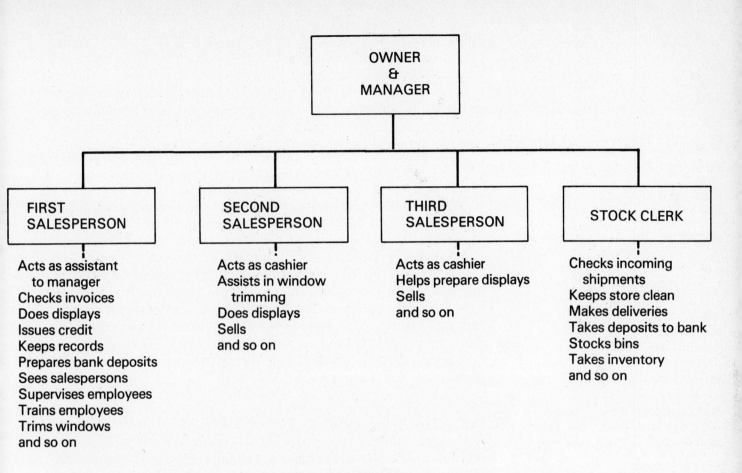

FIGURE 9–2. Organization chart of a small retail company.
*Owner can now devote more time to the *buying* and *control* functions. In addition, he or she must now *oversee all* employees. The owner begins to rely more heavily upon the first employee to train and supervise the others.

the small business manager ought to be familiar with the dimensions which are more frequently discussed by organizational theorists.

Employee Goals Can Be at Odds with Company Goals. You should recognize at the outset that people working in your organization are there primarily to satisfy their own needs. Either they want security and income or the feeling they have a place within a group, or they need to be recognized as somebody important, and so on. Although they will work willingly toward your firm's objectives, this occurs only if their own personal aims remain attainable through employment with you. Their goals and yours are not identical; at times, differences between individual and group goals will result in conflict. For the sake of internal harmony, you must concentrate on reconciling any differences which arise.

A Need for Departmentation. As anyone in business realizes, there is a wealth of activities that need to be performed by your employees. Handling this bulk is made easier by classifying the many work details into departments. Departments are segments of the business whose work functions are interrelated and so can be grouped together under the supervision of a single specialist. In addition to the sales, production, and bookkeeping departments, other departments commonly seen in business include purchasing, shipping, receiving, payroll, advertising, and the like.

Line and Staff Personnel. Most organizations have been arranged according to the "line-and-staff" concept. As the terms are used, line people both give and receive orders along the chain of command from the head of the company down to the lowest level worker. People in staff positions, on the other hand, are outside this chain of command. They are present to aid and support the line personnel. Examples of these staffers include administrative assistants, legal advisors, personnel departments, and other supportive service workers. These people possess a much more limited kind of authority. Within their own specialized areas of responsibility, they direct their own departments' personnel. You may have to cope with internal friction which can result from this type of organization.

Should Your Organization Be Flat or Tall? As a business grows, the organizational structure shows layers of authority—top, middle, and lower (supervisory) management; communication barriers tend to form between the layers. People at the top of the hierarchy tend to have little contact with people at the bottom. In the traditional "tall" structure, people become relatively confined within their own specialized positions and dissatisfaction begins to emerge from persons in middle and lower positions. Broadly interpreted, their feeling is that they are not really making a significant contribution to the business. This attitude spreads or deepens and decisions tend more and more to be made at the top and filtered down to the bottom levels.

Furthermore, management positions multiply. The organization gradually becomes laden with many chiefs and higher salaries. A kind of rigidity sets in that mitigates against creative problem-solving and results in an overabundance of red tape.

On the other hand, in the "flat" type of organization, there are only one or two levels of management. The supervisory leadership exerted by the executives is of a more personal nature, with more fact-to-face contact. People in lower management niches take on more responsibility for their efforts and make more decisions. The fact that these individuals are closer to the action than higher management and are permitted to make decisions on the spot makes for increased initiative and higher morale.

One Boss or More?   The "unity of command" principle is one policy which should seldom be violated. Most workers would agree that no employee, indeed no executive, should have to answer to more than one superior. More than one boss can cause confusion, as, for example, where an employee working within a partnership arrangement is given two opposing directives by the partners.

How Many Subordinates Can You Handle?   The principle here is referred to as "span of control". The average manager finds it relatively easy to supervise one to several workers on the job, to watch over them, to train them, to direct, and to guide them. As the number of subordinates increases it becomes more and more difficult for the supervisor to devote enough attention to each person.

The number of people a person can supervise depends upon several factors: the supervisor's capabilities; the abilities and characteristics of the subordinates; and the nature of the work being performed. The greater the span of control (that is, the number of people under one superior), the fewer the number of supervisors and departments necessary. A narrow span, however, enables supervisors to work more closely with their people.

The average small business owner can usually manage up to six or eight subordinates before things become too unwieldy.

Decentralization.   As business grows, the mass of work details increases. Yet, it's hard for the entrepreneurial personality to delegate, to let go of the responsibilities so far handled alone, and now to assign them to people who are less capable and less motivated.

Some managements keep a firm grasp on everything. They maintain home offices where power, authority, and tight supervisory controls are centralized. Others decentralize to the point where a capable group, to a large degree autonomous, manages each major division of the business. The concept of decentralization, organizing a firm around self-governing "profit centers" banded together in a loosely controlled federation, maximizes individual initiative, ensures localized decision-making, and facilitates the pinpointing of responsibility.

Methods for Delegating Work.   One day the very existence of your business will depend on relinquishing some of the details to assistants. You will be faced with the delegation problem. Here are some guidelines suggested by the SBA to assist the small business owner in delegating work.

- Do it slowly
- Give your employee facts to work with
- Share your knowledge
- Add responsibility gradually
- Hold a loose rein
- Give authority
- Tolerate mistakes
- Train the employee well

DIRECTING

After you've prepared the plan and organized the five "Ms" (manpower, machinery, money, methods, and materials), you initiate the third step in the administrative sequence—directing the plan.

This area really tests the mettle of the operating executive. This is the "hands-on" point. Until now the administrative activity has been mostly in the mind of the planner(s). Now you're involved in a one-to-one contact sport. The people in your organization must be motivated, persuaded, led, coordinated, encouraged, ad infinitum. Involved here are concepts like teamwork, supervision, and productivity. For the most part, these concepts constitute the subject matter of the next chapter ("Leadership")—and so little more needs to be said at this point.

CONTROLLING

An analysis of the controlling function would seem to indicate the need for measuring results all along the way while the plan is unfolding, as well as the necessity for making adjustments where and when needed. Logically, the control function cannot be separated from the planning function; they are interdependent, much like the two sides of the same coin.

The control process includes analysis, setting standards, monitoring, securing feedback, and taking corrective action.

1. *Analysis:* Study and compare, for quantity and quality, the output of people and machines, the products made, the systems employed, and so forth. Examine everything with an eye to standards and decision-making.
2. *Setting Standards:* As a result of analysis, establish acceptable standards of performance in all areas. In turn, these standards become control valves, quantitative and qualitative measurements for future performance, guidelines for projecting cost, time, and sales.

3. *Monitoring:* You need regular inspection and performance checks to note exceptions to the standards you've set and possible reasons for the deviations.

4. *Securing Feedback:* A foolproof system for reporting deviations from standards must be established so that the proper people are notified regularly and promptly.

5. *Corrective Action:* Finally, all exceptions to the established standards must be acted on. Adjustments need to be made promptly so that contingent outcomes are brought back on target.

All areas of a business must be subject to this control function. You might think quite readily of inventory control, order processing, quality control, and production control. Yet, controls are just as necessary in the personnel area (for example, in performance evaluation), in the financial end of things (where ratios can be used to investigate a variety of problems), in the long-term planning of projects, and so forth.

For control is, in essence, self-discipline.

THE ROLE OF COMMUNICATION

Business runs on communication. Prospective customers are located, contacted, and persuaded to buy products and services through communication. Similarly, employees are found, hired, trained, and directed; departments are managed; machines are manned and operated. Communication is the oil that lubricates the various gears and cogs in the free enterprise system.

Let's examine the process of communication in business. There are a number of components involved. Indeed, communication in business appears to be a closed system with all parts interacting in synergistic fashion. The major elements are discernible in Figure 9–3, which simplifies a company's external communications with its customers.

Some essential parts of the communication system are:

- *source:* the sender or originator of the messages,
- *messages:* information emitted by the source and directed to the receivers,
- *media:* the various carriers or transmitters of the messages (such as radio, newspaper, billboards, and the like),
- *receivers:* those for whom the messages are intended, and
- *feedback:* customer reactions, demographics, and other facts returned by or drawn back from customers to assist management in its decision-making.

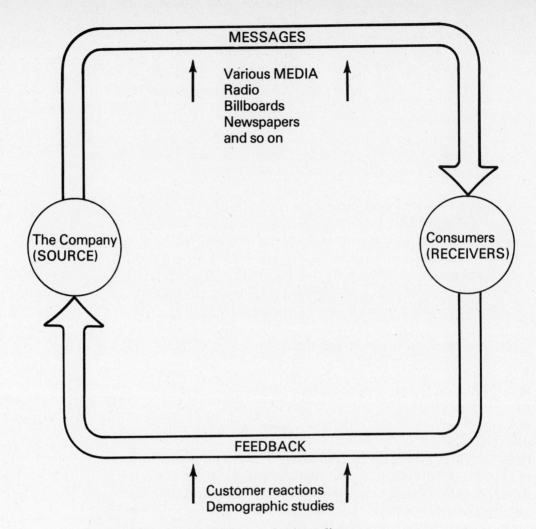

FIGURE 9-3. External communications diagram.

Improvements within any of these areas—for example, in the quality of messages sent, in the selection of more appropriate media, or the refinement or elaboration of the feedback system—improves the productivity of the entire system.

Applied to a firm's internal organization, the communications picture looks something like the diagram in Figure 9–4. Messages (orders, etc.) are passed down from the owner to lower levels, through verbal and written communications. Feedback moves upward, completing the system. Of course, the effectiveness of the system is based on unimpeded horizontal communication on each individual level.

Unfortunately, poor communication is frequent within organizations, perhaps due to the pressures of day-to-day details which make communicating on a one-to-one, face-to-face basis nearly impossible. As business owner, make certain that all orders, instructions, and other messages to employees are couched in

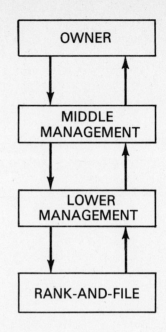

FIGURE 9–4. Internal communciations.

terms that can be clearly understood and that convey your exact meaning. To accomplish this, learn to look at things from the employees' point of view and become familiar with their vocabulary. Moreover, listening is an important asset in communication; half-hearted listening interferes considerably with your effectiveness. Encourage your people to listen, too. Make sure they understand your instructions. Encourage them to ask questions.

As a final point, train all your supervisory personnel to be effective communicators too.

FOR FURTHER INFORMATION

Books

Albrecht, Karl. *Successful Management by Objectives.* Englewood Cliffs, N.J.: Prentice-Hall, 1977.

Coventry, W. F., and Burstiner, Irving. *Management: A Basic Handbook.* Englewood Cliffs, N.J.: Prentice-Hall, 1977.

Donnelly, James H. Jr., Gibson, James L., and Ivancevich, John M. *Fundamentals of Management: Functions, Behavior, Models.* 3rd ed. Dallas: Business Publications, 1978.

Giegold, William C. *Management by Objectives: A Self-Instructional Approach.* New York: McGraw-Hill, 1978.

Koontz, Harold, and Fulmer, Robert M. *A Practical Introduction to Business.* rev. ed. Homewood, Ill.: Irwin, 1978.

Rachman, David J., and Mescon, Michael H. *Business Today.* New York: Random House, 1976.

Reitz, H. Joseph. *Behavior in Organizations.* Homewood, Ill.: Irwin, 1977.

Sisk, Henry L. *Management and Organization,* 3rd ed. Cincinnati: South-Western, 1977.

Terry, George R. *Principles of Management,* 7th ed. Homewood, Ill.: Irwin, 1977.

Williams, J. Clifton. *Human Behavior in Organizations.* Cincinnati: South-Western, 1978.

Free Materials from the Small Business Administration

Management Aids

    # 179—"Breaking the Barriers to Small Business Planning"

    # 218—"Business Plan for Small Manufacturers"

    # 233—"Planning and Goal Setting for Small Business"

Small Marketers' Aids

    # 150—"Business Plan for Small Retailers"

    # 153—"Business Plan for Small Service Firms"

10

Leadership in Management

You cannot be a leader unless you have someone to lead. This is self-evident. Equally true is the corollary: Where there is a leader, there are followers (at least *one*). Consequently, *your* leadership skills will not flourish until you've hired your first employee!

THE DYNAMICS OF LEADERSHIP

Social psychologists tell us that leadership is a process involving certain types of interpersonal behavior. Acts of leadership exert influence upon other people. Verbs usually associated with leadership—guiding, motivating, instructing, encouraging, and the like—imply a sense of purpose, of movement, of action.

Studies of work groups in action suggest that much of the behavior of leaders falls into one of two categories:

149

1. the action is oriented toward completing the work group's assigned tasks, or
2. the behavior shows consideration for and support of the members of the group.

The first type is practical, getting a job done; the second is more personal, involving the care and nurturing of human needs. Put together, these two dimensions define the job of the manager. The manager works with people and with things to get the job done.

Leadership—the "Three Skills" Concept

More than two decades ago, a now-classic article in the Harvard Business Review described the skills any good administrator ought to possess. A well-expressed and illuminating concept, it is certainly worthy of the attention of the small business entrepreneur.

According to the author, Professor Robert Katz, the effective administrator needs proficiency in three skill areas: human, technical, and conceptual.

Human Skills. Certain human skills or talents are necessary for any manager to work successfully with other people and to build teamwork. At the core of this set of abilities is skill in communicating. You must be able to communicate in order to administer; skill in this area is needed to train employees for new tasks, to encourage them to work harder and smarter, and to supervise on-the-job performance. Both oral and written communication skills are involved here, as well as listening skills and nonverbal communication (gestures, grimaces, body language, and so forth).

Administrators need a solid grasp of adult psychology to understand what makes people tick, to interpret their actions, and to be familiar with various human needs, wants, and drives. Further, leaders need to know about attitudes and their formation, the place of value systems in people's lives, what personalities are like and how they differ.

Other human skills are important for success as an administrator—among them, tact, diplomacy, and empathy. You must cultivate the talent of seeing things from others' points of view, in short, be able to wear someone else's hat in order to obtain a different perspective.

Technical Skills. Usually, people obtain technical skills through education in a formal school setting or through on-the-job training. These are the skills they need for successful performance in a chosen specialty. For example, the accountant, lawyer, teacher, or other professional receives the necessary technical training before launching a career. The apprentice electrician or plumber learns to work with the problems and tools of those crafts while serving an apprenticeship.

As a rule, managers are fairly well versed in their specialties (as opposed to the human or conceptual skills which need to be carefully cultivated). Yet, excelling as a manager or leader most certainly requires an above-average technical proficiency in the chosen field.

Conceptual Skills. Many people say this is the area that truly distinguishes the wheat from the chaff, the men from the boys and the women from the girls! Because abstract ideas are involved here, this is the most difficult of the three skill groups to define.

An individual with well-developed conceptual skills has the capacity for visualizing an entire organization as one pulsating, vibrant system with a great many interdependent parts held in equilibrium. This person can perceive the relationships that bind all segments, and the places and functions of the components—people, machines, systems and procedures, finances, and so forth.

Tied into this ability are foresight and vision, and a capacity for structuring and for setting priorities. The conceptual skills include the capacity to analyze and to solve problems.

Conceptualization is the very opposite of small or "bit" thinking.

LEADERSHIP STYLES

In summary, leadership involves interaction. It is a way of behaving—of persuading and inducing, of guiding and motivating. A totally rounded leadership form calls for a mastery of certain skill areas, the creation of the right climate within which the work group can function properly, and the direction and control of group activities.

Leadership style is often a reflection of personality. However, a single, consistent type of behavior may not always be applicable or desired. What works well with one individual (or group) may not necessarily work at all with the next. Individuals as well as groups are extremely varied. Consequently, effective leadership requires an eclectic approach, taking into account the three-way match between leader, group members, and the situation at hand. Most people tend to use, over the long pull, the style that yields the best results.

The Autocratic Leader

At one end of the leadership continuum is the authoritarian type. He or she tends to rule with absolute power, commanding obedience through domination, intimidation, and threats. This person insists on complete compliance with orders, yields no authority to anyone else, and makes decisions alone. Usually, this type of person is production-oriented in thinking (that is, people exist for the sake of performing the required work).

This is the "boss" type of leader. Some individuals, for various reasons, both need and want this kind of leader. Perhaps they had a domineering parent or became conditioned to autocratic bosses in past jobs, or for some other reason put up with an autocratic boss. These employees are usually reluctant to shoulder responsibility; they like to be told what to do, preferring the kind of boss who is an exacting task-master, gets things done, protects workers against outsiders, yet can mete out punishment when warranted.

Undoubtedly, autocratic leadership behavior can occasionally be of value, as when coping with impending peril or in emergencies. Nevertheless, an autocratically run group shows evidence in time of some undesirable types of behavior, such as, for instance, demonstrations of aggression and internal conflict within the group. This kind of employee behavior probably stems from unanswered, ongoing frustrations and from the stifling of individual creativity.

Some autocrats exhibit parental behavior; they infantilize their subordinates, treating them in the same way some fathers and mothers raise young children. Depending on the circumstances, this type of boss wavers from being indulgent and permissive to firm and unyielding. Such treatment of adults can weaken individual initiative and make the workers ever more dependent upon their leader.

The Democratic Leader

The democratic type obviously possesses a broader view of the leader role. This person realizes that people are needed to help get the job done and accepts the fact that they are people, not machines. Moreover, a democratic leader realizes that people have separate and distinct personalities, needs, wants, and drives that must be met if they are to function well. This leader's overall attitude centers on ways to create a climate wherein all do their best to meet both group and company objectives.

A democratic-type boss knows that the most successful approach is to develop employees over time to the point where they can ably function on their own. Consequently, this person exhibits an openness at all times, remains accessible, and is eager to communicate freely with others. This wise leader keeps employees informed about ongoing conditions and about any impending changes that may affect them. Decisions are arrived at with the group's fullest input. For the most part, the carrot-and-stick principle is eschewed out of respect for the individuals; they are encouraged to exercise self-direction and make decisions on their own.

More than any other leadership stance, this type of administration produces workers who are motivated self-starters. As a result, productivity will edge upwards.

Leader Characteristics

Most of us are guilty of holding stereotypical notions about leaders. To many, a good leader is one who commands respect, who electrifies the atmosphere when entering a room, who is, without a doubt, aggressive, domineering, able at manipulation, a skilled communicator, an extrovert, and so on. Our concepts even go beyond personality to physical attributes; we think that a good leader usually is taller and heavier (and more attractive) than the rest of us.

Strangely, some of the greatest leaders in world history, and many capable managers of major corporations, have been quiet, unassuming, introspective, short, and thin people.

In fact, leaders can be just like you and me—or anyone else. Management experts have often theorized about the kinds of personal traits necessary for effective performance in the leader role. Studies have compared the qualities evidenced by top executives with those demonstrated by unsuccessful leaders in order to uncover the characteristics that differentiate the two. Yes, several distinguishing attributes keep showing up; but bear in mind that leadership has three dimensions—the leader, those who are led, and the individual situation. Consequently, whether you rate high or low in these attributes does not necessarily make you a good (or bad) leader.

Perhaps you'll find it helpful to review the following list of personal traits which can be valuable in dealing with others.

adaptability	openmindedness
alertness	optimism
confidence	patience

communication skills	persuasive powers
creativity	poise
curiosity	resourcefulness
dependability	sensitivity to others
drive	supportiveness
enthusiasm	teaching ability
evaluation skills	tolerance
flexibility	warmth
human relations skills	willingness to listen
maturity	willingness to take chances

Inasmuch as leadership activity also has a task-oriented, impersonal dimension, certain additional skills and abilities must be developed. Among these are:

- the ability to establish priorities,
- a capacity for giving credit when it is due,
- skill at planning and scheduling,
- a talent for analyzing situations,
- proficiency in problem-solving, and
- a willingness to delegate responsibility to others.

UNDERSTANDING YOUR PEOPLE

People are complex. This statement, of course, doesn't surprise you at all! Yet, it's so important to bear in mind in your relationships with your employees. Each individual is multifaceted; among his many sides are the intellectual, the physical, the emotional—and the economic, social, political, ethical, and moral as well. So it isn't surprising that people's behavior can be as complex and as difficult to interpret as people are themselves.

This section contains basic adult psychology—and social psychology as well (that's the psychology of people in groups) which can help you in your role as leader.

People hold values. Values are concepts people come to accept over the years as they interact with others and with environments.

People form attitudes. Attitudes serve as vehicles for organizing knowledge, for adjusting to the world around them, for shielding them from confusion and pain, and for orienting them toward things that are pleasurable.

People develop response traits. People have habitual ways of responding to and dealing with others.

Personality is an amalgam of values, attitudes, and interpersonal response traits.

You might prepare yourself by reading a basic psychology textbook which will give you many insights into what makes people tick. In turn, this could possibly lead to an increased capability on your part to motivate and direct your employees.

What Motivates People

Motives are the energizing forces that drive all of us and are behind most behavior. Many of our actions result from the interplay of several motives. Some motives are largely rational; this means that logic is behind them. For example, you probably avoid speeding in your automobile because (1) you may be involved in an accident that can endanger your vehicle or your life and (2) you may receive a speeding ticket. These two motives are clearly logical.

On the other hand, many motives are of an emotional (or non-logical) nature. Consider the urge to place a $10 bet on a particular horse in the third race at the track. Logically, your chances of winning are less than fifty-fifty, yet you have a "feeling" you might win.

The line of demarcation between rational and emotional motives is rather hazy. You might avoid speeding because of an emotional motive—fear of being ticketed, or of having an accident, and so on. Similarly, there can be a rational motive for the gambling situation, for example, if you need considerably more money for a vital purpose than you have in your pockets at the time.

Furthermore, what motivates one individual does not necessarily budge the next. The same motive can lead to varied behaviors in different people. The same behavior in different people can result from different motives.

All of us are driven by many motives: economic motives, safety motives, social motives, and so forth. Some of our motives derive from drives that are born in us, like hunger, thirst, the need for sleep, and sex. The majority of our motives, however, are based on learned drives—those which we develop as we interact with our environment.

Levels of Human Needs

One way to understand better this subject of human needs and wants is to review a notable theory proposed many years ago by the eminent psychologist Abraham Maslow. He postulated that man is a perennially wanting animal, that man's needs can be arranged on different levels according to their "potency" for influencing behavior, and that all of us are constantly struggling upwards to attain higher rungs on this "pyramid of needs" until we reach its pinnacle. From time to time, most people are restrained from proceeding up the hierarchy or are knocked down to lower levels by outside conditions (or, perhaps, by inner forces).

Needs at the lowest level—and therefore the most powerful of all—are the ones Maslow describes as the physiological, or bodily, needs. These include hunger, thirst, and sex. Once these needs have been largely satisfied, the human being will want still more, and move up to the next level of the pyramid, to the safety needs. On this level, people think of their safety, of gaining shelter from the elements and protection from accidents and other threats to well-being. If a person can provide for these needs, other wants soon develop; these were termed by Maslow as the love and belongingness needs.

At this point, the individual needs love and affection and actively seeks friends, a mate, and groups for affiliation. (As a note, Maslow pointed out that in the American culture, most people have largely satisfied the two lower levels—physiological and safety—and it's the thwarting of needs at the third level that is mostly responsible for the rather high incidence of psychological troubles in the population at large.)

When this level has been successfully attained, people still want (naturally!) more, and they move up to the esteem needs. Here, the individual wants to be respected by others, to be noticed and acclaimed, to build a reputation. By this time, the person has almost everything: income, a sense of security, family and friends, and is acquiring a reputation and the respect of others. Yet he or she still feels an inadequacy, a sense of missing out on something, a feeling that there is still something more needed.

To the fifth—and highest—level of the pyramid of needs, Maslow affixed the name "self-actualization." He explained this as the highest level of aspiration—to become in actuality that which an individual was designed to be. Only then, he claimed, was the individual truly "matured." That is the supreme goal which all of us are climbing toward, all our lives.

Interpreting Maslow's Theory in Practice

Translating Maslow's concepts into modern personnel thinking, you can expect your employees to seek things as follows:

Level 1 (Physiological Needs): a decent salary—enough to keep the wolf from the door, to keep the refrigerator well-stocked, and to maintain a comfortable dwelling place.

Level 2 (Safety Needs): job security and safe working conditions. This need perhaps includes getting life insurance protection for spouse and children.

Level 3 (Love and Belongingness Needs): the feeling of being part of an organization and having a place in the group; acceptance by coworkers and employer, a friendly environment.

Level 4 (Esteem Needs): ego satisfaction, recognition (an occasional pat of the back), authority and status within the group; the belief that the person's work is both responsible and respected.

Level 5 (Need for Self-Actualization): a chance for growth and the opportunity to demonstrate initiative; encouragement for the individual to participate and contribute to the fullest.

Practice pegging the positions of your employees on Maslow's pyramid. It will do wonders for your understanding of their behavior.

Employee Characteristics

What will *you* be looking for in your employees? Here is a representative list of characteristics that are valuable in an employee.

- a fair shake
- a good level of productivity
- consistency
- honesty
- loyalty
- no rocking the boat
- pleasant personality
- promptness
- proper behavior on the job
- regular attendance
- respect for authority

SUPERVISING YOUR PEOPLE: SOME SUGGESTIONS

It is only natural for your employees to regard you as their mentor, guide, leader, and counselor. If you set high standards for yourself as well as for them, if you continually demonstrate good human relations, and if you treat your employees as people—and not like pawns—your skills as a supervisor will be above-average. Following the "Do's" and "Don'ts" suggested below helps to increase your leadership ability.

Do:	Don't
be consistent	be argumentative
be fair	be autocratic
be honest	be overly demanding
build enthusiasm among your people	be unreasonable
encourage them to ask questions	conceal the truth
encourage them to make their own decisions	discourage initiative
instill confidence in them	discourage new ideas
keep an open door	do their thinking for them
listen attentively to what they have to say	fail to clarify your instructions
recognize individual differences	play favorites
set a personal example for them	reprimand an employee in front of others
show consideration for the feelings of others	think small

DECISION-MAKING

In the small business, most decisions are made by intuition. The owner appears to fly by the seat of his (or her) pants in much the same way that Charles Lindbergh flew over the Atlantic Ocean more than fifty years ago,—without the benefit of the vast array of intricate instruments that decorate the cockpit of today's jet aircraft.

Intuitive decision-making stems partially from a lack of familiarity with problem-solving techniques and partially from the realization that extensive resources—time, energy, and funds—should only be diverted to the most serious and complex problems. Happily, these major problems do not occur very often in a small business. When they do, the owner is often better off relying on the assistance of an experienced consultant, such as when contemplating major relocation of a factory or designing a new system.

Luckily, most problems in business repeat themselves, and so once a satisfactory solution has been worked out (or accidentally hit upon), the entrepreneur knows how to solve the problem the next time it pops up. It's only the new, infrequent, unique problems that present a strong challenge.

Decision-making is but one step in the problem-solving process. It is the last step, where you choose the one alternative that seems best. When you are confronted with any problem that merits your time and energy, try applying the following steps (which precede actual decision making) to solving it.

1. First, diagnose exactly what the problem is all about. On a sheet of paper, write down a clear statement of the problem's "essence"; this helps you keep the pinpointed problem clearly in mind as you work on its solution. Many problems are quite complex; often, you need to go further and break down the original problem statement into its major parts. Each part should then be summarized and written down as a "sub-problem" statement.

2. Another useful trick is to draw a simple diagram of the problem making certain you put in all the elements involved.

3. Hunt for pertinent information to help you solve the problem. (Facts are not only available from internal records, external sources of data, and primary research; they are also readily obtained from people.)

4. Develop a number of alternative solutions to the problem. (Creative thinking can help here. See Chapter 11 for approaches to use in generating new ideas by the dozen.)

5. Evaluate the alternatives according to various criteria, for example cost, time, judged effectiveness, effect on you, company resources, and the risks involved.)

6. If some criteria are more important to you than others (for example cost), then accord more "weight" to those in your analysis.

7. Finally, evaluate each of the alternatives against your set of criteria, and select the best one(s). You have now made your decision.

8. Translate your decision into action.

Of course, many more sophisticated techniques are currently in vogue for solving business problems. For the most part, these techniques are used by the larger companies and not by the small entrepreneur. There are methods that take into account "chance" or probabilities, those that use mathematics and statistics, those that require computer programming, and so on. You may have read or heard about some of the following terms: game theory, decision trees, decision matrices, queueing theory, simulation, and linear programming.

If you become interested, at a later date, in learning more about such approaches. a number of good books are available on the topic of decision-making in business and industry.

FOR FURTHER INFORMATION

Books

Bittel, Lester R. *Improving Supervisory Performance*. New York: McGraw-Hill, 1976.

Boyd, Bradford. *Management-Minded Supervision*. New York: McGraw-Hill, 1976.

Dowling, William F., Jr., and Sayles, Leonard R. *How Managers Motivate: The Imperatives of Supervision*, 2nd ed. New York: McGraw-Hill, 1978.

Eden, C. and Harris J. *Management Decision & Decision Analysis*. New York: Halsted Press, 1975.

Fulmer, Robert M. *Practical Human Relations*. Homewood, Ill.: Irwin, 1977.

George, Claude S., Jr. *Supervision in Action: The Art of Being Effective*. Reston, Va.: Reston, 1977.

Gordon, Gilbert and Pressman, Israel. *Quantitative Decision-Making for Business*. Englewood Cliffs, N.J.: Prentice-Hall, 1978.

Haimann, Theo and Hilgert, Raymond. *Supervision: Concepts and Practices of Management*, 2nd ed. Cincinnati: South-Western, 1977.

Harrison, E. Frank. *The Managerial Decision Making Process*. Boston: Houghton Mifflin, 1975.

Lundgren, Earl F., Engel, William J., and Cecil, Earl. *Supervision*. Columbus: Grid Publishing, 1978.

Sartain, Aaron and Baker, Alton W. *The Supervisor and the Job*, 3rd ed. New York: McGraw-Hill, 1978.

Steinmetz, Lawrence L. and Todd, H. Ralph, Jr. *First-Line Management: Approaching Supervision Effectively*. Dallas: Business Publications, 1975.

Terry, George R. *Supervision*, rev. ed. Homewood, Ill.: Irwin, 1978.

Thomas, Howard. *Decision Theory and the Manager*. New York: Beekman, 1972.

Todes, Jay L.; McKinney, John; and Ferguson, Wendell, Jr. *Management and Motivation: An Introduction to Supervision*. New York: Harper & Row, 1977.

Free Materials from the Small Business Administration

Management Aids

    #191 "Delegating Work and Responsibility"

    #208 "Problems in Managing a Family-Owned Business"

Available from the Superintendent of Documents

Nonseries Publications:

    "Managing for Profits" Stock #045-000-00005-2, 170 pp., $1.90.

    "Strengthening Small Business Management" Stock #045-000-00114-8, 158 pp., $2.25.

11

Marketing— and Product Management

Regardless of the nature of your new enterprise, the managing of the marketing function demands more creativity and more astute judgement than any other single phase of the business. Your warehouse may be jammed to the rafters with inventory, your new machines may be churning out thousands of merchandise units each day, your store's shelves may be crammed with goods, yet all can come to naught if sales are not consummated. The end purpose of all this activity and preparation is the accomplishment of those exchange transactions called "sales," where your firm receives customer dollars in exchange for its products.

THE MARKETING CONCEPT

In contrast to the old-fashioned accent on production that characterized American business only a few decades ago, today's healthy small firm is one that is, first and foremost, oriented

161

toward the customer. This contemporary approach is simple to learn: (1) identify your intended customer groups, (2) find out all you can about their needs and wants, and (3) try to satisfy them with the right products and/or services, supported by the right communication or promotion, and available at the right time and location.

Under this modern "marketing concept," an alert entrepreneur designs the company's organizational structure so as to give the marketing component its deserved prominence. The marketing function is fully integrated with other traditional divisions of the business such as finance and production, and placed in a position to coordinate them. The firm's marketing strategies and tactics are purposeful, well-organized, and projected years into the future. Furthermore, within a marketing-oriented company, planning responds to sociocultural and even natural environmental changes, and displays abundant flexibility.

Therefore, in directing your company's marketing efforts, bear in mind that there is little you can do about certain elements in the environment, for example, the legal framework within which your firm must operate or the general business conditions of the economy. Only four factors are truly within your control, and you must learn to skillfully manipulate them to compete successfully in the marketplace. These controllable elements are: *products, pricing, promotion,* and *distribution.* Together, they are commonly referred to as the firm's "marketing mix."

Each of these major factors in marketing decision-making is sufficiently important to be treated in a separate chapter. This chapter deals with the first of the four elements; the next three chapters are devoted to in-depth presentation of the other elements.

PRODUCT MANAGEMENT

Of the four constituent factors in the marketing mix, *products* (or the "product line") probably presents the major challenge facing your company. The other three ingredients are usually only support activities which, when carefully planned, will facilitate the movement of your goods into the hands of your customers. Products are the items which you *produce* (if you are a manufacturer) or *select and buy* (in wholesaling or retailing) to fulfill the needs and wants of your customers.

To manufacturers and middlemen alike, effective management of the product sphere is crucial. Product line management involves many things: how to find and select the proper items to carry, how wide or narrow a line to offer, when to discard or retain an item, and when to add new products to the line.

What IS a Product?

To the layperson, the word "product" generally signifies the actual, physical object offered for sale. Modern marketing approaches the product as much more than a simple, three-dimensional object. It's as though this "thing" designed to satisfy customer needs were surrounded by an intangible, invisible aura (or "frame of reference") which includes other attributes not easily discerned: the reputation of the producer or seller, the style of the packaging, past messages conveyed by advertisements of the product, other people's impressions and opinions about the item, and so on. As such, a product is much more than an object. It is an intricate mental concept, rich in connotations. It reflects an "image" that literally comprises a total package of satisfactions for the intended user.

Products do not exist by themselves, frameless and within a vacuum. A pair of Florsheim shoes, an electric toaster emblazoned with the Proctor or General Electric label, a Gucci pocketbook, a tube of Colgate or Crest toothpaste—each of these articles is positioned within a frame of reference which differentiates it from competitive products.

CLASSIFYING PRODUCTS

You may find it useful to know how marketing specialists assign products to categories, since these classifications provide an orderly basis for product management. The following are common product classifications:

- industrial and consumer goods,
- necessities and luxuries,
- durables and nondurables,
- convenience, shopping, and specialty goods, and
- staples and fashion items.

These labels by no means exhaust the possible approaches; however, they are sufficient to provide a basic grasp of product classification. Each sample category is discussed briefly below.

Industrial and Consumer Goods

This product class is based on the user for whom the products are intended. The merchandise used by industry, commerce, government, and middlemen of all types in the ordinary conduct of their operations is referred to as *industrial goods.* Partially finished as well as completely finished products may be included in this category: lumber, industrial chemicals, tools and machines, supplies, and the like. *Consumer goods* are the finished goods intended for use by the final consumer.

Necessities and Luxuries

This grouping classifies products according to the urgency or lack of urgency people show in their buying habits. This type of "consumer behavior" is tied to the concept of *discretionary* purchasing power. Obviously, categorization in this manner is sometimes misleading in that one person's luxury might be another's necessity. A new IBM Selectric typewriter purchased by a salesclerk, high school student, or automobile mechanic is most likely considered a *luxury good,* yet the identical machine is probably a *necessity* to a writer of fiction, a college professor, or a business executive.

Durable and Nondurables

The word "durable" means "of a lasting quality." Merchandise which lasts a long time (or has other want-satisfying attributes) such as pocket calculators, clothing, television sets, and pots and pans are called *durable goods.* The contrasting term, *nondurable goods,* refers to items that provide temporary satisfaction; foodstuffs, meats, and many services come under this category.

Convenience, Shopping, and Specialty Goods

Here again, products are looked at from the standpoint of the consumer, taking into consideration the time and effort expended in shopping around for the items. People generally spend almost no time shopping for items like chewing gum, sugar, and butter, and so these are designated *convenience goods.* Such merchandise is readily available at many locations; there is little product difference but often substantial differentiation of one brand from the next.

Furniture, jewelry, fashionable clothing, carpeting, and the like, are called *shopping goods* because they require more time and effort by the shopper. Here, the customer usually wishes to compare the item with other similar offerings with regard to product attributes like price, quality, and style before making a choice.

Prospective buyers expend even greater effort before purchasing *specialty goods* such as custom-made products, special brands, and the like. Of course, there could be a good deal of overlapping here, depending on individual consumer motivation and "search behavior." A convenience item for one person may be a shopping good—or even a specialty item—for the next.

Staples and Fashion Items

Staple goods are those that enjoy a widespread and generally continuous demand over time. Examples include men's socks, razor blades, fresh eggs, and butter. When demand is erratic and subject to wide fluctuations, as with "nonstaple" style merchandise (men's shirts, ladies' shoes and sportswear, and the like), the products are referred to as *fashion goods*.

MANAGING THE PRODUCT LINE

The first requirement in product management is to reach a consensus on specific product objectives which are then followed as guidelines. Among those commonly encountered in business are: increasing sales, enlarging the firm's market share, fully utilizing manufacturing capacity, matching new or improved products of competitors, and changing methods of distribution. Before deciding on such objectives, management should do some diligent soul-searching and ask questions like these:

- What kind of business are we in?
- Which segments of the general market are we catering to?
- Which new segments can we service in the future?
- How well do our current products meet the needs of our customers?
- Are there other items we ought to be carrying?
- Are there items in our line we should drop?
- Is each of our products compatible with the others in our line?

THE PRODUCT LIFE CYCLE

The concept of the "Product Life Cycle" is of special importance in the first steps of marketing strategy, and has been well publicized over the years in the marketing literature. This strategy attempts to describe the performance of any successful new product from the point when it's first introduced into the marketplace through its final demise. Except for fashion merchandise and fads, most products appear to pass through four stages before reaching obsolescence. These are the *introductory, growth, maturity,* and *decline* stages of the "Product Life Cycle."

Introductory Stage

When a new product is introduced into the marketplace, it is unknown to most of its targeted purchasers. Obviously, some groundwork has to be prepared for the "launching." During this first stage of the product cycle, the innovating firm must invest substantial funds in promotional activities of the "pioneering" type in order to carry the "product story" to prospective customers. Once they've provided the product information, the company must ensure that consumers will be able to purchase the item at convenient locations. So, manufacturers need to consider what distribution channels to employ in order to reach those prospects.

For the truly innovating firm, this first stage is a costly one. The producer must absorb the initial costs involved in designing the product, in gearing up the machinery and internal systems for its manufacture, in promoting the item, and in securing enough initial distribution points to generate product viability in the marketplace.

Often, the manufacturer seeks to recover a lot of this investment by placing a higher-than-ordinary price tag on the item. The company might seek mass distribution instead, by pricing the product somewhat "below-the-market" in order to secure a strong foothold. In either case, little or no profit is usually accrued during this introductory stage. Frequently, the manufacturer encounters losses, sometimes severe.

Growth Stage

Provided these initial efforts result in gradual customer acceptance, more and more people will learn of the new product, try it, and (if satisfied) continue purchasing and using the item. As greater effort is exerted in distribution, merchandise is increasingly available at more locations. Sales volume starts to climb. After the starting-up costs are substantially absorbed by early sales, the additional sales resulting from increased market penetration lead to a sharp rise in company profit. For the manufacturer, this stage generally bears the highest profit margins. During this stage, manufacturing methods are generally refined as production gears up to meet demand. This, in turn, results in even lower per unit costs.

Advertising is increased to support product growth, but now a broader sales base exists which supports advertising expenditures. For the small new company, it might be advantageous at this juncture to expand the number of purchase points, simply to keep costs within a reasonable range.

Wholesalers and retailers who handle the new product begin to enjoy the fruits of this increasing demand; they order more heavily as they experience a higher stockturn rate. Additional product variations may be launched—new sizes, new colors, new materials, and the like. It should be noted, that even at this comparatively early point in the product life cycle, when profits peak, competition begins to enter the picture, seeking to emulate the evident success of the pioneering manufacturer.

Maturity Stage

Eventually, the ascending growth curve begins to level off (although this might not occur for years). By this time, the product has found widespread consumer acceptance, and a number of competitors offering similar products have appeared on the scene. For the originating firm, the environment is then a highly competitive one; and competitors' prices are sometimes substantially lower. The manufacturer is frequently compelled to step up promotional efforts, perhaps differentiating the product from competitors' in order to protect the initial advantage and share of market so assiduously cultivated. Naturally, such tactics tend to force costs upward. In turn, profits begin to shrink. At best, efforts like these constitute a delaying action, although they can occasionally extend this particular stage for a long period of time.

The majority of products now in the marketplace are most likely in the maturity stage of their respective life cycles.

Decline Stage

In the face of declining profits, manufacturers sometimes make last-ditch efforts to resuscitate the item. These include approaches like new packaging, special promotions, new versions, price changes, and so on. Though it's often difficult to discard an item, sooner or later, as sales continue to decline, the decision has to be faced. In this final stage, appropriate steps include planning to phase out the product, tapering down gradually on inventory, working out equitable arrangements with middlemen so they don't suffer losses along the way, disposing of excess inventory, and so forth.

THE "EIGHTY-TWENTY PRINCIPLE"

A practical "rule-of-thumb" you can apply in a variety of ways to your marketing planning is the so-called "Eighty-Twenty Principle." For example, if a manufacturer lists all of its customers according to their annual purchases, chances are that the firm will discover as much as 80 percent of its total annual sales coming from about one-fifth of its customers.

Similarly, a company maintaining a sales force of around fifty sales people can analyze each employee's sales productivity according to this same principle. More likely than not, management will learn that the major portion of sales has been brought in by as few as nine or ten star performers.

The Eighty-Twenty Principle can also be applied to product line management. One firm, a wholesaler of janitorial supplies, maintained a huge inventory of over 8,000 items in order to suply hundreds of regular customers. Sales results for a two-year period were analyzed by computer, on an item-by-item movement basis. Management was surprised to learn that 1,700 items accounted for over three-fourths of their annual sales. Needless to say, the line of products was drastically reduced by more than 50 percent over the next few months. This resulted in a savings of $250,000 in capital formerly tied up in inventory. Although sales initially dropped by 4 percent, fewer salespeople could thereafter devote more time to fewer products (and the firm's mail-order catalog accented the more popular merchandise) resulting in an overall sales increase of more than 15 percent by the end of the year.

NEW PRODUCTS

From time to time, the progressive small company considers introducing one or more new products into its line. A number of reasons could account for this: a desire to enhance the firm's reputation as an innovator in its industry; the need to stimulate sales, replace products in a decline, or outperform a serious competitor; or, more simply, to take advantage of occasional, special deals.

Where to Find New Products

New item concepts are available from a variety of sources: the company's suppliers and their salespeople, customers and prospective customers, company personnel, trade journals and general publications, and competitors.

Of course, the bulk of ideas for new products or services can and should be generated internally, especially if the organization has a "product development section" or committee. In an "open" organization, where all are encouraged to come up with helpful ideas, there should be no lack of new product concepts. Certainly, a simple suggestion box system, reinforced by efficient follow-through procedures, will be of considerable value. For the retailer, a "want-slip" system can serve the same purpose.

Creative Thinking Approaches

The internal team in charge of generating new product ideas can be quickly indoctrinated in some of the more popular "creative thinking" techniques. Among others, these include brainstorming, attribute listing, "running the alphabet," and checklists. Each of these approaches is described below in brief detail.

Brainstorming. This is a group procedure (it can be used by individuals as well) generally enjoyed by participants and providing the benefits of a highly motivating atmosphere. The group, usually small, meets for the purpose of coming up with ideas in quantity within a short time-span—perhaps ten or fifteen minutes. There are no holds barred in that participants are encouraged to let their imaginations run wild; at the same time, all criticism or judgment is withheld. Ideas flow so fast at times that the use of a tape recorder is recommended. Over the following two or three days, ideas generated from the "brainstorm" can be typed up for thoughtful analysis; a set of previously established criteria is then applied and the more promising alternatives are selected.

Research has demonstrated conclusively that significantly more good ideas are produced when following brainstorming procedures (either individually or in groups) than under more customary approaches to idea generation.

Attribute Listing. As the name suggests, this technique involves preparing a list of the significant characteristics of a product that, combined, will differentiate it from other products. Let's say your company is in the business of manufacturing ordinary pencils and you are hunting for new, unique products to add to your line. You begin by describing the pencil itself: its color(s), its size and shape, its substances and constituent materials; and its function(s)—to write and maybe erase. Each of these characteristics then becomes a logical candidate for change or variation.

For example, the color *yellow* could be changed to dozens of other colors or, to *striped, polka-dotted,* or *transparent.* Other attributes, such as size, shape, material, function, texture, odor, taste, and so forth, can be used to originate hundreds of variations. Changing the function of a pencil, for example, from *to write* to something else, like *to play with, to eat,* or *to use as a weapon* (or a myriad of other possible functions) might lead to pencil-shaped objects that are toys, or of chocolate, or designed for self-defense!

Obviously, the manufacturer of luggage, giftware, or small appliances can employ the same approach to new product ideas.

"Running the Alphabet." Also referred to as the "ABC Method," this approach borrows liberally from the word association tech-

niques of psychologists. Essentially, it consists of preparing in advance a list of words beginning with the letter "A," then "B" words, and so on through the alphabet until fifty or more words have been listed. From a practical point of view, it's desirable to work mostly with nouns. The words selected are then used to "mine" for ideas.

Here is a hypothetical example of the technique in action: A canned soup manufacturer wanted ideas for new soups in order to increase its share of the market. Here's a sampling of the list prepared under this creative approach:

abalone	bronze
Africa	Brooklyn
alligator	bubble
apple	cabana
apricot	calliope
Aquarius	camera
aspirin	carousel
badge	circus
ball	cognac
banquet	crystal
blossom	

The manufacturer considered the words one by one, and came up with many new ideas, including: abalone soup (and other fish soups), fruit soups, soups for medicinal purposes, and so on. Edibles such as fruits, vegetables, meats, fish, and so on, are rather amenable to the "soup" concept. In this respect, then, the ideas may not be all that original or new. More likely than not, some competitive firm already succeeded in linking several of the more likely concepts to new soup possibilities; indeed, the competitor may be on the verge of launching the new product in the marketplace.

It is in the "mental manipulation" of the "non-edibles" on your list (for example, *Aquarius, blossom,* or *cabana*) that the true worth of this technique emerges. It's easy to see how the ideas generated *via* these unorthodox associations can result in truly innovative suggestions.

Consider, for instance, the word Aquarius. One immediately conceives of a soup designed specifically for people born under this sign, and by logical extension, a dozen items in a new line of "astrological soups." If you can't imagine what could be included in such products, you could begin with (at the very least) the more familiar alphabet soup—replacing the letters with miniature symbols of the Zodiac.

Of course, this technique (like "Brainstorming" and "Attribute-Listing") can be applied to a variety of business problems ranging from artwork and copy for advertising to choosing a packaging style, planning major promotions, and producing names for new items. For example, in hunting for ways to motivate your salespeople, you might come across the "B" words *badge* and *ball*. These words could trigger ideas like issuing merit badges (or by extension, certificates) to outstanding performers of the month or quarter, perhaps an annual ball for employees who surpass their quotas (or an outing at a ball park), and so on.

Checklists and "Other Pump-Primers."   Checklists are used daily in business for purposes of measurement and/or control, and, sometimes to insure thoroughness in planning. A checklist is also a valuable device for triggering the imagination, although it is seldom used in this creative capacity.

Consider, for example, the familiar "Five Ws" of the journalist: *Who? What? Where? When? Why?* (A sixth question—"How?"—is usually added to this mini-checklist.) The "Five Ws" can be of extraordinary value in investigating and analyzing many types of business problems, such as declining sales, loss of market share, the proper deployment of company resources, and the like. The "Five Ws" are also useful in planning: for promotion campaigns, for expansion, and so on.

One famous checklist in "creativity" literature was devised by Alex Osborn, the "Father of Brainstorming." Essentially, it is a series of nine groups of questions all designed for the purpose of generating new product ideas from existing products. Some examples are: "How can this product be adapted to other uses? What else can we add to (or subtract from) it? Can we arrange any of its components? Can the item be enlarged or reduced?" and so on.[1]

In addition to checklists, there are other "pump-primers" to prod our imaginations. The classified telephone directory, for instance, can be used as a source of "leads," new prospects for a salesperson to go after. The daily newspapers and business publications are also excellent sources of ideas for your day-to-day business activities.

NEW PRODUCT DEVELOPMENT

For the manufacturing firm, the process of new product development involves a logical sequence:

[1]See pp 286–287 in Alex F. Osborn, *Applied Imagination* 3rd rev. ed., New York: Charles Scribner's Sons, 1963.

1. the emergence of the "raw" idea;
2. a "screening" procedure where the idea is evaluated, along with others, against previously established criteria;
3. the tedious research and development period during which the idea is gradually refined, a prototype of the item is made, cost analyses are worked up, production methods are devised, marketing factors such as price and packaging are considered, and estimates are made of demand and expected profits;
4. the testing stage where the product's performance in one or several areas is carefully watched; and, finally
5. full-scale introduction on the market.

The criteria mentioned above in the second stage are, for example: the size of market for the item, the product's potential contribution to company profits, the uniqueness of the item and its effect on other products in the line, and how easily it can be integrated into the total production load.

Generally, the expenditures required to develop a single new product are substantial, to say the least. This fact, coupled with the recognition that most new products fail, is a serious warning to the recently-established small business to think twice (or more) before embarking on this path. Until the firm is well established, management is wiser to consider a different strategy in its product line management—waiting until a competitor has a substantial degree of success with a product, and then producing its own improved version (thus riding "on the bandwagon").

Perhaps there is more sanity and less risk in striving to be second than in being first!

A FINAL NOTE: PACKAGING AND BRANDING

Along with the development of a new item, the manufacturer must think about enclosing the product in some type of package or container for purposes of protection. Of course, the product must be packaged so it can be easily handled, cartoned off, shipped, stored, and eventually placed on shelves or on display, all with an eye to avoiding damage to the contents. Additionally, modern packaging helps to sell the merchandise it contains, through a combination of factors that include design, color, materials used, and others. Moreover, the package identifies the producing company.

In this respect, the selection and subsequent popularization of a brand name, trademark, or other identifying device is important to a company seeking to differentiate its merchandise from competitors'. Over time, the brand name will establish a vital "sales personality" for the product. Hence, extreme care should be exercised at the outset in the selection of a name. The name should be simple—easy to spell and easy to pronounce. Often, the name chosen is simply the firm's name, like General Electric, Heinz, or Remington. At times, brand names reflect the benefits promised to users of the product or imply its important qualities.

As a general rule, unless the new firm has based its entire marketing effort on a single innovative product (which is usually not the case), the choice of brand name is relatively unimportant. In the long run, the popularization of a company name is more significant. In time, the company name can be successfully used to "brand" its products.

FOR FURTHER INFORMATION

Books

Boone, Louis E. and Kurtz, David L. *Contemporary Marketing*, 2nd ed. Hinsdale, Ill.: Dryden, 1977.

Brannen, William. *Successful Marketing for Your Small Business*. Englewood Cliffs, N.J.: Prentice-Hall, 1978.

Constantin, James A., Evans, Rodney E., and Morris, Malcolm L. *Marketing Strategy and Management*. Dallas: Business Publications, 1976.

Cundiff, Edward W. and Still, Richard R. *Basic Marketing: Concepts, Decisions and Strategies*, 2nd ed. Englewood Cliffs, N.J.: Prentice-Hall, 1971.

Kotler, Philip. *Marketing Management: Analysis, Planning, and Control* 3rd ed. Englewood Cliffs, N.J.: Prentice-Hall, 1976.

McCarthy, E. Jerome. *Basic Marketing: A Managerial Approach*, 6th ed. Homewood, Ill.: Irwin, 1978.

Nickels, William G. *Marketing Principles: A Broadened Concept of Marketing*. Englewood Cliffs, N.J.: Prentice-Hall, 1978.

Rosenberg, Larry. *Marketing: An Introduction*. Englewood Cliffs, N.J.: Prentice-Hall, 1977.

Schwartz, David J. *Marketing Today: A Basic Approach*, 2nd ed. New York: Harcourt, Brace, Jovanovich, 1977.

Spitz, A. Edward, ed. *Product Planning*. Princeton, N.J.: Auerbach, 1972.

Stanton, William J. *Fundamentals of Marketing*, 5th ed. New York: McGraw-Hill, 1978.

Free Materials from the Small Business Administration

Management Aids
82—"Reducing the Risks in Product Development"
194—"Marketing Planning Guidelines"
203—"Are Your Products and Channels Producing Sales?"
216—"Finding a New Product for Your Company"

Small Business Bibliographies
  # 75—"Inventory Management"

Available from the Superintendent of Documents

Small Business Management Series
  # 39—"Decision Points in Developing New Products." Stock #045-000-00146-6, 64 pp., 90¢.

12

The Management of Prices

The pricing area is of no less stature—and possibly greater—than the other ingredients of the marketing mix, and it requires consummate managerial skill on your part. How a firm handles its pricing frequently signifies the difference between marketing success and failure. Business survival and growth depend upon proper pricing practices.

THE MEANING OF PRICE

Clearly, the price concept is closely affiliated with products and product management; indeed, these two "Ps" are often handled in tandem, although this should not be the case. Price, you see, has many facets:

- Price facilitates the buying and selling process.

- Price is affected by the interplay of demand and supply.
- Price is a useful tool in promotion.
- Price can help—or hinder—sales.
- Price ties into methods of distribution.
- Price can affect your "bottom line" figure for better or for worse.
- Price has to do with costs and profits.
- Price can be an extremely valuable tool when used as a competitive weapon.
- Price can be manipulated strategically from one stage of the product life cycle to the next.

To the consumer, the price of a product (or service) represents nothing more than the seller's interpretation, expressed in monetary terms, of the product's utility value—its ability to satisfy a buyer's wants or needs. Consequently, consumers regard the price of an item as *fair* (congruent with his or her perception of its worth in dollars and cents) or pegged higher or lower than "fair." If considered too high, customers resist purchasing the item; if the price is considered low, then it becomes a "bargain" (although a low price can cause consumers to doubt the quality of the product).

So for most products there appears to be an acceptable "price range" instead of a specific and exact price point. Bear this in mind when you are pricing your goods.

To manufacturers, price is a more complex affair. Indeed, producers regard their "manufacturer's price" as a composite designed to cover, at the very minimum, all of the following: the cost of the raw materials that went into the product, the cost of labor required for manufacture, part of the manufacturing overhead and the administrative and selling expenses, plus a margin of profit to make it all worth while.

Middlemen (wholesalers and retailers) approach pricing in much the same way, except that the "cost of goods purchased" is substituted for materials and other manufacturers' expenses.

Most small businesses use this "cost-plus" approach to pricing. Nevertheless, prices should not be formulated solely in this manner. The perceptive entrepreneur sees a built-in inconsistency here: the method pays no attention whatever to the *demand* for the product. When the demand for an item is heavy and people are clamoring for it, the majority of consumers will tolerate an increase in the regular (list) price. While some customers will refuse to purchase the item, most will buy it anyway, and the resulting sales will generate a good deal more profit overall. Further, when demand is light, maintaining the usual price of an item may lead to a decrease in sales volume.

In pricing your merchandise, then, you should take into consideration other pertinent factors:

- competitors' prices,
- desired return on your investment,
- economic conditions,
- level of demand,
- location of your business,
- market factors,
- product factors,
- seasonal factors, and
- the "price/quality relationship" (and other psychological factors).

PRICING POLICIES

Work out in advance, and to your own satisfaction, a number of specific pricing policies for every aspect of your company's marketing activities. For example, mull over the best pricing strategy to employ with relation to your competition. Logically, there are only three ways to go: (1) set your prices on a level with those of your competitors; (2) deliberately price above the competition (a wise move if you seek to build a quality image for your firm) and use pricing to differentiate your product from competitors'; or (3) undercut your competitors (to secure a foothold in a brand-new market, to create a "discount" image, to obtain a heavier-than-average sales volume, and so on).

Other marketing areas for establishing a pricing policy include:

1. the marketing channels employed (setting manufacturer's, wholesaler's, retailer's, and consumer's prices);
2. the stage of the product life cycle (as an example, the introductory stage, when a company has the choice of adopting a "skimming" policy where the price is set high in an attempt to "skim the cream" off the market, or a "penetration" policy with a low price in order to establish a strong foothold within short order in the marketplace);
3. the promotion mix area (the use of such devices as specials, cents-off (or dollars-off) sales, leader items, and the like);
4. discounting, arranging terms of payment, and so on.

THE "COST-PLUS" APPROACH

Business costs are traditionally broken down into *fixed* and *variable* costs (although some firms go further in their accounting procedures and use terms like "semivariable costs"). The term "fixed" encompasses all costs which remain approximately the same whether, for example, ten pieces or ten thousand pieces of Item X are produced each day in the plant. In other words, the costs do not vary along with the ebb-and-flow in the production rate. This "fixed" costs category includes rent, heat, insurance, depreciation, executive salaries, interest on loans, taxes on property, and so forth.

Expenses that *do* vary along with output are labeled variable costs; these include: the cost of raw materials (or semi-processed materials and components if used), wages earned by the production workers (direct labor), warehousing and shipping costs, sales costs (commissions), and so on.

Markups/Markons

When you set the selling price of any item you should not only try to cover all relevant per unit costs but also tack on an appropriate amount so you end up with some profit for your firm.

Take the situation where the owner of a small gift shop purchases two dozen decorative ashtrays from a jobber at $24.00 a dozen. Individually, the ashtrays have cost $2.00. The retailer decides to put them on display at $3.75 apiece. So, the owner has decided to ask $1.75 more than the original cost. Is this amount all profit? Not really, if you are thinking in terms of "net" profit, for a store owner must also consider operating expenses: rent, electricity, insurance, labor, advertising costs, and the like. So the $1.75 is really a *contribution* toward overhead. Hopefully that figure also contains some profit, too.

The $1.75 represents the retailer's *markup*. Markup is the difference between the cost of an item and its selling price. It is generally defined as the amount of "gross" profit earned on the article of merchandise when it is sold. Usually, markup is expressed as a percentage—either of the selling price (commonly in retail businesses) or of the cost (usual in manufacturing and wholesaling). *Markon* is another term used fairly interchangeably with markup in business, because the gross profit margin is "marked on" to the cost to arrive at the selling price.

Although this difference in terms could be regarded as hair-splitting, markons ought to be relegated to the manufacturing and perhaps wholesaling sphere, leaving markups to the retailers. For the manufacturer generally approaches the pricing of products by totaling each item's direct costs and then marking on a fixed percentage of the costs as a contribution to overhead and profit. The knowledgeable retailer, on the other hand, thinks first in terms of the overall percentage of sales needed in order to cover operating expenses and to yield the planned (net) profit margin, and then adds on this percentage to the costs of the hundreds of items brought in at all different costs.

An Illustration

Let's attempt to work this through: Assume that an item costs the manufacturer $.50 to produce. This cost figure is arrived at by combining the cost of materials per unit ($.20) with the direct labor cost ($.30). Seeking $.30 as a contribution toward other expenses and toward profits, the manufacturer decides to offer the product at $.80 per unit to the wholesaler. This represents a desired markup on cost of 60 percent ($.30 divided by $.50).

After buying the article at $.80, the wholesaler prices it for sale to the retailer at $1.04, apparently looking for a markup (on cost) of 30 percent. This markup covers expenses, and profit for performing wholesaling services as the goods travel along the marketing channel toward the consumer. (See the section on "Marketing Channels" in Chapter 14.)

Markups in Retailing

The majority of small retailers approach the pricing problem in the same way. Jewelry stores, for instance, traditionally use a "keystone" markup in pricing merchandise—they simply double their costs. If a gold wedding band costs a jeweler $40, the item is usually offered to the consumer at the retail price of $80. This earns the jeweler a 100 percent markup (markon?) on the cost.

There is a better way: You can follow the pricing procedures of department stores and large chain operations. They plan in advance: their sales, stock, expenses, profits, and so on. The planned sales figure is regarded as the basis for their calculations; all other areas are then tied in—expressed as some percentage of the sales. Although it's true that a department store carries literally thousands of different items, the average retail shop might carry only hundreds. (Compare this "product line" to that of the small manufacturer producing only a few different items.) It's difficult for the small store owner to keep abreast of all the separate costs, expecially since the cost of a single item may vary throughout the year and from one supplier to the next. However, maintaining all paperwork (inventory records, accounting statements, and the like) on a retail valuation basis, the small store owner can employ this information for decision-making as skillfully as department store management. Using the net sales figure atop the annual income statement, a retailer can readily calculate the year's total operating expenses as a percentage of sales; then, planning for the following year a smaller percentage of sales can be appended to a projected sales figure reflecting the new profit target.

Let's return to the earlier illustration of the item that cost $.50 to manufacture and wound up being offered to the retailer (by the wholesaler) at a cost per unit of $1.04: Suppose you are the retailer in this case, and you have calculated that your operating expenses total 32 percent of sales. For next year, you would like to shoot for an 8 percent profit goal (before taxes). Putting the two percentages together, you now have a 40 percent-of-sales figure that must be "covered" over and above the original cost of all your merchandise. Since you do need an overall markup of 40 percent of sales on goods sold the following year, you try to price most items you purchase for resale with that figure in mind. The item which costs you $1.04 then, should sell at about $1.73-⅓ (Note: to obtain the proper selling price, divide the cost price by the *complement* of the markup. This is what you have left after you subtract the markup, whatever it may be, from 100 %. In this case, we have 100% − 40% = 60%. If you divide $1.04 by .60, you will come up with that $1.73-plus figure.)

Of course, this figure doesn't seem quite right for a selling price, and so the retailer most likely pegs the price at $1.75 or $1.79 (which seems psychologically like a better figure).

Also, the retail price might vary somewhat from the 40 percent markup figure since some items can sell for more money because of their appeal while others may have to be placed on sale for less. What's important here is that the retailer attains the targeted 40 percent (at least) on an overall, maintained markup basis.

BREAKEVEN ANALYSIS

The "breakeven point" is a vital piece of information you should understand completely before your business even gets off the ground. It's the point at which the sales you are able to generate exactly cover all costs. If sales don't reach that level, your firm will find itself "in the red." However, once that point has been passed, your profits will start to mount.

If you own a small factory that manufactures a single product, you may also want to know just how many units of that item must be sold before you can reach your breakeven. Here is the way to find out:

1. Remember: At the breakeven point, there is no profit, no loss, but costs are exactly equaled. This indicates that whatever approach we use to arrive at a breakeven figure, all costs must

be taken into consideration. Hence, we can use the following formula:

Breakeven Point (in units)
$$= \frac{\text{Total Fixed Costs}}{\substack{\text{Per Unit Contribution} \\ \text{toward Fixed Costs}}}$$

2. Let's assume your total fixed expenses for the year are estimated to run $110,000. You have pegged your variable costs on a per-unit basis at $.88, and your price to the wholesaler will be $2.70 per unit. This means that every unit you sell will make its tiny contribution of $1.82 ($2.70 − .88) toward your fixed expenses.

3. Substituting those amounts for the terms in the formula above, we have:

$$\text{Breakeven Point (in units)} = \frac{\$110,000}{\$1.82} = 60,440 \text{ (approx.)}$$

In short, you will need to produce approximately 60,440 units before you reach your breakeven. After that profits should be coming in.

4. To determine the sales volume you must reach in order to attain your breakeven, simply take the number of units required to be sold and multiply by the selling price: $60,440 \times \$2.70 = \$163,188$.

The manufacturer will often engage in breakeven analysis by considering what the various breakeven points would be at different selling prices. This analysis aids in determining how to price products.

Another Approach to Calculating Breakeven

Assume you're thinking about launching a retail business such as the Two Sisters' Dress Shoppe in Chapter 6. You can figure your breakeven right from the *proforma* income statement you prepared for your first year of operation. Simply follow the procedure below:

1. Add up all your expected operating expenses, both fixed and variable, for the year. (Let's say this totals $45,000.)

2. Decide on the average retail markup you can expect to maintain during the year, expressed as a percentage of the sales. (For example, if we assume a 40 percent markup, then what we're really saying is that $.40 out of every dollar taken in will be gross profit,

and that the balance ($.60) of that dollar will be paid out for the merchandise you purchase for resale.)

3. Divide the total expenses (No. 1 above) by the *per-dollar gross profit* figure (No. 2 above) to find your breakeven point. (In this case, it amounts to $45,000 divided by $.40 which is $112,500.)

4. You might want to go further and find out what your store must produce in sales in order to break even on a *monthly* basis. One way is to simply divide the yearly figure by 12. Of course, you ought to bear in mind that some months (like December) are busier than others, and so you can only discuss the "average" month in this situation.

5. If you want to calculate your *daily* breakeven figure, count up the number of days your store will be open during the month, and divide the monthly figure (No. 4 above) by the number of days.

GLOSSARY OF PRICING TERMS

Advertising allowance. A contribution made by a manufacturer or distributor toward the costs incurred by another channel member to induce the latter firm to advertise the former's product(s).

Bait pricing. An illegal promotional practice whereby a retailer prices an item at a bargain price (with no intention of selling the item) and then advertises the offer in order to bring people into the store.

Bait-and-switch. The "follow through" on the bait advertising technique mentioned above. Once the seeker of the advertised "bargain" is in the store, the retailer attempts to switch the customer to another, higher-priced brand or type.

Bid pricing. Estimating, then setting the price for an individual job to be performed (as in construction work) in order to bid against competitors for the work.

Brokerage allowance. The fee or commission earned by a broker for the role he plays in bringing together buyer and seller.

Cash discount. A reduction in price, usually expressed as some percentage of the total, granted to encourage the prompt payment of a bill.

Competitive price. A price designed to meet those of competitors.

Cost-plus pricing. The most frequently used approach to pricing, this method involves adding to the total cost of merchandise some percentage of the overhead expenses and also a profit margin.

Customary price. The price which purchasers are accustomed to paying for a particular product or commodity.

Discount. Any reduction from the regular or list price, usually expressed in terms of a percentage of the selling price.

Early-bird discount. A form of discount offered in advance of a seasonal or other major promotion to encourage early purchase.

Geographical pricing. Any of several distribution-oriented approaches to price determination designed to encompass solutions to the freight problem. Among them are zone, FOB-Factory, and uniform delivered pricing.

Guarantee against price decline. A tactical decision of management designed to contribute toward good channel relationships where, for example, a manufacturer will try to protect his wholesalers against falling prices in industries (or commodities) when prices fluctuate excessively during the year.

Introductory discount. A reduction in the regular price to induce middlemen or consumers to buy a particular (usually new) product.

Leader pricing. A favorite technique of retailers, this involves lowering the customary selling price of one or more usually popular articles of merchandise in order to attract customers to the store. Although the store will earn a lower-than-ordinary markup on the goods, it still enjoys some gross margin.

List price. The price customarily quoted for a particular item to the customer. Also known as the "basic list price."

Loss leader pricing. A variant of leader pricing, where the selling price of an article of merchandise is reduced even more drastically, to the point at which it is offered at below original cost. The technique, illegal in many states where unfair sales practices laws are in effect, is employed at times for a dual purpose: to clear out stocks while simultaneously increasing store traffic.

Markdown. A reduction from the selling price—a popular and useful maneuver for the retail enterprise. Items are marked down to clear out goods that are soiled or damaged, to sell off end-of-season merchandise, to push slow-moving items, and so forth.

Markon. Another word commonly used in place of markup—the difference between the cost of an item and its price.

Markup. The difference between the cost of an item and its selling price. It may be expressed in dollars or as a percentage of either cost or selling price.

Market price. The price of any article or commodity, fixed by the interaction of demand and supply.

Multiple pricing. A promotional pricing technique designed to induce the customer to buy two or more units of a product at one time by affording some savings, such as "3 for $1.00."

Odd-and-even price endings. A pricing concept with psychological ramifications. Despite the fact that research in this area has been inconclusive, many retailers prefer to use prices that end in odd figures, such as $.99, $3.95, and $12.75. On the other hand, there are some who prefer even-dollar amounts or even-figure price endings and price their merchandise accordingly.

One-price policy. As contrasted with a variable-price policy, here the company mandates that prices be held firm and that all customers should pay the same price for the item (under the same terms and conditions). This may be especially important at the retail level for instilling customer confidence.

Penetration pricing. A marketing tactic most often used at the introduction stage of the product life cycle with a low-priced good. Here, a low price is deliberately set in order to assure ready acceptance and to gain extensive distribution.

Premium. Something offered at a reduced price or given away free with the purchase of an article of merchandise or a service.

Prestige pricing. A firm deliberately employs higher-than-customary prices for its offerings in order to differentiate its image from those of its competitors. This has the psychological effect of inducing people to regard the merchandise (and store) as better in quality.

Price lining. A technique which seeks to make it easier for customers to select merchandise and, at the same time, simplifies stock planning for the retailer. Here, the number of choices made available to the consumer is reduced by grouping similar items within a few, rather than many, price lines. For example, a men's habadashery might group its neckties at $3.50, $5.00, and $8.95, depending upon quality and appearance of the goods.

Price reduction. A markdown from the original—or perhaps subsequent—selling price.

Promotional allowance. See "advertising allowance."

Promotional price. A special, lower-than-usual price introduced to help move the product.

Psychological pricing. Any of several pricing tactics employed by firms to create consumer interest in the product by appealing to certain beliefs which consumers hold, for example, prestige pricing or using odd-price endings.

Push money. Commonly called "PMs" in the business world, this term refers to the promotional technique of paying a small commission to the salesperson to push the sale of a particular article of merchandise.

Quantity discount. A reduction in the normal selling price of merchandise to induce purchasers to buy in quantity. It is generally expressed as a percentage of the selling price.

Resale price. The selling price placed on an item by the retailer after adding the desired markup to the cost.

Resale price maintenance. The controlling of retail prices on products by manufacturers in some states (where fair-trade laws are on the books).

Retail price. The selling price—the price at which an article of merchandise is offered to the customer.

Return-on-investment pricing. Also known as "target pricing," this is where the firm will calculate alternative outcomes at different prices of various quantities and select the one that will offer the best return on their investment in the merchandise.

Seasonal discount. A reduction in selling price that is offered to encourage customers to purchase products in advance of a forthcoming season.

Selling price. The current list price which the customer is asked to pay.

Skimming price. A tactical price employed by a company pioneering a new product at the introductory stage of its life cycle. Here, the firm uses a higher-than-customary price and aims at prospects who would be receptive to such a price in order to recover some of the developmental and initial promotional costs involved.

Suggested price. Generally, a price recommended by the producer of a product for the retailer to follow.

Target pricing. See "return-on-investment" pricing.

Trade discount. Any reduction from the regular list prices of goods which is offered to middlemen as compensation for the functions they perform along the channel structure. Usually expressed as some percentage off the quoted price as, for example, $72.00 per dozen, less 45 percent.

Trade-in allowance. A deduction from the selling price of an article based upon the turning in of an old one of the same type.

Uniform delivered pricing. A form of geographical pricing where all customers are charged the same price even though they may be in different geographical areas. Here, the firm has calculated in advance the effects of differing freight charges and "built them in" to the price through some over-all adjustment for freight.

Unit pricing. Marking the price for differently-sized packages of the same product in terms of some basic unit of measurement (such as pounds or quarts) so that consumers are enabled to make more valid choices through comparison.

Variable pricing. A flexible pricing approach which permits the retailer to adjust his prices upwards or downwards (as in bargaining with a customer). A commonly used technique in the selling of used cars.

Wholesale price. The price at which a product will be offered by the wholesaler to the retailer.

Zone pricing. A form of geographical pricing, for instance, where a manufacturer sells its product at one price to all purchasers East of the Mississippi—and at another price to those West of the Mississippi. (An excellent example of zone pricing is that engaged in by the United States Post Office, in its handling of parcel post.)

FOR FURTHER INFORMATION

Books

Alpert, Mark I. *Pricing Decisions.* Glenview, Ill.: Scott, Foresman, 1971.

Haynes, W. Warren. *Pricing Decisions in Small Business.* Westport, Conn.: Greenwood, 1973.

Lere, John C. *Pricing Techniques for the Financial Executive.* New York: Wiley, 1974.

Marting, Elizabeth, ed. *Creative Pricing.* New York: American Management Associations, 1968.

Oxenfeldt, Alfred R. *Pricing Strategies.* New York: American Management Associations, 1975.

Simon, Sanford R. *Managing Marketing Profitability.* New York: American Management Associations, 1969.

Tucker, Spencer A. *Pricing for Higher Profit: Criteria, Methods, Applications.* New York: McGraw-Hill, 1966.

Free Materials from the Small Business Administration

Management Aids
> # 193—"What Is the Best Selling Price?"
>
> # 206—"Keep Pointed toward Profit"
>
> # 226—"Pricing for Small Manufacturers"

Small Marketers Aids
> # 25—"Are You Kidding Yourself About Your Profits?"
>
> # 105—"A Pricing Checklist for Managers"
>
> # 158—"A Pricing Checklist for Small Retailers"

Available from the Superintendent of Documents

Small Business Management Series
> # 25—"Guides for Profit Planning," Stock #045-000-00137-7, 59 pp., 85¢.

13

Promotion Management

"Persuasive communication" is an apt synonym for promotion. It is through well planned and coordinated promotional activities that consumers are attracted to your products or informed about your services, persuaded to try them, and ultimately become your regular customers.

The general purpose of this chapter is to bring that esoteric world of account executives and Madison Avenue down to a more practical reality which enables you to run this phase of your business with the same professionalism you need in other areas.

PROMOTIONAL OBJECTIVES

While promotional activities may be varied and subject to change, they do have to be congruent with the firm's long-range objectives. They must also be flexible enough to sometimes admit tactical maneuvering and, less frequently, allow broad changes in strategy as your company copes with competitors' moves and environmental dynamics. Common promotional objectives include:

- attracting new customers,
- establishing brand differentiation,
- building company (or store) image,
- increasing store traffic,
- introducing new products,
- obtaining additional distributors,
- opening up new territories,
- selling products or services,
- supporting the company's salespeople, and
- sustaining brand loyalty.

THE BUDGET FOR PROMOTION

To the average firm, setting the annual expenditure for promotion represents a complex challenge. There is no one pat approach here; management is generally unable to assess the consequences of allocating x dollars to next year's promotional activity. Most budget decisions in this area are judgmental in the nth degree. Often, they are preceded by an investigation (generally unscientific) which raises questions like:

- How much can we afford to allocate to promotion?
- Can we learn from our competitors? How much do they spend annually, on the average?
- What was the total dollar amount we spent last year, and how did it help our sales?
- Would we be better off putting some of our promotion money into new equipment or machinery? Office help? Additional salespeople?
- Are there particular promotion areas which need to be beefed up?

In planning the promotion budget, firms follow diverse strategies, perhaps gravitating from one to another every two or three years. A few are indicated below:

1. Allocating a small percentage of overall sales volume, usually matching the trend within the particular industry;
2. Defining the job that needs to be done and then estimating how much is required to accomplish the job;
3. Holding down next year's budget to the amount which will be spent during the current year (or making a minuscule adjustment in the percentage, upward or downward);

4. Going overboard for one year in order to match the estimated promotional expenditure of a leading competitor; and

5. Preparing several alternative budgets (low, medium, high) forecasting the expected return on investment for each, and then selecting the most promising one.

THE PROMOTION MIX

Promotion's first objective is to initiate demand for the company's products and services. Here the small business owner should think in terms of planning the blend or mixture of several basic ingredients, much like mixing a cocktail. This deliberate "mix" always encompasses three major ingredients (although the proportions vary depending on the nature of the job): *direct (personal) selling*, *advertising*, and *sales promotion*—with a dash of *publicity*.

DIRECT (PERSONAL) SELLING

For the small manufacturer or wholesaler, there's no doubt that energetic direct selling efforts constitute the most critical aspect of promotion. This is also true for the retail firm, though to a lesser degree. Retail selling differs radically from other forms of personal selling in that there is little need to "prospect" for customers in the usual sense, much less call on them to promote your wares. Good salespersonship is brought into play once the prospect enters the store.

So, this section is not addressed to retailers, but to the sales efforts of manufacturers, agents and brokers, and wholesalers.

Partnerships are frequently formed in which one partner has experience in plant operation and the other in sales, and in this case, the sales-oriented partner makes the necessary contacts and visits. More commonly, however, the young manufacturing company contracts with a selling agent for its particular product or product line.

Manufacturers' agents (or "reps") are "middlemen" in the channels of distribution who can offer the small firm quick entry into a territory by providing an experienced sales staff and ready-made customers. In brief, sales representatives can bring in orders for your company shortly after you sign up with them.

Generally, a sales rep is compensated on a commission basis, earning a small percentage of the total billings facilitated through his or her efforts. This approach enables you to calculate your sales costs with comparative ease.

For help in locating suitable agents, contact MANA (Manufacturers' Agents National Association) of Irvine, California[1], the National Council of Salesmen's Organizations in New York City[2], or your trade association.

Engaging a sales rep to promote your product has obvious advantages in cost and time; however, there are several drawbacks as well. Your representative also assists other clients, making it impossible to work 100 percent of the time on your behalf. In addition, if you don't renew your agreement when it expires, your rep may take along some of your customers to your competitor. Moreover, you might find your selling expenses running rather high if your sales volume increases substantially.

However, as sales volume continues to expand, management may eventually decide to take a giant step forward—initiating a sales force of its own.

SALES FORCE MANAGEMENT

Once this decision is reached, a number of problems have to be resolved, ranging from the kind and number of salespersons required, through developing training programs and plans for compensating salespeople to methods of deployment and supervision.

The productivity of the small firm's salespeople is of paramount importance in its attempt to secure a foothold in the competitive environment. The salespeople are its battle troops directly on the firing line; in fact, they are the very lifeline of the business.

There are literally hundreds of kinds of selling positions. Some require little in the way of ingenuity or sales ability, like that of the route salesperson who, while making rounds, routinely notes orders for milk, pretzels, potato chips, and other items onto a preprinted order form. Other selling jobs are more demanding, requiring a high level of creativity. Examples include the selling of life insurance, group pension plans, swimming pools, and retirement homes.

[1]P.O. Box 16878, Irvine, Calif. 92713.
[2]127 John Street, New York, N.Y. 10038.

Personnel Aspects

Evidently, good salespersonship is more of an art than a science. The expert practitioner needs to possess not only good communication skills but also a thorough understanding of the psychological processes underlying human interactions. Salespersons are not born with these capabilities; such skills are developed and enhanced through practice and training.

Few star sales performers are out of work. Consequently, it's difficult for the small company to locate unemployed top salespeople, much less hire them. It generally makes more sense for the young firm to hire "green troops"—potential salespeople—and then develop that potential through training. The company should search for individuals who display characteristics commonly found in successful salespersons: good communicative ability, empathy, drive, good appearance and posture, emotional balance, and so forth.

Before initiating a brand-new sales force to promote the product line, a company ought to make a careful appraisal of the characteristics and needs of its targeted prospect groups. In so doing, the company will gain insights into the type and caliber of salespersons needed to do the job well. (For details on how to recruit, train, and supervise employees, see Chapter 18, "Personnel Management.")

Organizational Structure

Sales forces are usually structured according to geographical requirements, along product lines, by customer type, or via some combination thereof. Of course, the right kind of internal organization is affected by a number of variables, most importantly: the product line, the amount of capital, the desired scope of sales activity, and the nature of the customers. In the earlier stages, the salespeople should be directed by the owner(s) of the business; later on, management may consider adding a sales manager to the organization for better results.

It is essential for outside salespeople to be backed up by: an efficient inside sales office, a failsafe order-processing and delivery system, diligent credit supervision, competent management, and good two-way communication.

How to Pay Your Salespeople

Logically, a major thrust behind any plan for compensating sales efforts ought to be the stimulation of sales productivity. What—and how—you pay your people should also be competitive, to deter them from leaving your employ to sign up with another company offering a more attractive arrangement. Naturally, any plan you select should be simple for your bookkeeping section to administer, and all details should be perfectly clear (and acceptable) to your sales personnel.

Three basic compensation plans are available for your purposes: the regular ("straight") salary approach, the "commission-only" plan, and the "combination" plan.

Regular Salary. This is the most frequently used method of compensating retail salesclerks; it's also favored for many other types of selling positions, especially for new salespeople. Management often prefers the regular salary plan because it then knows its sales costs exactly. Salespeople like the sense of security derived from a steady income for food, rent, and other bills. With this method, management feels reasonably assured that its sales representatives will avoid being too aggressive, often to the displeasure of clients. Under this approach, it's also relatively easy to shunt sales personnel into other activities, such as preparing sales analyses and projections, paperwork, and other office routine.

On the negative side, paying a steady salary does little to encourage above-the-median sales effort. When an individual's salary remains the same regardless of the amount of sales produced, there obviously exists little incentive to "try harder." (Of course, if an employee is too far under par, the possibility of losing the job does provide some motivation to work at an acceptable level!)

Another disadvantage of a regular salary is that selling costs remain the same whether the company's sales are on the upswing or going down. This can prove expensive to the firm when sales are depressed because sales costs increase percentage-wise. Moreover, salaried individuals do expect, over time, periodic pay increases; therefore, your sales costs are forced upwards over the years with this method of compensation. It's likely that the "hungry" or money-oriented salespeople won't be attracted by the regular salary plan, and, you may end up with a large percentage of mediocre producers on your sales force.

"Commission-Only." Some firms follow the philosophy that the salesperson ought to be paid only if he or she delivers sales. The rate of commission paid is dependent on (among other variables) the type of industry and the nature of the selling job required. The major advantage of the commission approach is that it provides a substantially high level of motivation for many

salespeople. While the sales cost tends to fluctuate with economic conditions and with productivity, paying more dollars in commissions can only mean that the company is earning higher profits simultaneously. Expressed as a percentage of sales, this cost remains a constant.

Top producers seem to like this approach. Indeed, many don't want to work on any other basis.

Of course, there are some minuses to be considered: When earnings depend entirely on sales productivity, people on a commission-only basis sometimes tend to sell more aggressively, possibly generating unfavorable customer reaction. Under this compensation plan too, a firm may find it more difficult to get its salespeople to perform other necessary, nonselling activities.

More properly classified as a "combination plan," a variation of the commission-only approach is the "guaranteed draw-against-commission", where a firm is willing to advance x amount of dollars to a salesperson in order to impart that needed sense of security to meet daily expenses.

Combination Plans. These approaches are designed to incorporate the more desirable features (from management's point of view) of both the regular salary and the commission-only plans, in an attempt to have the best of both worlds. Though there are a number of variations, the most common is the "salary-plus-commission" plan. A basic, steady salary designed to meet the salesperson's needs is furnished weekly, and a small percentage of actual sales is earned as a commission. This latter amount is often paid monthly. The thinking behind the combination approach runs this way: (1) it guarantees the salesperson some funds for paying current expenses, and (2) it provides some type of override which will induce the salesperson to try harder.

What to Do About Travel Expenses

The salesperson incurs expenses while wending his or her way from one account to the next. Included are the costs involved in traveling by rail, air, or automobile; meals on the road; overnight lodging; telephone calls; and the like. In the majority of instances, such expenses are reimbursed by the company.

Some firms, however, arrange to have their sales representatives pay their own expenses without reimbursement, usually by setting them up in a self-employed "independent contractor" type of relationship. Automobiles may be purchased or leased by the firm for their salespeople's use; other companies require the salesperson to use his or her own vehicle. Either approach has its benefits and drawbacks; your accountant, who knows *your* business, can give you advice in this area.

In setting up an expense-reimbursement plan, you should have your people report their expenses to you on a regular basis, preferably weekly. Check these expense reports carefully to insure that they reflect a relatively accurate picture; your position ought to be that your people will neither gain nor lose.

As a general rule, salespeople on the road should not expect to stay overnight at exclusive luxury hotels (with certain exceptions—specific industries, higher-level salespeople, and so on). Neither should they be expected to stay at rundown rooming houses. Indeed, the same type of accommodations are called for as if he or she were traveling for personal reasons. Likewise, reasonableness should be the keynote for dining out; these days, a daily "cap" of $25.00 for meals is ample. (Of course, this does not refer to taking prospects to dinner. That's entertainment!)

Deploying Your Troops

If you have the usual type of sales organization, you should consider assigning your salespeople to "manageable" territories. This approach permits you to pare travel costs substantially and to cover each area more intensively, thereby insuring better service to your firm's accounts. This arrangement also lends itself quite well to the fixing of responsibility; you will find it easier to hold your people accountable for both sales production and sales expenses.

In the selling game, a lot of time is frittered away on traveling to, from, and between accounts; waiting in outer reception areas until purchasing agents can be seen; doing paperwork and keeping records; and so forth. Proper attention to the scheduling and routing of your salespeople can reduce much of these wasted efforts.

Training Your Salespeople

In a healthy sales organization, training is a continuous function, with initial training when the employee first joins the company, and follow-up or refresher training later on. The content of beginning training programs should encompass topics like the history of the company, the product line, pricing, the demographics and other characteristics of the firm's clientele, internal systems, and sales instruction. More advanced training is often oriented toward improving sales performance: methods of prospecting, how to make more effective presentations, ways of handling objections, how to close a sale, and the like.

Available training methods run the gamut from formal classroom lectures to programmed instruction and self-study. Included here are small-group discussions, role-playing, demonstrations by top salespeople, films and other audiovisual material and equipment, attending salesmanship classes at local universities, and so forth.

ASSESSING SALES PERFORMANCE

Evaluations of sales personnel have at least two primary purposes: (1) to provide management with information for decision-making in this particular promotion area, and (2) to improve the performance of salespeople over time. While continuous training for people in the selling operation is admittedly essential—not only for improving sales skills but also for teaching self-management—the gathering of comparative data does enable supervisory management to pinpoint deficiencies and correct below-par performances.

Both subjective and objective approaches should be used to assess selling performance. Subjective observations include: the salesperson's extent of company knowledge and product knowledge, familiarity with competitive organizations and their offerings, the ability to communicate effectively, good personal appearance and proper attire, steady work habits, and the like; objective evaluation mainly consists of comparing the "input-output" statistics of fellow salespeople. Among the more useful ratios and indexes in this connection are: the number of orders secured each month related to the number of calls made, the average sales volume per order, the number of new accounts landed per the number of visits made, and so on.

The booklet "Measuring the Performance of Salesmen" is of particular assistance to the small business person (Free from the Small Business Administration). Figure 13–1 reproduces two helpful aids from this booklet.

ADVERTISING

For many small manufacturers advertising constitutes the bulk of the total promotional effort. In contrast to personal selling, advertising is simply paid communication designed to influence prospects and customers en masse.

Effective management of this area of your business requires attention to specifics like selecting (and then researching) market segments, setting advertising objectives, conceptualizing plans, constructing messages and advertisements, selecting the media for reaching your targets, and so on.

One basic principle to follow here is to reach as many of your "preselected" audience as you can at as low a cost as possible. This may be accomplished through a variety of media—newspapers, magazines, radio, television, billboards, subway and bus cards, direct mail, circulars, and the like. Of course, it's difficult (if not impossible) to assess the effectiveness of your firm's advertising. Mail order and direct mail advertising are an exception: Responses to your advertisements can be keyed or couponed and some evaluation made of results.

Types of Advertising

Depending upon how you look at it, advertising may be classified in a number of ways:

1. According to the firm's position along the channel of distribution, either *manufacturer*, *wholesaler*, or *retailer* advertising (Where the cost of advertising is shared by two channel members, this is referred to as *cooperative* advertising.);
2. According to the intended geographical coverage, that is, *national*, *regional*, or *local* advertising;

SOUND CRITERIA FOR MEASURING PERFORMANCE?

Which of the following are sound criteria for measuring the performance of salesmen?

1. Volume of sales in dollars.

2. Amount of time spent in the office.

3. Personal appearance, for example, clothes, style of haircut, cleanliness, and neatness.

4. Number of calls made on existing accounts.

5. Number of new accounts opened.

6. Completeness and accuracy of sales orders.

7. Promptness in submitting reports.

8. Dollars spent in entertaining customers.

9. Extent to which salesman sells his company.

10. Accuracy in quoting prices and deliveries to customers.

11. Knowledge of the business.

12. Planning and routing of calls.

FIGURE 13–1a
Reproduced from "Measuring the Performance of Salesmen" (Management Aids No. 190) (Washington, D.C.: Small Business Administration, 1975), p. 6.

GUIDE FOR IMPROVING A SALESMAN'S PERFORMANCE

One goal of measuring a salesman's performance is to help him improve. The three steps in bringing about improvement, when, and if, it is needed are: planning, measuring, and correcting.

PLANNING

• Get the salesman's agreement about what he is to attain or exceed for the next year:
(1) Total profit contribution in dollars.
(2) Profit contribution in dollars for:
Each major product line.
Each major market (By industry or geographical area).
Each of 10–20 target accounts (for significant new and additional business).

• Get the salesman's agreement about expenses within which he is to stay for the next year:
(1) His total sales expense budget in dollars.
(2) His budget in dollars for: travel, customer entertainment, telephone, and other expenses.

• Have the salesman plan the number of calls he will make to accounts and prospects during the next year.

MEASURING

• Review at least monthly the salesman's record for:
(1) Year-to-date progress toward his 12-month profit contribution goals.
(2) Year-to-date budget compliance.

CORRECTING

Meet with salesman if his record shows that he is 10 percent or more off target. Review with him the number of calls he has made on each significant account plus what he feels are his accomplishments and problems. In addition, you may need to do some of the following to help him improve his performance:

• Give salesman more day-to-day help and direction.

• Accompany salesman on calls to provide coaching.

• Conduct regular sales meetings on subjects which salesmen want covered.

• Increase sales promotion activities.

• Transfer accounts to other salesmen if there is insufficient effort or progress.

• Establish tighter control over price variances allowed.

• Increase or reduce selling prices.

• Add new products or services.

• Increase salesman's financial incentive.

• Transfer, replace, or discharge salesman.

FIGURE 13–1b
Reproduced from "Measuring the Performance of Salesmen" (Management Aid No. 190) (Washington, D.C.: Small Business Administration, 1975), p. 7.

3. By the media employed, either *television*, *radio*, *print* (newspaper, magazine), *outdoor* (billboard), *car card* (subway, bus), *direct mail*, or *mail-order* advertising; and

4. By what is being advertised, that is, *product*, *brand*, or *institutional* (company, industry) advertising.

The Media

Where to advertise?

Proper media selection is a most difficult task for the entrepreneur. For optimum yield, specialized knowledge is a must. If you envision a moderate-sized advertising budget for your new business, you are strongly urged to enlist the services of a small advertising agency willing to take on your account and grow along with you.

Some factors to take into account in making media choices are: the appropriateness and size of each medium's audience or readership, comparative media costs, production costs, and the relative rapidity of results you can expect. Each medium has its own particular attributes, negative as well as positive.

Where speedy action is wanted, television, radio, and the daily newspaper lead all other media. Reaction to advertising in these three media is almost immediate; 70 to 80 percent (if not more) of the results will be in within the first week. Consequently, these are the favorite choices for retailers; indeed, most of your newspaper's advertising is local store advertising. Television is only occasionally resorted to by the smaller retail firm; the preparation of even a 30-second commercial is expensive. This is why television is primarily the domain of the larger, mass merchandising companies.

Local radio is relatively more feasible for the smaller company, and of value in reaching specific segments of the market or for offering special "deals" or promotions. Of course, radio copy can be written for you by your local station representative.

In small towns, the local newspaper is a valuable medium for the majority of businesses. In a metropolitan area, however, much of the newspaper's circulation is "waste" simply because a substantial majority of the readers lives or works miles away from the location. Unless the "drawing power" of the advertisement is exceptional, it's doubtful that many of those people would come down to the store. On the other hand, weekly area newspapers—or small-space classified advertisements used on a regular basis—can be of value. A listing in the yellow pages of the local telephone directory can also reach customers.

You should know that newspapers can assist you in preparing copy as well as layout for your purposes. Often they are able to furnish standard illustrations or cuts for a more effective presentation.

Magazines and trade journals can be effective media when used for expanding your distribution, securing additional dealers for your products or services, recruiting salespeople in different territories, or selling merchandise by mail order.

For retail store owners, the handbill or flier is a relatively inexpensive, yet often effective medium. I'm not referring to simplistic printed announcements but to well-conceived and imaginative messages aimed at motivating people to visit your store.

Here's a case in point: A young technician completed an excellent course of training in television repair and servicing and then opened a small repair shop. His was an "off-main-street" location, one that carried a low monthly rental. However, the area was literally saturated with block after block of apartment houses. For a rather low investment (about $75), he printed up 2,000 handbills which he managed to personally distribute to occupants throughout the buildings. Because the sheet offered a free service call (at no charge) and suggested that the apartment dwellers keep the flier handy "just in case," he was able to build a substantial clientele within a few months.

This leads us to the following suggestions for your advertising messages:

Messages

Any advertising for your own company should be designed primarily to inform people about your products or services and to persuade them to buy. Hence, whatever the medium you select, each "message" ought to reflect all of the following characteristics:

- It should be clear, and couched in the targeted customers' vocabulary
- It should provoke interest
- It should appeal to people's wants and needs
- It should stress desirable features of the product
- It should sound believable
- It should motivate prople to buy
- It should tell them where they can buy

In addition to the copy, artwork and layout are also essential elements in preparing newspaper advertisements. Artwork and layout complement and reinforce the copy while at the same time attract the attention of more readers. In this respect, large black type (or unusual type faces), borders around the advertisement, illustrations, and halftones (photographs) will not only contribute to the total message but also result in expanded readership. Yes, a picture may indeed be worth a thousand words (or more!).

As a general rule, doubling the size of the advertisement does not by any means trigger an automatic 100 percent increase in the number of readers; often, only an additional 10 or 15 percent readership can be expected. Given the erratic, though perfectly normal behavior of the fallible human memory, there is far more value in the design and use of an "advertising campaign" than in scheduling a single, one-shot advertisement, no matter how large, in the newspaper. Preferably, one ought to think in psychological terms—the reinforcement of learning that takes place in the regular reader's mind as a result of "frequency of exposure."

SALES PROMOTION

Sales promotion is a composite of activities that round out the personal selling and advertising components of the company's promotion mix. It mainly seeks to stimulate sales—at the point of purchase (when selling consumer goods and services through retail stores and service shops), and by assisting the middlemen (wholesalers and retailers) as they move these products toward the targeted purchasers. In addition, sales promotion aids both manufacturer and distributor handling industrial goods.

Among the techniques employed are: catalogs, reprints of advertisements, special displays and display fixtures, banners and signs, exhibits and trade shows, and the like. Their major contribution is in the areas of training, supporting, and otherwise helping along the efforts of the salespeople involved.

Promotion at the Point of Purchase

The sales promotion tools wielded by today's retailers are legion; a few of the more popular techniques are indicated below:

contests	giveaways
coupons	premiums
demonstrations	PMs ("Push Money")
displays	sales

endorsements	sampling
fashion shows	special offers
free goods	tie-in promotions
games	trading stamps

In the listing above, *displays* are the single most significant category for the retail store.

Display. The majority of retail firms rely on window displays to attract the attention of passersby, to hook their interest, and induce them to enter the store. Once inside, they can be persuaded to make purchases through good salespersonship on the part of the clerks, aided by additional (interior) displays.

While a detailed treatment of this important area is beyond the scope of this chapter, here are some basic pointers to provide general directions for window displays:

1. Shoppers will regard your store front and show window as the "face" of your retail business. Therefore, the window treatments should always convey the impressions of quality, style, and distinctiveness which you would like to project.

2. Displays should be kept clean and neat in appearance at all times. A crowded display contributes nothing but clutter; instead, use air (or "breathing") space between merchandise groupings.

3. Whether you engage the services of a professional window trimmer or you do the displays yourself, your windows should be changed frequently. At least 10 to 15 changes each year are recommended. (Hint: You might be able to hire someone with window display training from the local high school's distributive education program.)

4. Window displays are generally more effective when built around a single, unifying theme (Going-Back-to-School, Mother's Day, Christmas, Springtime, Vacation Fun, Travel, and so on).

5. Merchandise, materials, display stands, mannequins (if required) and signs or posters should be carefully selected and prepared ahead of time so that the window may be completely trimmed without incident within a few hours' time.

6. In selecting appropriate merchandise to put into the window, pay careful attention to the seasonality factor, to product sales appeal, and to individual gross markups.

7. Color is an essential ingredient of display. The color combinations used in the window should be attractive and harmonious.

8. Window bases (platforms) are usually covered with appropriate materials which contribute to the overall effect of the display—satins, netting, burlap, paper, artificial grass mats, and so forth. The retailer ought to build up a stock of such materials, over time.

9. All point-of-purchase materials, such as sign tickets, posters, banners, and the like, should look professional and be kept perfectly clean.

10. Special effects, such as motion, lighting, and sound, can be used profitably in connection with your display to draw attention to the window. As a simple example, motion can be imparted to a section of your display through use of a small electric (or battery-operated) turntable or ceiling turner.

A Word or Two About Public Relations

The phrase "Public Relations" is a catch-all sort of term. Narrowly interpreted, it seems to imply no more than a stream of news releases emitted by the company over time that manage to find their way into print—or over the radio. Such an interpretation leads many business executives to consider "P.R." as tantamount to free, unpaid advertising.

These kind of news release are more in the realm of "publicity" than of public relations.

More properly defined, public relations is a broad area of company behavior, expressive of the firm's attitudes toward others. In the main, it consists of meaningful, two-way communication between the company and its many publics: internal (employees, supervisors, executives) as well as external (customers, prospective customers, suppliers, competitors, government agencies, and so on).

Every company has public relations; the P.R. may be good, fair, or poor. A good public relations program starts with the firm's owner(s) and reflects its way down throughout the organization: in good employee relations as well as in good company relationships with the outside world. Good P.R. has to do with observing guarantees on products, acting aboveboard in conducting business, showing courtesy in the treatment of all, answering complaints promptly, and so forth.

Books

Baer, Earl E. *Salesmanship*. New York: McGraw-Hill, 1972.

Caples, John. *Tested Advertising Methods*, 4th ed. Englewood Cliffs, N.J.: Prentice-Hall, 1974.

Dodge, H. Robert. *Field Sales Management: Text and Cases*. Dallas: Business Publications, 1973.

Engel, James F., Wales, Hugh G., and Warshaw, Martin R. *Promotional Strategy*, 3rd ed. Homewood, Ill.: Irwin, 1975.

Johnson, H. Webster. *Creative Selling*, 2nd ed. Cincinnati: South-Western, 1974.

————. *Sales Management: Operations, Administration, Marketing*. Columbus: Merrill, 1976.

Kirkpatrick, C. A., and Russ, Frederick A. *Salesmanship,* 6th ed. Cincinnati: South-Western, 1976.

Kurtz, David L., Dodge, H. Robert, and Klompmaker, Jay E. *Professional Selling*. Dallas: Business Publications, 1976.

Pederson, Carlton A., and Wright, Milburn D. *Selling: Principles and Methods*, 6th ed. Homewood, Ill.: Irwin, 1976.

Robeson, James F., Mathews, H. Lee, and Stevens, Carl G. *Selling*. Homewood, Ill.: Irwin, 1976.

Russell, Frederic A., Beach, Frank H., and Buskirk, Richard D. *Textbook of Salesmanship*, 10th ed. New York: McGraw-Hill, 1978.

Stanley, Richard E. *Promotion: Advertising, Publicity, Personal Selling, Sales Promotion*. Englewood Cliffs, N.J.: Prentice-Hall, 1977.

Stanton, William J., and Buskirk, Richard H. *Management of the Sales Force*, 5th ed. Homewood, Ill.: Irwin, 1978.

Stroh, Thomas F. *Managing the Sales Function*. New York: McGraw-Hill, 1978.

Ulanoff, Stanley. *Advertising in America*. New York: Hastings House, 1977.

Wright, John S., and Warner, Daniel S. *Advertising*, 4th ed. New York: McGraw-Hill, 1977.

Free Materials from the Small Business Administration

Management Aids

#178—"Effective Industrial Advertising for Small Plants"

#187—"Using Census Data in Small Plant Marketing"

#188—"Developing a List of Prospects"

#190—"Measuring the Performance of Salesmen"

#192—"Profile Your Customers to Expand Industrial Sales"

#200—"Is the Independent Sales Agent for You?"

#230—"Selling Products on Consignment"

Small Business Bibliographies

> #20—"Advertising—Retail Store"
>
> #29—"National Mailing List Houses"

Small Marketers' Aids

> #111—"Interior Display: A Way to Increase Sales"
>
> #113—"Quality and Taste As Sales Appeals"
>
> #121—"Measuring the Results of Advertising"
>
> #161—"Signs and Your Business"

Available from the Superintendent of Documents

Small Business Management Series

> #27—"Profitable Community Relations for Small Business," Stock #045-000-00033-8, 36 pp., $1.50.
>
> #36—"Training Salesmen to Serve Industrial Markets," Stock #045-000-00133-4, 85 pp., $1.15.

14

Distribution Management

The area of distribution is still another major constituent of the marketing mix. Involved here are the logistics necessary to deliver the company's products and/or services to the right places at the right time in the right quantities, and at the lowest costs. For the most part, distribution management encompasses the concept of "marketing channels" through which the merchandise moves, both storage and transportation aspects of marketing, and the allocation of inventories.

Visualize a small factory that produces inexpensive ladies' slippers: The slipper manufacturer brings in raw materials and perhaps semi-finished goods, slipper components, packaging materials and other supplies, and then manufactures the finished products on his machines, packages them, cartons the packages, and ships the lot off "to market." Unless the producing firm wishes to assume the burden of selling the slippers by the pair in a door-to-door canvassing operation, the services of one or more intermediaries, called "middlemen," are required. The merchandise is funneled into a kind of pipeline, and then propelled through to the customers. In actuality, this "pipeline" is a set of component companies, linked together to form a "marketing channel."

MARKETING CHANNELS IN THE ECONOMY

Without a sales contingent of its own, the small manufacturing firm will probably resort to consigning its output to an "agent" for the purposes of securing distribution. In turn, the agent might call on various local wholesalers—or operate on a more expanded scale if the output is large—to interest them in taking on the new line of products. As alternatives, the manufacturer may decide to deal directly with one large distributor which maintains a sizable sales force, or opt instead to sell directly to a number of large retail outlets in his area.

Evidently, the "more cooks are in the broth," the less control the producer can exercise over the product line. Of course, adding intermediaries necessitates building a cost structure to compensate each of the channel members for the part it plays in the total distribution process. The small business and its management must carefully assess the benefits and drawbacks of the various alternatives, each of which may yield a different payoff for the manufacturing company. Figure 14–1 contains a diagram of the customary channel choices.

SOME NOTES ON CHANNEL MEMBERS

"Intermediaries" are those firms that play roles within the channels of distribution between the producing company and the ultimate consumer; they are commonly called "middlemen." Most people are familiar with the role of the retailer within the economy, and so it won't be treated in this section. Most of us, however, have not had substantial contact with wholesaling institutions.

Wholesalers

The Federal Government traditionally describes the activities and contributions of wholesale enterprises in five separate categories, as follows:

- wholesalers,
- agents and brokers,

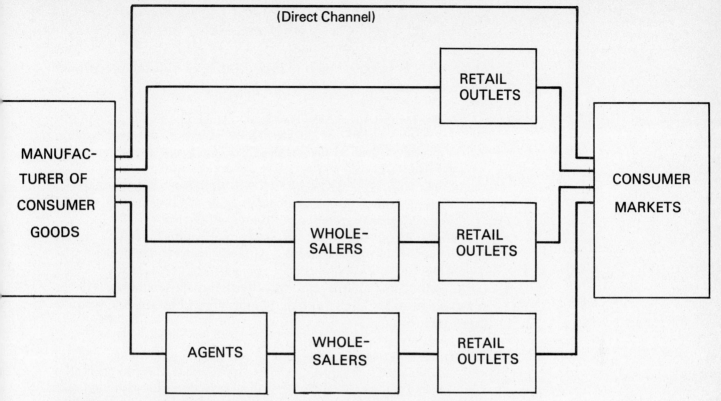

FIGURE 14–1 Distribution channels for a manufacturer of consumer goods.

- manufacturers' sales branches,
- petroleum bulk plants and terminals, and
- assemblers.

Probably only the first two categories are of interest to the majority of people reading this book, and so the other categories won't be discussed further.

The majority of wholesaling firms fall into the "regular" or "merchant" wholesaler category. Such companies purchase materials and merchandise in large quantities, warehouse them, then break them down into smaller shipments for distribution to retail firms. Other terms for "wholesaler" include "distributor" and "jobber."

Most regular wholesalers are termed "full-service" or "full-function" because they perform all the necessary functions of wholesalers in the marketing channel: buying, selling, storage, distribution, extending credit, providing sales information and assistance, and so forth. Some, on the other hand, are known as "limited-service" wholesalers because they do not perform all of the services which are expected. For instance, some types do not extend credit to their customers but require cash on delivery; others will not store the merchandise.

Full-Service Wholesale Firms.   Three types of full-service wholesalers are found:

1. *The General Merchandise Wholesaler.* Much like a general store that carries a variety of different lines of goods, this type of firm provides "general merchandise" to larger and departmentalized retail stores.
2. *The Single Line Wholesaler.* A firm equipped to supply its retail clients with a complete, in-depth stock in one particular line of goods, such as groceries, hardware, and the like.
3. *The Specialty Wholesaler.* A company that usually handles a small number of products within a particular merchandise line.

Limited-Function Wholesalers.   Middlemen in this category are far fewer in number than regular wholesalers. The more common types include:

1. *The Cash-and-Carry Wholesaler.* Often a chain operation, this distributor sets up outlets at convenient locations where local retailers may come in, purchase needed merchandise with cash, and take the goods out with them. Common examples are those selling bottled/canned beverages and grocery items.
2. *The Drop-Shipper.* Found most frequently in the coal, lumber, and metals industries, this type of wholesaler usually purveys raw materials or bulky products of a low unit price to industrial users, though not limited to such products or markets. This middleman does not take physical possession of the merchandise at any point, nor puts it in a warehouse, but rather arranges for the producer to ship the goods directly to the customer. This type of firm (sometimes a one-person operation, commonly called a "desk jobber") is billed directly by the producer, and in turn, sends an invoice to the customer, for payment. The customer must be billed at a price high enough to incorporate a margin of profit for the middleman.
3. *The Mail-Order Wholesaler.* This type of company offers smaller retailers merchandise for resale, characteristically through the medium of printed catalogs issued periodically.
4. *The Rack Jobber.* This name is earned by the wholesale business involved in distributing specialized lines of soft-cover books and magazines, toys, health and beauty aids, novelties, household items, and the like through supermarkets and other high-traffic stores. The goods are merchandised with the aid of many types of display racks frequently placed on consignment within a store. It's the jobber's responsibility to keep the racks well-stocked and fresh-looking.
5. *The Truck Jobber.* Commonly encountered in the grocery trade, this type of distributor services retail outlets directly from a truck with fast-moving products and perishable goods. In addition to fresh fruits and vegetables, the truck jobber handles dairy products, cookies, frozen foods, and similar items.

Agents and Brokers. These middlemen, found in many lines of business, are mostly specialized individuals and small enterprises. Essentially, their business activity consists of buying and selling on behalf of others (principals), thereby earning commissions or fees. Apart from well-known types such as real estate and life insurance agents, there are two major classifications for the business person to become familiarized with: the *manufacturer's agent*, and the *selling agent*. The label depends on the scope of activities the agent performs on behalf of the principal.

The manufacturers in search of distribution in a specific geographical area (who do not have their own sales force) contract with an agent to represent the company in the selected area. Hence, the oft employed synonym "manufacturer's representative" or more simply, "rep." Usually the rep is assigned an exclusive territory to operate in. He or she handles only a portion of the total output from the manufacturer and may also represent other producers (usually with complementary lines) in the same area. Reps are asked to sell an entire "package" handed over to them by the manufacturer; there is little or no discussion over details like prices, terms, quantities, and such.

On the other hand, the manufacturer gives the "selling agent" extensive authority over the details of prices, terms, customer selection—the entire production of the plant. Sometimes called a "commission agent," this middleman often maintains a sizable, effective sales force. The relationship between this agent and the principal is a close one; indeed, it may even call for the agent to extend financial aid to the principal when imperative.

Finally, the "broker" functions as an intermediary between buyers and sellers, bringing together the two parties while representing either side (not both at once, of course!).

TRANSPORTATION

This is a major decision area for manufacturer and wholesaler, as the costs of transportion can range from a mere fraction of the item's selling price (the case with grain, coal, gravel, and other bulky commodities) to as much as 40 percent and even higher. Consequently, transportation (or "traffic") management must focus on two major objectives: (1) minimizing costs and, at the same time, (2) insuring speedy, reliable delivery of the merchandise.

Goods are moved about by land, water, or air through a variety of transportation modes employed singly or in combination, and with the assistance of several supporting agencies.

Major Transport Modes

Materials and products move overland by means of trucks, trains, and pipelines. Goods are also moved by air (airmail, air freight) and by water (inland waterways, ocean transport). A brief overview of these five major modes of transportation follows:

1. *Truck Transport.* The shipping method most frequently employed by small business (and often by large businesses as well) trucks offer faster and more frequent delivery to more destinations in the country than any other mode. They are particularly useful for short-distance shipments.

2. *Trains.* The railroads offer regular service to more distant areas and are especially valuable in transporting machinery, heavy equipment, cattle and livestock, commodities, and so forth. Over their lengthy history of service to the nation, the railroads have developed a number of customer benefits which are peculiar to this mode. Examples of such services include in-transit privileges, diversion-in-transit, demurrage and others.

3. *Pipelines.* This method is generally confined to the movement of petroleum products.

4. *Air.* A more costly method of transporting merchandise, shipments by air are customarily of value for the rapid movement of highly perishable goods (exotic plants, sea food, and the like) and items of a high unit value, such as diamonds, jewelry, expensive drugs, rare paintings, and so forth.

5. *Water.* Moving material by barge along the nation's inland waterways is a low-cost method of transportation. Ocean transport, of course, is significant to the import and export trades.

Auxiliary Services

Several important transport services assist in the movement of goods. These include the freight forwarders, shippers associations, and the United Parcel Service. In addition, the U.S. Post Office forwards small shipments through their Parcel Post service.

WAREHOUSING

Moving the goods or materials from one stop to the next along the marketing channel is one major facet of distribution; another important aspect is the temporary storage, or warehousing, of merchandise. There are labor-saving approaches to materials handling, warehousing methods, and inventory procedures all of which merit managerial attention.

Companies that require warehousing facilities must decide to either (a) maintain their own, strategically-located depot(s) or

(b) resort to holding their goods in public warehouses. In contrast to the older, multi-story structures which dot metropolitan areas around the country, today's modern warehouse is commonly a long, low one-story building located outside a city (with access to a major highway) where land costs are substantially less. With this type of construction there is no need for installing and maintaining freight (and passenger) elevators, or building staircases and stair wells, and no concern (or added expense) is necessary for floor load limits, and the like. Furthermore, the internal flow of stock can run a straight course instead of proceeding up and down a number of levels; merchandise comes in at one end of the rectangular structure, is stored in the center, and then departs through the other end. Because of excellent warehouse layout and operation—including wide aisles and skids (or pallets) on which cases of goods are stacked—heavy machinery such as fork lifts can easily move the merchandise.

Receiving and Shipping

Ideally then, goods are brought in through truck bays onto receiving platforms where they are accepted by the Receiving Department. Here, each incoming delivery is recorded in the "Receiving Log," a register where data such as date and time of shipment, name of supplier, name of transporting agency, invoice number, number of cartons or cases received, and so forth are recorded. The delivery is unloaded and checked against the accompanying bill of lading for quantities, contents, possible damage, and the like. The goods received are then consigned to specific locations within the warehouse proper, as reserve stock for future shipment.

When orders are received by the Shipping Department from the sales division, order pickers in the warehouse select the merchandise specified, assembling them in a staging area where they are shipped out. Of course, shipping times and routing are worked out in advance with an eye to transportation capability and costs.

Inventory Control

A vital phase of warehouse operation is the inventory procedure established to keep track of the merchandise. You can keep a running "book inventory" of all receipts and withdrawals, either by hand or by mechanical or electronic means; however, no method is as accurate as the taking of physical inventory on a periodic basis (weekly, monthly, quarterly, or otherwise). This involves counting directly all cases, cartons, and individual pieces of stock throughout the building, including both the receiving and shipping departments. Physical inventory is usually accomplished by a team: one individual checks out every nook and cranny of the premises, calling out the count to a second person who enters the quantities onto a preprinted inventory sheet. Totals and extensions (translating the totals into dollar figures) are done later on in the bookkeeping section.

FOR FURTHER INFORMATION

Books

Ballou, Ronald H. *Basic Business Logistics*. Englewood Cliffs, N.J.: Prentice-Hall, 1978.

Bowersox, Donald J. *Logistical Management*. New York: Macmillan, 1974.

Mallen, Bruce. *Principles of Marketing Channel Management*. Lexington, Mass.: D.C. Heath, 1977.

Michman, Ronald D. *Marketing Channels*. Columbus: Grid, 1974.

Smykay, E. W. *Physical Distribution Management*, 3rd ed. New York: Macmillan, 1973.

Walters, C. Gleen. *Marketing Channels*. New York: Ronald Press, 1974.

Free Materials from the Small Business Administration

Management Aids:
#199—"Expand Overseas Sales With Commerce Department Help"

#200—"Is the Independent Sales Agent for You?"

#203—"Are Your Products and Channels Producing Sales?"

Available from the Superintendent of Documents

Nonseries Publications:
"Export Marketing for Smaller Firms," Stock #034-000-00112-1, 134 pp., $1.65.

15

Marketing Research

Marketing success is largely realized through: (1) carefully and continually appraising the total environment, internal as well as external; (2) setting realistic marketing objectives based on sound judgments; (3) providing structures for reaching these objectives; and (4) assessing the results of marketing efforts so that further improvements can be made.

The first step in the process implies *knowing* before *doing*, and knowing is therefore basic to marketing management. Far too often, small business is conducted by intuition, probably because the majority of problems repeat and once solved, provide direction for decisions in the next similar situation. Nevertheless, it makes good sense to carefully investigate new problems—and more complex problems—before making decisions, and certainly before coming up with marketing plans.

Here's an illustration: Do you recall the last time you were in the market for a new automobile? Most likely, you visited a showroom where you were promptly greeted by a salesperson. Think back to that meeting; try to recall the conversation between the two of you. Isn't it true that what the salesperson talked about and did in those first few minutes with you were more attuned to "reading" you as a prospective customer than to anything else? This was important, simply because the sales presentation could be tailored directly to you and your needs, increasing chances for a sale and a commission.

In that transaction, you witnessed the "exchange process" in action: Your money was exchanged for the ownership of the car. Remember, too, that communication was involved, on a one-to-one basis (the most persuasive way to communicate).

It is no different with any company that seeks to sell its products or services. Remember: The primary purpose behind a firm's promotional activities is to make sales. Again, this is done through communication, whether on a one-to-one basis as in personal selling, or indirectly through advertising and/or sales promotion. The key thought here is: the more a company knows about its prospects, the better it can tailor its messages to reach those prospects and induce them to become customers.

At any event, it should be clear to you now that attempts to "read" or "research" prospective customers can be of help to you in your own business.

NATURE OF MARKETING RESEARCH

Marketing research is a collective term; it embraces all the activities that assist management in reaching marketing decisions. In reality, it's nothing more or less than a logical, orderly approach to fact-finding. Marketing research reduces unknowns to knowns, thereby reducing risks, and enables management to make more rational choices among alternatives.

It should be understood from the outset that no planning is 100 percent infallible. No one can predict the future with certainty. To put it differently, all that research can do (if done properly) is increase your chances of coming up with better decisions. Don't think of it as a substitute for your business acumen, but simply as an additional managerial tool for you to use.

To the small business owner, marketing research appears to be a "frill"—something which only the larger corporations can afford to pursue. The entrepreneur rarely gets involved in this form of activity. What holds him or her back, apparently, are: (1) a lack of familiarity not only with the methods and techniques of research but even with its purposes; (2) the realization that outside research services are costly; and (3) an inability to evaluate such costs in concrete terms, such as return on investment.

When you get right down to it, all business executives conduct research on occasion, usually without realizing that's what they're doing. Comparing yesterday's sales figures with those of the same day or date last year, and drawing conclusions (which may be correct or erroneous) falls into the research category. Simple business research includes: telephoning a sampling of your customers to ask their opinions about a new product or service you are offering, carefully checking through the rate schedules and readership data of various magazines in order to determine the best place for your one-column advertisement; or studying the "production" ratios of your six salesmen (number of calls made per day, number of sales per 100 calls, and so on) for the purpose of discovering who may need more training or assistance.

Like any other form of activity, research can be performed in a careless, slipshod manner or in a more disciplined fashion. Of course, the way you conduct it influences the extent to which you find the results useful.

It goes without saying that the large-scale, formal type of study cannot be undertaken on a regular basis in the small company. There just isn't that kind of room in the operating budget. However, both the brand-new as well as the established small business need to carry on simple research from time to time in such vital areas as sales, market analysis, company growth, and the like.

A SIMPLE APPROACH TO FOLLOW

If you've had any military training in your past, you are more than familiar with the "by-the-numbers" learning technique. Here is a simple approach to use when you need to gather information to help you solve a business problem:

1. Try to clarify the problem in your mind by attempting to put down on paper a clearcut statement of it, preferably in the form of a question. Some examples of common problems might be: "What method can I use to control my inventory?... How can

we increase sales by 10 percent in New Jersey?... Through what channels should we distribute our products?... How can we motivate our salesclerks?"... and so on.

2. Next, do some investigating: Examine past records of your company that may pertain to the problem at hand, speak with knowledgeable people who might be able to shed some light on the subject, and try to find out if any informaton has been published in the particular area which you are investigating. During this "searching" stage you may encounter several possible solutions to your problem; if one or more of these seem applicable, you need go no further.

3. Should you decide you need more details, and if it's worth your time, effort, and the expense involved, then you can proceed to a more sophisticated level. You may want to set up a simple questionnaire, to be mailed out to your customers, your suppliers, or to specific groups in the general population, depending upon the nature of your problem. For faster results you can query some of these people over the telephone. (Both of these approaches are treated at greater length in a later section of this chapter.)

4. Finally, for an occasional problem that resists your best efforts at solving, you might consider hiring a research firm to handle the project, provided it's worth the costs involved. Turn things over to specialists who are thoroughly familiar with suitable study designs, how to select sample populations, collecting data, and how to analyze the findings statistically.

Later on in this chapter, there is a section entitled "A Simple, Inexpensive Research Tool for the Small Business." You can use it to tap the opinions, attitudes, likes, and dislikes of your customers about your company, your products and prices, your promotional efforts, and so forth. In brief, it can produce effective "customer-oriented" facts for making decisions in business. It also has a good many other applications.

TYPES OF MARKETING RESEARCH

Here is a convenient classification of the more common types of studies used in business to help managers make better decisions.

1. *Market Research*   Ascertaining the needs and wants of prospective customers, assessing the potential of specific market areas, studies of competition, and so on.

2. *Product Research*   Research into new product development, testing the prices of products to determine whether they are too high or too low, and other investigative activities.

3. *Promotion Research*   Checking the effectiveness of displays or advertising copy, comparing different newspapers and magazines as to costs involved and numbers of readers reached, and similar research.

4. *Sales Research*   Evaluating the performance of salespeople, studies of sales expenses and sales, territory analysis, and the like.

5. *Company Research*   Checking business trends for the industry and the firm, investigating the firm's "image," studies of employee morale or facility locations.

HOW TO GATHER INFORMATION

In the process of collecting information for decision-making, it is prudent to think in terms of two general categories of information—"primary" and "secondary." Primary information is those facts which are not available and which therefore require of the investigator considerable initiative and effort; secondary information encompasses facts which are normally available, although they necessitate some searching around. The trick with "secondary data" is to know the sources you can go to—how and where to locate the information desired.

Chances are that most of the "fact-finding" you'll be doing in your small business will involve secondary data; hence, this category is discussed first.

Secondary Data

Here, several cautions need to be borne in mind: the reliability of the source, the possibility of bias on the part of the collecting agent, the fact that the information is obviously dated, the applicability of the information to your specific problem since the facts may have originally been gathered for a completely different purpose, and so forth.

Among the many sources of secondary information are internal company records of all kinds, government compilations of statistics, trade associations, public and university libraries, research organizations, business and scholarly journals, and reference works such as encyclopedias. In the majority of instances the two most fruitful sources for solving your business problems will be the internal records of your company and government statistics.

Company Records. In the established firm, there are abundant records available of every type. These include historical sales data on a daily, weekly, and monthly basis; records of inventory levels and flow; financial statements; purchasing records; personnel files; and so on. Often, what's involved here is rearranging or reordering the facts so sense can be made out of them, and then applying the findings to the problem at hand.

Let's assume, for example, that you own a men's haberdashery and that it reflects a departmentalized layout: sport jackets in one section, slacks in another, shirts and ties in a third, and so forth. Assume further that you would like to investigate the sale of these various merchandise classifications, perhaps so you could organize a more effective store layout. "After all," you reason, "if I do 20 percent of my business in sport jackets, perhaps I should devote about that much of a percentage of my store's selling area to that particular classification."

Obviously, you need to ascertain the sales volume enjoyed by each class. You must "attack" your in-house records, breaking down both inventory and purchasing records by merchandise classification. Further, you might want to analyze these categories not only by total dollar sales volume but also by the number of units sold. This study of company records will provide further insights to help you in thinking through your decision.

Government Statistics. The Government is a formidable supplier of information of every type and description for the business world. The Department of Commerce is probably the most important government source at the federal level. This department compiles statistical data obtained periodically through its Bureau of the Census (*Census of Population, Census of Manufactures, Census of Business, Census of Agriculture,* and so on.). In addition, the Department issues an annual summarizaton of the economy in its *Statistical Abstract of the United States* (to be found in most public libraries). On a monthly basis, it publishes the *Survey of Current Business*.

Other departments, such as the Department of Labor (with its *Monthly Labor Review*) and the Department of Agriculture, issue reports periodically.

Other Sources. There are a good many other sources of information for the alert business manager. These include newsletters and occasional reports issued through a number of organizations including the Federal Reserve banks, both the Federal Communication and Federal Trade Commissions, and various state and county agencies. Familiarize yourself with the indexes usually available in the public library, such as the *Business Periodicals Index,* the *Wall Street Journal Index,* and the *New York Times Index.* Other indexes are available in fields such as personnel administration, psychology, chemistry, sociology, and so on.

Then there are the trade reference works which are valuable to businesses, including those issued by Dun and Bradstreet, the Thomas' Register of Manufacturers, and other trade books. Such periodicals as Dun's, Forbes', Fortune, Business Horizons, the Harvard Business Review, and various journals (Journal of Marketing, Journal of Retailing, Journal of Business, and the like) make for additional worthwhile reading.

Primary Data

The collecting of primary information in marketing research usually involves one of two approaches: (a) asking people (the *survey method*) or (b) watching people (the *observation method*). There is a third approach seldom used by marketers; it is called the experimental method. These methods are explained below:

Survey Method. Because surveys are relatively inexpensive and are adaptable to a wide range of problems, they seem to be by far the most popular device for gathering primary information. Essentially, the survey seeks answers to specific questions through personal interviews, telephone interviews, and/or mail questionnaires. In one form or another, the survey technique can be of value in gathering information for any of the five types of research listed earlier in this chapter.

The preparation of a good interview guide or questionnaire is difficult; it requires good thinking and planning. Consideration should be given to the wording and sequencing of questions, how easily the results can be tabulated, the validity of the questions, and so forth. Mail and telephone surveys are generally less expensive than personal interviews. Of the three types, the telephone will produce the most immediate response. Of course, there is no substitute for the personal interview (when conducted by a competent interviewer) to extract the maximum amount of information from the person interviewed, and to probe specific areas in depth.

Observation Methods. As the name itself suggests, this technique involves observing people's behavior, such as their facial expressions or movements in reaction to something presented to them (for example, observing or filming customers in the act of making a purchase). In this kind of study, mechanical equipment such as cameras (often hidden from view), tape recorders, and the like are used to gather information needed to solve the problem at hand.

The major flaw with this technique is that we can only observe behavior; we cannot ascertain what goes on within people's minds.

Experimental Method. This approach involves the deliberate setting up of an experiment under well-controlled circumstances. As an illustration, a chain store retailer might wish to try out a new gift item at several different selling prices before making a decision as to the one price which would yield the best possible combination of unit volume and gross profit. This person might then try to locate among his or her retail outlets three stores which are roughly equivalent in terms of store size, clientele, type of neighborhood, and monthly sales volume. The retailer is attempting here to "control" some of the other factors that might affect the outcome of the experiment, in brief, trying to keep all other things equal. Identical displays of the new item are set up in each store and put on sale on the same day in all three locations. There is one difference, however, from store to store: At Store A the price tag reads "$4.50"; at Store B, "$5.50"; and at Store C, "$6.50."

At the end of two or three weeks, a comparison of the sales data on the item from store to store should prove illuminating!

Of course, there are many other ways to set up experiments, or "experimental designs" as they are called. Further discussion of such designs, however, is beyond the scope of this book.

A SIMPLE, INEXPENSIVE RESEARCH TOOL FOR THE SMALL BUSINESS

One variation of the survey method that appears to bear many possibilities for the small firm bears the technical name "The Semantic Differential."[1] "Semantic" of course has something to do with words, and "differential" with differences. So that the technical name need not throw you. It is a simple-to-use research

[1]William A. Mindak, "Fitting the Semantic Differential to the Marketing Problem," *Journal of Marketing*, 25 (April 1961), 28–33.

tool which can be used to tap people's impressions of, opinions about, or attitudes toward objects, concepts, or things.

Basically, it consists of a number of pairs of adjectives and/or short phrases printed on a sheet of paper. These pairs, called "polar" words or phrases, are opposite to each other in meaning. Examples include "Good/Bad, High-priced/Low-priced, Cold and businesslike/Warm and neighborly," and the like.

The two opposites that form a pair are set off from each other by a number of dashes; the entire line thus formed is referred to as a "semantic differential scale."

To ascertain a person's opinions about any particular object, you ask them to check off the one word or position on each of the several scales that most nearly coincides with the way the person feels about the object.

A sample of a semantic differential containing eight separate scales of this type is shown in Table 15-1. The form asks for people's impressions about a particular company. The individual who feels that the ABC Company is an *extremely progressive* firm places a check mark over the dash in column *1*. On the other hand, a person who believes that the same firm is *very backward* would check column *6*. The fourth column represents a neutral position.

Once shown how to enter opinions onto the form, it should take the average person no more than two or three minutes to complete a sheet that contains up to fifteen scales.

To illustrate the use of this technique, let's take as an example a distributor of giftware who wishes to gather information regarding the attitudes customers (retailers) hold toward the company. The distributor can use the semantic differential presented in Table 15-1, substituting the right firm name for the "ABC Company". The distributor then prepares a mailing to all customers which includes the semantic differential, a letter of explanation, and a stamped (or metered) return envelope. To insure that the customers will indicate their true feelings towards the company, they'll be advised in the letter to return the sheet *anonymously*.

In the event that this distributor has a lengthy customer list, the cost of this research can be reduced by limiting the mailing to 10, 20, or 30 percent of the customers. This is often done when conducting a survey. In such cases, it's wise to try to select the

TABLE 15-1.

QUESTION: What are your impressions of the ABC Company?

	(1) Extremely	(2) Very	(3) Somewhat	(4) DON'T KNOW	(5) Somewhat	(6) Very	(7) Extremely	
Progressive	___	___	___	___	___	___	___	Backward
Cold and businesslike	___	___	___	___	___	___	___	Warm and neighborly
Reliable	___	___	___	___	___	___	___	Unreliable
High-priced merchandise	___	___	___	___	___	___	___	Low-priced merchandise
Poor credit policies	___	___	___	___	___	___	___	Good Credit policies
Wide variety	___	___	___	___	___	___	___	Little variety
Poor customer relations	___	___	___	___	___	___	___	Good customer relations
Little-known company	___	___	___		___	___	___	Well-known company

"sample" on a *random* basis so that every firm in the list has an equal chance of being selected. An easy approach is to select every third, fifth, tenth, etc. name from the entire list and mail to those selected names only.

Tallying up the responses for any number of people is relatively simple. Each scale (the two opposite words or phrases plus the spaces in between) is treated separately. You add up the total number of individuals who have checked off Column 1, Column 2, and so on. Then, you multiply the number of individuals per column *by the number at the top of the column* to obtain a *total* score. This total score is then divided by the total number of people who have responded in order to obtain an *average* score for the entire group.

This may sound somewhat complicated, so let's use a concrete example—the 100 returns received by the giftware wholesaler mentioned above. The following distribution of check marks was observed on the first scale, "Progressive/Backward":

Number of Column	Number of People Checking Column
1	2
2	3
3	12
4	9
5	31
6	26
7	17

The first step in analyzing the results is to obtain a total score by multiplying the number of individuals who have checked off each column by the number of the column. In brief, we must multiply 2 by 1, which yields 2; then 3 by 2, yielding 6; next, 12 by 3, to obtain 36; and so on to the last entry. Then, total all the sums. In the above distribution, the total score amounts to 510. Then divide this total by the number of people who responded to the scale; in this case, it was one hundred. Dividing 510 by 100, we come up with an average "rating" of 5.1 for the entire group. This would indicate that, as a whole, the one hundred people who completed the semantic differential scale regarded the giftware firm as being "Somewhat Backward."

It's just as easy to translate these average (or "mean") scores into pictorial form so that management can readily grasp their significance. Take a new blank sheet containing the semantic differential and mark off for each scale the approximate position where the group's mean score falls. Then, connect all of the marks with straight lines. What then emerges is a "profile" or "image" of the group's collective response to the various scales of the semantic differential.

By way of illustration, Figure 15-2 shows the profile of customer reactions to the salesclerks of a medium-sized retail store.

Not only is this procedure valuable for obtaining insights into people's attitudes toward your business but it can also be useful in ascertaining their opinions about your competition. All you need do is repeat the process, asking others to rate your major competitor. (Of course, the proper way to conduct this kind of survey is to make certain that the people you survey do not know *who* is behind the survey. This way, you are more likely to receive unbiased opinions!)

By placing the two profiles side by side on a single page, you are

Figure 15–2.

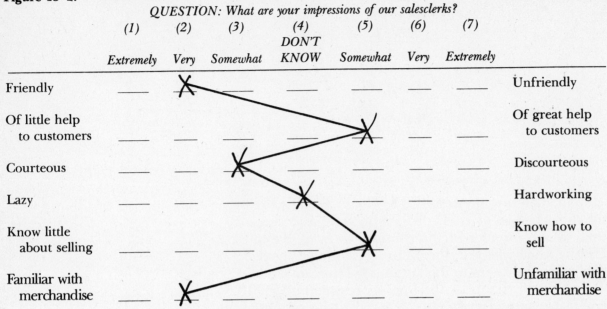

QUESTION: *What are your impressions of our salesclerks?*

	(1) Extremely	(2) Very	(3) Somewhat	(4) DON'T KNOW	(5) Somewhat	(6) Very	(7) Extremely	
Friendly		X						Unfriendly
Of little help to customers					X			Of great help to customers
Courteous			X					Discourteous
Lazy				X				Hardworking
Know little about selling					X			Know how to sell
Familiar with merchandise		X						Unfamiliar with merchandise

able to view rather graphically your company's strengths and weaknesses vis-a-vis those of your competitor. This can lead to your taking steps to bolster your weak points, and to publicize your strong ones to greater avail.

There is one problem with the semantic differential: the difficulty of selecting the right adjectives or phrases to fit your particular needs. To help you, three lists of suggested scales have been appended to this chapter for use by small manufacturers, wholesalers, and retailers. These are not meant to be all-inclusive; however, they should provide enough material to yield some useful information for your business.

APPENDIX

Semantic Differential Scale Suggestions for the Small Manufacturer:

progressive . . . backward
cold and businesslike . . . warm and neighborly
wide variety of products . . . little variety of products
unreliable firm . . . reliable firm
low prices . . . high prices
good customer relations . . . poor customer relations
fast deliveries . . . slow deliveries

poorly advertised . . . well advertised
excellent product quality . . . poor product quality
hard to deal with . . . easy to deal with
excellent service . . . poor service
unpopular styles . . . popular styles
liberal credit policies . . . stringent credit policies

Scale Suggestions for the Small Wholesaler:

(These are for use in addition to many listed above for manufacturer.)
salesmen are helpful and "low key" . . . salesmen are aggressive and pushy
good adjustment policies . . . poor adjustment policies
too many "out-of-stocks" . . . merchandise is readily available
provides excellent sales assistance . . . provides poor sales assistance
salesmen are unfamiliar with product line . . . salesmen are knowledgeable about products
provides excellent help with advertising . . . does not provide advertising help

Scale Suggestions for the Small Retailer:

(Use these in addition to many listed in the above categories.)
attractive displays . . . unattractive displays
quite a shabby place . . . store is spotlessly clean
ordinary, run-of-the-mill salesclerks . . . topnotch salesclerks
poor store layout . . . excellent store layout
convenient store hours . . . store hours are inconvenient
a comfortable place to shop . . . an uncomfortable place to shop
sensitive to customer needs . . . insensitive to customer needs
slow checkout . . . speedy checkout
easy return privileges . . . strict return privileges

FOR FURTHER INFORMATON

Books

Bellenger, Danny N., and Greenberg, Barnett A. *Marketing Research: A Management Information Approach.* Homewood, Ill.: Irwin, 1978.

Boyd, Harper W., Jr., Westfall, Ralph, and Stasch, Stanley F. *Marketing Research: Text and Cases,* 4th ed. Homewood, Ill.: Irwin, 1977.

Breen, George Edward. *Do-It-Yourself Marketing Research.* New York: McGraw-Hill, 1977.

Clover, Vernon T., and Balsley, Howard L. *Business Research Methods,* 2nd ed., Columbus: Grid Publishing, 1978.

Green, Paul E., and Tull, Donald S. *Research for Marketing Decisions,* 3rd ed. Englewood Cliffs, N.J.: Prentice-Hall, 1975.

Free Materials from the Small Business Administration

Management Aids
 # 192—"Profile Your Customers to Expand Industrial Sales"

Small Business Bibliographies
 # 9—"Marketing Research Procedures"
 # 18—"Basic Library Reference Sources"

16

Production Management

Here is a sampling of small businesses, selected at random:

- manufacturing cleaning compounds
- glasscutting for windows
- dressmaking
- assembling pocket radios
- printing circulars and business cards
- handcrafting beaded flowers
- molding plastic toys
- canning preserves
- building houses
- tool and die-making

What do they all have in common? *Production*. Production is an activity which converts materials into forms which are useful. A great deal of activity must take place in order to produce useful things. Management must plan, organize, direct operations, and control the overall situation. The materials involved may be raw materials, semi-processed or semi-finished goods, even finished products. Machinery and equipment, methods and processes are commonly required.

Traditionally, manufacturing processes are considered to be of four different types:

- Analysis. The breaking down of raw materials, such as crude petroleum, into their components.
- Extractive Process. The removal of substances from other materials, as in the extraction of copper from ore.
- Fabrication. Changing the form of materials in some way such as by pressing, weaving, cutting, and the like. Examples include the manufacture of clothing, shoes, metal bolts, and the like.
- Synthesis. The combining of materials to form new products, as in the manufacture of glassware, metal products, synthetic fibers, and so forth. Another kind of synthesis is *assembly*, where various fabricated parts are placed together to form a new product (as in the manufacture of appliances and automobiles).

Among small businesses, synthesis and fabrication are by far the most common types of manufacturing.

PROCESSES IN PRODUCTION

Production can be either *continuous* or *intermittent*. In the first type, often called "flow production," materials are brought uninterruptedly to the machines, the equipment runs smoothly for long periods of time, and standard products roll off the machines to be stored in the warehouse as reserves against future orders. Good illustrations of factories in continuous production are television assembly plants and automobile plants. Of course, a completely automated factory is ideal for this type of production.

Intermittent production is often referred to as "job" or "job lot" production (and where "less intermittent," as "batch" production). This type characterizes most small manufacturing businesses. Machinery (or hand labor) "runs" are characteristically short—"interrupted" as opposed to continuous. The materials flow varies; that is, frequent changes in setting up, dismantling, or changing the equipment are necessary. The products turned out are usually in the nature of custom-made products. A printing shop is an excellent example of intermittent production.

Production Methods

Before the advent of factories, early manufacturing processes combined manual skills with small hand tools to produce useful objects. Although handcrafted items are still with us, production today is infinitely more machine-oriented than ever, and this tendency toward automation becomes more pronounced with each passing decade. Today, we have machines that:

stamp	affix
heat	turn
sift	carry
chop	roll
sort	weld
melt	blow
lift	shape
cut	pour
mix	move
mill	depress
press	

Nowadays, there are machines designed to duplicate nearly every imaginable function formerly performed by hand—even machines that "think."

But a factory is more than its machinery. The typical production plant could be compared to a large, activity-choked arena. To run this arena profitably, all the major resources of the firm must be drawn together in a logical, businesslike way: management, money, machinery, materials, manpower, and methods. Here's a brief explanation of several of these "Ms":

Management. One or more layers of management is needed to set objectives and then to formulate plans in line with those goals, to marshal and organize all the other resources in order to accomplish those objectives, to direct operations, and to control all elements of this giant jigsaw puzzle.

Machinery. This includes all the power equipment and tools (both those which are permanently positioned and those which are portable), the hand tools and equipment, and auxiliary equipment such as dies, gauges, jigs, fixtures, and the like. In addition to running the machines, important activities here include purchasing, maintaining, and replacing the equipment.

Manpower. A manpower support system is required to operate not only the machinery but *all* production activities. In any factory there are many specialized functions to manage. This leads to the principle of *specialization of labor* and to the setting up of an organizational structure designed to accomplish the various jobs. Consequently, both semi-skilled and skilled workers may be needed as well as a variety of functional departments, such as purchasing, receiving, production, stockkeeping, quality control, and so forth.

Methods. Because of the intricate nature of the production process, methods and systems used in a factory setting are many and varied. Some examples include methods for production planning and production control, the setting of detailed procedures, the fixing of standards, the designing of layouts, and the like.

Production Scheduling

The Small Business Administration puts out an excellent eight-page folio which has this to say about production scheduling:

> Some small manufacturers take production schedules for granted because bottlenecks are few and far between. Minor problems are easily ironed out, and orders are delivered to customers on time.
>
> Other small manufacturers are not as fortunate. Scheduling in their plants is complicated by the nature of the process, the complexity of the products, and frequent changes in quantity requirements.[1]

This booklet suggests that the small plant production scheduler should be familiar with these important factors before lining up production: production layout, factory workload, factory capability and versatility, existing standards, systems and procedures. The booklet goes on to say that before actual scheduling everything which needs to be done must be spelled out:

> PRODUCT DESCRIPTION. The product description describes individual parts as well as the finished product. One part of this is the bill of materials. It lists all of the items needed to produce a part, or in total, the final product. Prints and drawings depict the parts, showing much detail as to their physical characteristics. Specifications describe in detail the allowable tolerances in dimensions, sizes, and finishes.
>
> PROCESS DESCRIPTION. The process description is concerned with the steps needed to produce individual parts of the complete product. It will list the operations sequences, the machines to be used, the amount and kind of labor, and the estimated time involved. Additional data may include machine set-up instructions and inspection instructions.
>
> Another phase of the process description is the route sheets. These are operation sequence outline forms with an allowance for set-up

[1] John B. Kline, *Pointers on Scheduling Production.* Management Aids #207 Washington: Small Business Administration, June, 1977 reprint.

times and for movement of the job from one operation to the next. If your production is divided into departments, route sheets can be used by a department to schedule the time for a particular job, to monitor a series of jobs, and to tell where the part will go next.[2]

Functions in Production Control

In contrast to inventory management and control, production planning and control is a broad-scope set of operations concerned with work-in-process. The planning phases include routing, loading, and scheduling, followed by the dispatching and follow-up phases. Here is what these terms mean:

Routing.   This is initiated once the bill of materials for the product has been prepared and the process description completed. Each individual operation as a component of the total product is planned out; a sequence of steps is indicated; time and labor are apportioned to the various steps in the progression, and work-stations, machines, and departments are spelled out.

Loading.   This has to do with scheduling. The function involves computing the amount of time required for each operation and adding that to work already planned for each machine or work-station. This results in a "machine load chart" (traditionally, a bar chart).

Scheduling.   This function deals with the timing of production in order to meet deadlines and delivery requirements. It involves determining when each operation is to be performed, starting and completion times, and so forth. The operation and flow processes charts, the machine load chart, and the network (PERT) chart are the principal charts used for scheduling.

Dispatching.   This involves the authorization of operations in the shop through work orders (instructions).

Follow-up.   Also called "reporting," this function is normally the bailiwick of the dispatcher, who supplies information about work-in-progress. The reporting of delays and other problems can lead to rapid corrective action.

MAJOR DEPARTMENTS WITHIN THE PLANT

In addition to the primary production function, there are a number of other major functions which must be performed in a factory. These include purchasing, receiving, shipping, quality control, R & D (research and development), and maintenance.

[2] Kline, *Pointers on Scheduling Production.* p.4.

In the smallest manufacturing firms, of course, such functions are shared among the owners and a few employees. As the firm grows larger, specialists are eventually sought to manage those areas, and departmental divisions soon follow.

The Purchasing Function

This area of plant operations has to do with the procurement of all raw materials, components, machinery, equipment, supplies, and necessary services; eventually this area comes under the direction of a purchasing agent. Responsibilities assigned to this department include: cultivating of sources of supply for all items to be purchased; placing purchase orders (after securing quotations and working out prices and terms); following up on merchandise ordered; comparing invoice after receipt of goods with purchase order, and approving then forwarding invoices to the accounts payable department. The purchasing agent maintains a close liaison with the receiving department and is kept abreast of stock levels of all materials and supplies (the agent must keep a perpetual running inventory if there is no stockkeeping department).

The Receiving Function

All purchases of raw materials, semi-processed goods, equipment, supplies, and the like come into the plant through the receiving department (earlier mentioned in Chapter 14). Activities in the receiving section generally include:

1. Receiving onto the unloading platform all incoming materials, goods, and supplies, including returns from customers;
2. Checking all incoming merchandise for quantity, price, quality, and so forth against both the packing slip and the accompanying bill of lading. Further, checking each delivery against a copy of the original purchase order issued from the plant;
3. Routing and transporting all materials to the proper department or assigned areas of the warehouse;
4. Keeping records of various types, ranging from the receiving register ("log") where all pertinent details of each shipment are recorded, to the invoices submitted to the purchasing department for payment.

The Shipping Function

This department is similar to the one just described except that it lies at the other end (figuratively if not literally) of plant activities.

As with the Receiving department, I cannot overemphasize the importance of maintaining tight internal control (along with the necessary paperwork). Some of the major functions of the shipping section are:

- order processing,
- order picking,
- order assembly,
- order checking,
- special packing (where required),
- routing shipments,
- scheduling shipments, and
- following up on damage claims, and the like.

The Quality Control Function

This area of specialization, an essential phase of good factory management, ensures that established standards are observed, and that what is produced by the plant indeed conforms to customer (and company) specifications.

In a small factory, this function is often vested in a single individual who may also have other duties. However, where the products or the manufacturing processes are more complicated, a small department may be needed to inspect products and maintain effective control. An efficient factory operation regularly checks not only its output but also all incoming merchandise (whether raw materials, semi-finished components, or finished items such as supplies and the like).

Generally speaking, quality control involves sampling products from time to time, running tests, and using statistical methods. The point is to detect inferior or substandard products early in the game and then take steps to correct these deviations from the norm.

The Research and Development Function

A separate and distinct "R&D" facility is characteristic only of large corporations; rarely does a small manufacturer have an individual, let alone a section or department, dedicated to researching and developing new products, methods, machinery, and the like. Even among the larger firms, this function is most often found within companies which are committed to industry leadership and a policy of "being first in their field."

Consequently, this R&D function is not at all organized in a small manufacturing company, but is spread among the various people who comprise the firm; therefore, results emerge only occasionally, and in a serendipity fashion rather than from deliberate, planned effort.

In the average small firm, development comes about largely through trial and error.

The Maintenance Function

Usually, a well-organized factory is quickly placed under the capable administration of a skilled plant engineer. This is a logical step, because the breakdown or interruption of a machine, a boiler, a transformer, or any other important equipment can rapidly bring activities to a virtual standstill. Plant engineers must frequently have at their disposal other specialists—such as an electrician, a machinist, a plumber, and a carpenter.

The maintenance shop or section is responsible for keeping all machinery and equipment in top-notch operating condition, constructing new facilities when needed within the plant, moving machines from one location to another, assembling newly-purchased equipment, and so forth. It's extremely important to schedule any major maintenance efforts so as to avoid interfering in any way with the flow of production. Likewise, good plant maintenance is preventive in the sense that it inspects all equipment on a regular, scheduled basis to avoid a slowdown or stoppage.

The Stockkeeping Function

Materials supply is of paramount importance in the efficient operation of every stage of the manufacturing cycle. Raw materials must be readily available for scheduled production runs; semi-finished and fabricated components need to be in place when called for; finished products have to be warehoused as ready stocks until drawn against the customer orders.

So, overseeing great amounts of materials is a major, ongoing effort within a plant. It's often under the direction of a "storekeeper." In actuality, stockkeeping is the part of the overall inventory control system which deals with specifics like organizing and maintaining the storage area, placing and moving about the stored merchandise, protecting the materials, issuing merchandise from the storage area, and doing the necessary paperwork.

INVENTORY MANAGEMENT AND CONTROL

There should be little difficulty in understanding the significance of the inventory control concept in the manufacturing plant. Its purposes are simply to manage and control two varieties of inventories: (1) the *materials inventory* necessary to the production process, and (2) the finished *merchandise inventory* which is stored for eventual customer orders.

By logical extension this business of controlling your inventory embraces a number of activities including: the acquistion of materials (purchasing and receiving functions); the handling, internal movement, and storage of materials (stockkeeping function); and the physical distribution of materials (shipping function).

You realize, of course, that a firm's inventory represents a substantial financial investment on its part not only because of the initial purchasing costs of the materials but also for additional processing costs (labor, machines, other overhead expenses) and storage. Consequently, efficient management of this phase of your business requires continuous attention to planning and making projections, determining desirable inventory levels, ascertaining lead times for proper ordering, checking inventory methods and control systems, and other details. Here, the twin objectives seem to be (1) to meet the needs of plant and customers alike, and (2) to hold down inventory levels to their minimums.

Among the more important requisites for effective control are: setting up a good perpetual inventory system (maintained manually, mechanically, or electronically), taking occasional physical inventory counts, establishing minimum/maximum levels for all items inventoried, strategically using buffer or reserve stocks, and knowing the details of all pertinent costs. Recordkeeping is extensive in this area, and a great deal of direction for management can be derived from all this paperwork. Management can study, item by item, the "movement" or sales figures for all merchandise carried by a firm.

Further treatment of inventory control and other facets of production management will be found in Chapter 19, "Improving Results in Your Manufacturing Plant."

FOR FURTHER INFORMATION

Books

Ammer, Dean S., *Materials Management*. 3rd ed. Homewood, Ill.: Irwin, 1974.

Buffa, Elwood S., *Basic Production Management*. 2nd ed. New York: Wiley, 1975.

Lee, Lamar, Jr., and Dobler, Donald W. *Purchasing and Materials Management*, 3rd ed. New York: McGraw-Hill, 1977.

Lester, Ronald H., Enrick, Norbert L., and Mottley, Harry E., *Quality Control for Profit*. New York: Industrial Press, 1977.

Mayer, Raymond E., *Production and Operations Management*, 3rd ed., McGraw-Hill, 1975.

Monks, Joseph G., *Operations Management: Theory and Problems.* New York: McGraw-Hill, 1977.

Moore, Franklin G., and Hendrick, Thomas., *Production/Operations Management,* 7th ed. Homewood, Ill.: Irwin, 1977.

Starr, Martin K., *Production Management: Systems and Synthesis,* 2nd ed. Englewood Cliffs, N.J.: Prentice-Hall, 1972.

Free Materials from the Small Business Administration

Management Aids:
- \# 189—"Should You Make or Buy Components?"
- \# 207—"Pointers on Scheduling Production"
- \# 212—"The Equipment Replacement Decision"
- \# 217—"Reducing Air Pollution in Industry"
- \# 218—"Business Plan for Small Manufacturers"
- \# 219—"Solid Waste Management in Industry"
- \# 227—"Quality Control in Defense Production"

Small Business Bibliographies:
- \# 69—"Machine Shop—Job Type"
- \# 75—"Inventory Management"
- \# 80—"Data Processing for Small Businesses"
- \# 85—"Purchasing for Owners of Small Plants"
- \# 88—"Manufacturing Management"

Small Marketers Aids:
- \# 149—"Computers for Small Business—Service Bureau or Time Sharing?"

Available from the Superintendent of Documents

Small Business Management Series:
- \# 4—"Improving Material Handling in Small Business," Stock #045-000-00041-9, 42 pp., $.75.
- \# 21—"Profitable Small Plant Layout," Stock #045-000-00029-0, 48 pp., $.80.
- \# 28—"Small Business and Government Research and Development," Stock #045-000-00130-0, 41 pp., $.75.

17

Financial Management

In the frontier days of our economy, trappers and Indians brought furs and animal skins to the local trading post to barter them for foodstuffs and other products proferred by the settlers. Finished goods imported from Europe also found their way into these earliest retail outlets.

But bartering as a way of American life has long since vanished from the scene (except to reveal itself on occasion in "trading newspapers" where a person might exchange a thirty-year-old manual typewriter for someone else's used (and rusted) tricycle!).

Today, all business organizations, even the nonprofit type, run on money. Indeed, money is the fuel that fires up the business engine.

The inability to effectively interpret and control the financial factor is one of the prime causes of business failure. Efficiency in production, dynamic sales delivery, top-notch personnel administration, and adroit handling of other phases of your business—all of these activities take a distant second place to the necessity for consummate skill in managing a company's finances.

This brings us to the whys and wherefores of accounting:

SOME FUNDAMENTALS OF ACCOUNTING FOR THE SMALL BUSINESS OWNER

A brief consultation with Webster's Third International Dictionary reveals that accounting is a "system of classifying, recording, and summarizing business and financial transactions in books of account." This dictionary further specifies that the system involves "analyzing, verifying, and reporting the results."

If you mull over this reference, more likely than not you will realize the necessity for devising a systematic approach to money management in your business. You need a helpful set-up for feeding inputs and registering outputs so that a state of equilibrium can be maintained. Further, it's obvious that all the entries in and out of the system must be classified in a sensible, useful fashion so they can be "worked"—that is, added up, subtracted, and compared.

Accounting is not bookkeeping; bookkeeping is simply a necessary part of the firm's accounting system.

Here is what an accounting system helps us to do:

- interpret past performance,
- measure present progress,
- anticipate and plan for the future,
- control operations,
- uncover significant trends,
- compare results with similar firms, and within the particular industry,
- make decisions, and
- comply with the government regulations.

Your accounting system is based on a simple, balanced equation. This is it:

$$ASSETS = LIABILITIES + NET\ WORTH$$

The "Profit Equation" is another important equation you ought to become familiar with since it's important to all profit-oriented businesses:

$$PROFIT = SALES - COSTS$$

You've already run across these two basic equations (in different form) in Chapter 6.

Look up the Balance Sheet for the ADG-Tenafly Manufacturing Company in that chapter. Note how it's divided into two major sections: Assets and Liabilities + Capital (Net Worth). Both sections total up to $47,800. Notice that the sections conform to each other.

In the same chapter, refer to the Income Statement presented for The Two Sisters' Dress Shoppe. This is a detailed "expansion" of the Profit Equation.

RATIO ANALYSIS

The two major accounting statements above contain lots of information about the results of company operations and the current state of its finances. Company management can manipulate this information in ways which yield meaningful insights for decision-making; one of these ways is called "ratio analysis." Using this technique, you juxtapose one item of information to another, thereby forming something called a "ratio". A ratio is a proportion that expresses or implies some kind of relationship between two numbers. For example: "Your chances of losing in this game are about one out of three."

A ratio is like a fraction—a numerator placed over a denominator. Consequently, it's easily converted to a percentage by first dividing out the fraction and then multiplying the result by 100 percent.

As an example, assume your company earned $100,000 in sales last year, that your total labor costs reached $25,000, and that the rental for your premises came to $12,000. It's relatively easy to construct two helpful ratios here—namely, a "labor-to-sales" ratio and a "rent-to-sales" ratio. Here's how:

$$LABOR/SALES = \frac{\$25,000}{\$100,000} = \frac{1}{4} = 25\%$$

$$RENT/SALES = \frac{\$12,000}{\$100,000} = \frac{12}{100} = 12\%$$

You can now ascertain (from putting the two figures together in a meaningful way) that last year you paid out one dollar in labor for every four you took in, and twelve out of every hundred dollars in sales went for the rent. You can literally track your progress (or lack of it) from one year to the next by comparing these ratios and others. Of course, business people often find it more helpful to compare percentages over time, since they are easier to work with.

Now we can get on to the business of learning about the major (more commonly used) ratios which you can obtain from your Balance Sheet and Income Statement.

Liquidity Ratios

Here we are interested in learning just how "liquid" our company appears to be. Comparing liquidity ratios over a period of years is helpful in determining whether things are improving or deteriorating. A firm is said to be liquid when it has enough in assets to pay all its debts and still has a dollar or two left over.

The Current Ratio. Current assets divided by current liabilities gives you the "Current Ratio."

Look at the balance sheet of the ADG-Tenafly Manufacturing Company in Chapter 6. The firm's current assets are listed as $16,200 and its current liabilities as $4,500.

Therefore:

$$\text{CURRENT RATIO} = \frac{\$16,200}{\$4,500} = 3.6 \text{ to } 1$$

As a general rule of thumb, a current ratio of at least 2:1 (twice as much in current assets as in current liabilities) is desirable. This reflects a fairly sound financial situation for any firm. However, the safe current ratio will vary by industry, and it might be wiser to compare the current ratio with that of other firms similar to yours. Also, if your current ratio decreases over time, you may have a developing problem which you should look into.

The Quick Ratio. Also called the "Acid Test Ratio," this is a more significant indication of a company's ability to liquidate its debts. It is similar to the current ratio, except that the valuation of the merchandise inventory is omitted:

$$\text{QUICK RATIO} = \frac{\text{Cash} + \text{Negotiable Securities} + \text{Accounts Receivable}}{\text{Current Liabilities}}$$

Here is the quick ratio for the ADG-Tenafly Mfg. Co. discussed in Chapter 6.

$$\text{QUICK RATIO} = \frac{\$9,600}{\$4,500} = 2.13 \text{ to } 1$$

As with the current ratio, the higher the ratio the better. The quick ratio should be, as a minimum, 1:1; if it's less than this, the company may be headed for financially-troubled waters. Again it would be fruitful to not only compare your quick ratios for several years to watch for trends in direction, but also to compare your ratios to those of other firms in your industry.

Profitability Ratios

These ratios let you know how profitable (or unprofitable) your company's operations are. Of course, profits may be lined up and measured against a variety of data, such as sales, net worth, assets, and so forth. Generally, such ratios are expressed as percentages rather than proportions or fractions.

The Profit-to-Sales Ratio.   If you examine the data furnished on the Profit-and-Loss statement of The Two Sisters' Dress Shoppe (Chapter 6) you can see that for the month of March the store earned a net profit after taxes of $550, on a net sales volume of $11,350. Here's how you calculate the profit-to-sales ratio for this store:

$$\text{PROFIT/SALES} = \frac{\text{Net Profit (after taxes)}}{\text{Net Sales}} \times 100\%$$

$$= \frac{\$550}{\$11,350} \times 100\% = 4.8\%$$

This means that for every dollar of sales during March of 1978, the store earned 4.8 cents. You must remember that this particular ratio varies from one month to the next, because retail stores will not enjoy the same dollar sales nor the same expenses from one month to the next. December sales, for instance, may increase dramatically while the store's outlay for labor, advertising, and other expenses may constitute a less-than-usual percentage of sales. Generally, the true picture is reflected more accurately by semi-annual or yearly computations of this and other profitability ratios; the month-to-month fluctuations wash out over time.

Incidentally, for the majority of small retailers, the annual profit-to-sales ratio runs about 2 to 5 percent (higher or lower in individual cases).

Other Indications of Profitability   Additional ratios may be computed similarly. Here are two others frequently used by business people:

$$\text{PROFIT/NET WORTH} = \frac{\text{Net Profit (after taxes)}}{\text{Net Worth}} \times 100\%$$

$$\text{RETURN ON ASSETS} = \frac{\text{Net Profit (after taxes)}}{\text{Assets}} \times 100\%$$

Other informative ratios which can indicate profitability and are especially useful to retailers include: sales/square foot of selling space, average sale/customer, sales-to-inventory, and so forth.

"Stock turnover" is not directly a profitability ratio, but retail store owners make good use of it to ascertain how fast (or slow) their inventory is moving and to help them in ordering merchandise. Three different stockturn ratios are used:

$$\text{STOCKTURN IN UNITS} = \frac{\text{Number of Units Sold}}{\text{Average Stock in Units}}$$

$$\text{STOCKTURN AT COST} = \frac{\text{Cost of Goods Sold}}{\text{Average Stock at Cost}}$$

$$\text{STOCKTURN AT RETAIL} = \frac{\text{Retail Sales}}{\text{Average Stock at Retail}}$$

In all three instances, the figure for "average stock" is derived by averaging the number of inventory listings. For example, if a physical inventory is taken on January 1 and then again on December 31 (or on January 1 of the following year), there would be two listings. In this case, the value of both would be added together and then divided by 2 to obtain the average stock.

RECORD-KEEPING FOR YOUR COMPANY

Keeping books properly is essential to your firm's accounting system. Before you begin operating your business it's generally advisable to have an accountant set up your books according to the specific needs of your business. Thereafter, you can maintain your own books until the business can afford to pay for a full-time or even part-time bookkeeper. Another approach is to use the services of a firm in the "bookkeeping systems" business. For a fee, they maintain your books for you, although the Small Business Administration advises that you still need to maintain four (at the very minimum) basic types of records, regardless of whether you or someone else keeps your books.[1] These are:

[1]John Cotton, *Keeping Records in Small Business.* Small Marketers Aids # 155 Washington: Small Business Administration, 1974.

1. sales records,
2. cash receipts,
3. cash disbursements, and
4. accounts receivable.

If you decide to "do-it-yourself," there are simplified, one-book systems available at most business stationery stores. However, I still recommend that you seek the assistance of a qualified accountant; this person can set you up with a tailor-made approach designed not only for your accounting needs but also to provide information over time to help you make decisions.

As an overall guide, every single transaction should be entered in a journal on a daily basis. If this is done—if you keep copies of all bills, receipts, canceled checks, checkbook stubs, and so on—your bookkeeper will be able to make sense of it all.

With regard to how long records should be kept, it's customary to keep business tax records for at least six years, and your basic journals of original entry for about the same length of time. General ledgers, corporate minutes, leases, contracts, copyrights and patents, and other important documents should be kept indefinitely. It is also advisable to keep employee payroll records for at least five years (sometimes longer, depending upon the requirements of the state in which your firm is located).

CAPITAL BUDGETING

Budgeting today, of course, is a way of business life. In a healthy firm, budgets are strategically employed in every phase of the enterprise, for both planning and control purposes.

A capital budget involves setting aside monies each year for large investments that might need to be made. Throughout the lifetime of your business, you will occasionally be confronted with major decisions—for example, purchasing costly equipment or machines; expanding or relocating your business premises, instituting a complete internal reorganization, developing and launching a new product, and the like. Consequently, you need a logical method for evaluating alternatives.

Here, then, are some important "money" concepts to keep in mind:

- A firm's capital is always limited.
- Money borrowed for capital expenditures will cost more money.
- Today's dollar is worth one dollar-plus, in the sense that it can be held in a bank account and draw interest.

- Tomorrow's dollar will probably worth one dollar-minus.
- Money assigned to capital expenses may sometimes be put to different, more productive uses.

Capital Spending Decisions

Basically, capital investments are made for two reasons: (1) to lower operating costs, or (2) to increase sales. Any major commitment of your company's funds warrants due caution and consideration on your part. Indeed, a common blunder of many small businesses has been putting too many dollars into capital assets thereby precipitating a cash crisis which can immobilize operations and even cause bankruptcy.

Of course, such investments can be made directly from the company treasury through borrowed or equity capital and long-term leasing. Whatever the approach (or combination thereof) you will find the following procedure of value in making decisions of this nature:

1. List all of the alternatives on a sheet of paper. Remember also to list the one alternative that is always present in these situations: Do nothing.
2. Work up all the costs involved for each of the choices. Be sure to include estimates of details like the cost of borrowing additional sums of money if you don't have enough, and the value of leaving your firm's current dollars untouched and earning interest in a savings account.
3. Estimate the most likely results (outcomes), in dollars and cents, of each of the alternatives.
4. Select the best alternative, for example, the one with the greatest payoff (after subtracting the total costs from the most likely results).

EXPENSE MANAGEMENT

There are three major areas of internal activity within any company involved in the manufacturing and/or distribution of goods and services: (1) production and/or buying, (2) selling, and (3) the financial aspect. Simply by tackling each area one at a time and applying good sound business judgment, you should be able to increase your net profits over time.

When it comes down to brass tacks, there are only two ways to make more money in business. Either you:

1. increase sales while holding down costs, or
2. lower costs while holding up sales.

Expense management has to do with that second approach: lowering costs in every segment of your business.

Types of Business Expenses

Most small firms use what is called a "natural classification of expenses," assigning each individual cost incurred in operating the enterprise to a particular debit account. Below is a categorization of business expenses which is suitable for the average small company. It's spelled out by the Small Business Administration in one of their Small Marketers' Aids:[2]

Salaries and wages	Insurance
Contract labor	Interest
Payroll taxes	Depreciation
Utilities	Travel expense
Telephone	Entertainment
Rent	Advertising
Office supplies	Dues and contributions
Postage	Miscellaneous expenses
Maintenance	

If you scan the above list, you quickly see that many of the expenses lie within your control, that some of them are *fixed* (that is, they continue whether your sales volume increases or decreases), and that most of them seem to be *variable* in nature and fluctuate along with sales.

To hold down costs, your challenge is to work out a delicate balance between sales and costs all along the way, and in all areas of variable expense. Consequently, it's wise to constantly bear in mind the basic accounting formulas mentioned earlier in this chapter:

$$ASSETS = LIABILITIES + NET\ WORTH$$

and

$$PROFITS = SALES - COSTS$$

Many management tools are available to assist you in your endeavors, among them: ratio analysis, operational techniques (such as time and methods study, work simplification, value analysis, critical path method, PERT, and so forth), and budgeting. All of these approaches are quite useful in making comparative analyses of information, so arranged that you can compare the present period with past periods—that is, make projections, based on trend extrapolation, into the future.

A Word About Budgeting

Budgets are not found too often in small business, despite their

[2]Cotton, *Keeping Records* . . . p. 6.

value to a firm both as planning and as control devices. This is especially true for small retail organizations. Conjecturing as to the possible reasons behind the lack of "budget orientation," I can only surmise that (a) budgeting is an activity that runs contrary to the entrepreneurial personality, (b) the small business owner is not conversant with budgeting approaches, and/or (c) the preparation of budgets for various phases of a business consumes an inordinate amount of time (a commodity which the entrepreneur feels must be dispensed most frugally).

Nevertheless, a budget is a tool for planning, for anticipating what will be; it's a map for charting the future course of the firm. Budgets are detailed plans which represent objectives against which to measure results. Such blueprints are of immense value in the area of cost reduction.

CREDIT MANAGEMENT

Manufacturers and wholesalers find it imperative to offer credit terms to their customers along the marketing channels, simply in order to survive. Retailers and many service companies, on the other hand, generally operate on a cash basis. Yet, even these latter types are more and more resorting to extending credit to customers. Indeed, some of our larger department stores today boast that as much as 70 percent (or more) of their clients are charge-account customers.

There are two basic types of credit: trade and consumer. In either case, a firm which offers credit is engaged in more than a simple service; credit is a deliberate marketing strategy designed to stimulate business and give a firm a competitive edge.

Firms extend credit to other firms to give their customers some leeway in operating. A retailer who purchases goods for resale from a wholesaler might simultaneously owe substantial amounts of money to other wholesalers and to other creditors, such as the telephone and electric companies, the insurance company, the landlord, and so on. This retailer simply does not have enough cash on hand to pay all of the business' bills upon receipt of goods or services.

This isn't too different from extending credit to consumers. Similarly, individuals have to await the next paycheck before being able to pay various bills.

In the case of trade credit, a wholesaler ships goods to a retailer, sending along with the shipment an invoice indicating the terms of purchase. One common example is "2% – 10 days, Net 30."

This means that the retailer is permitted thirty days of credit from the date of the invoice. Further, if the bill is paid promptly, that is, before ten days have passed, the retailer is entitled to deduct 2 percent from the face amount of the bill.

Naturally, this kind of savings can mount up over the course of a full year.

Extending Credit

Each business, of course, must decide its own credit policies. While credit is a must for both manufacturer and wholesaler, other types of firms need to weigh the advantages and disadvantages of credit extension. Obviously, there are risks attached to the strategic deployment of credit as a sales-generating tool. Credit is an area of business operations which cannot be taken lightly. Indeed, it merits a well thought-out approach, careful and continuous monitoring, and occasional reappraisal.

Generally, a firm's credit approach involves:

1. setting policies, including standards for measuring each applicant;
2. devising a credit application form to be completed by the individual or firm applying for credit;
3. checking on the data provided on the application form;
4. approving the application;
5. setting a credit limit for the applicant;
6. careful monitoring of credit usage; and
7. establishing a collection policy for delinquent accounts.

The "Three C's of Credit"

Decisions to extend credit to any specific client are generally based on what's called the "three Cs of credit." These are:

Character. Since an individual's (or firm's) character (in the sense of personality or behavior patterns) is extremely difficult to appraise, much less define, character is usually translated to mean the applicant's willingness to pay bills when they're due. Hence, records must be studied to determine what kind of behavior was evidenced in the past by the applicant with respect to debts.

Capacity. This criterion refers to an individual's (or firm's) ability to pay debts out of current income.

Capital. Another indication of the applicant's ability to pay is, of course, his or her financial resources (or net worth, in the case of a business firm).

The information provided in the application form is then checked carefully by mail or telephone, and with a credit bureau or mercantile agency, such as Dun and Bradstreet.

Consumer Credit

Often, a retail enterprise tries to avoid unnecessary risk by signing up with one or more of the major credit card entities—for example, Visa, Master Charge, American Express, Diner's Club, and the like. While it's true that a credit card arrangement requires a business owner to yield a small percentage of sales volume to the agency (a fee often between 3 and 6 percent), offering such a service to customers generally results in an overall sales increase which more than compensates for the agency fee.

When retailers extend credit to consumers, it usually takes one of several basic forms:

Open Credit.   Also referred to as "open account," "open book," or "regular" credit, this form extends short-term credit to individuals without requiring any down payment and without adding either interest or carrying charges to the bill. It's usually extended for a thirty-day period.

Installment Credit.   Here, a customer is required to place a down payment on merchandise and then pay up the balance in full over a period of time in regular installments. Most often the customer signs a conditional sale contract and is charged for the service (frequently, 1½ percent per month on the unpaid balance).

Option account.   This type of credit permits a customer to charge up to a limit, and pay (if he or she so desires) within thirty days of the billing date without penalty. A firm can assign a carrying charge for any amount not paid within that time period, and release additional credit (up to the limit) as payments are made. Thus, the features of both open credit and "revolving charge" credit are combined in the one plan. (The latter refers to the continuous releasing of credit to the credit ceiling as payments are made.)

Collections

No matter how tightly supervised your credit activities may be, there will still be some customers who pay their bills late and other who won't pay them at all. The structuring of a good collection procedure helps to reduce "delinquency" to an appreciable degree. A working policy might include the following steps:

1. Institute some kind of "red flag" bookkeeping technique to alert you when an account is tardy in payments.

2. Mail a duplicate invoice—stamped "past due," "second notice," or some similar phrase—to the customer shortly after discovering an amount overdue.

3. After several weeks elapse without you receiving a response, send out the first in a series of form letters (prepare these long in advance). The first letter should be pleasant in tone and suggest that the customer may have accidentally overlooked payment of such-and-such an amount. (You might consider placing a telephone call in between the first and second letters to find out what has been happening.)

4. If you hear nothing further, send out the other letters, each of which becomes progressively stronger. These should be spaced so that they reach the addressee about every ten days or two weeks. Your last letter in the series should emphasize the fact that you are about to turn the delinquent account over to your attorney.

5. Give the matter over to your attorney.

FOR FURTHER INFORMATION

Books

Beckman, Theodore N., and Foster, Ronald S. *Credits and Collections: Management and Theory,* 8th ed. New York: McGraw-Hill, 1969.

Dyer, Mary L. *Practical Bookkeeping for the Small Business.* New York: Contemporary Books, 1976.

Engler, George N, *Business Financial Management,* rev. ed. Dallas: Business Publications, 1978.

Haynes, W. Warren, and Henry, William R. *Managerial Economics: Analysis and Cases,* 3rd ed. Dallas: Business Publications, 1974.

Hobbs, James B., and Moore, Carl L. *Financial Accounting.* Cincinnati: South-Western, 1974.

Horngren, Charles T. *Accounting for Management Control: An Introduction,* 3rd ed. Englewood Cliffs, N.J.: Prentice-Hall, 1974.

Schattke, Rudolph W., Jensen, Howard G., and Bean, Virginia L. *Managerial Accounting: Concepts and Uses.* Boston: Allyn and Bacon, 1974.

Free Materials from the Small Business Administration

Management Aids:
- \# 170—"The ABC's of Borrowing"
- \# 174—"Is Your Cash Supply Adequate?"
- \# 176—"Financial Audits: A Tool for Better Management"
- \# 206—"Keep Pointed Toward Profit"
- \# 210—"Records Retention: Normal and Disaster"
- \# 212—"The Equipment Replacement Decision"
- \# 220—"Basic Budgets for Profit Planning"

229—"Cash Flow in a Small Plant"

Small Business Bibliographies:
15—"Recordkeeping Systems—Small Store and Service Trade"
31—"Retail Credit and Collections"
87—"Financial Management"

Small Marketers Aids:
107—"Building Strong Relations with Your Bank"
110—"Controlling Cash in Small Retail and Service Firms"
126—"Accounting Services for Small Service Firms"
130—"Analyze Your Records to Reduce Costs"
139—"Understanding Truth in Lending"
146—"Budgeting in a Small Service Firm"
147—"Sound Cash Management and Borrowing"
155—"Keeping Records in Small Business"

Available from the Superintendent of Documents

Small Business Management Series:
9—"Cost Accounting for Small Manufacturers." Stock #045-000-00115-6, 163 pp., $1.60.

#15—"Handbook of Small Business Finance," Stock #045-000-00139-3, 63 pp., $.75.

20—"Ratio Analysis for Small Business," Stock #045-000-00150-4, 65 pp., $1.80.

25—"Guides for Profit Planning," Stock #045-000-00137-7, 59 pp., $.85.

32—"Financial Recordkeeping for Small Stores," Stock #045-000-00142-3, 135 pp., $1.55.

18

Personnel Management

In the beginning, the prudent entrepreneur operates alone, perhaps with the assistance of only one or more family members. The new business owner is usually apprehensive about adding employees, realizing that to do so would add substantially to the overhead costs which he or she is trying so hard to hold down (at least until securing a comfortable foothold). Indeed, when the situation finally does demand additional help, often the entrepreneur's immediate reaction is to hire part-timers.

Personnel is, of course, one of the firm's major resources. Hiring the right people—and training them well—can often mean the difference between scratching out the barest of livelihoods and steady, continuous business growth.

Incidentally, personnel problems do not discriminate between small and big business; you find them in all businesses, regardless of size. Usually, a small business owner has had little prior experience with any personnel activities; staffing is often done purely on the combined bases of personal judgment and intuition. A new entrepreneur has probably had little exposure to good supervisory practices unless, by chance, he or she is fortunate enough to have worked under an excellent supervisor in some past position. Most likely, a new business owner is totally unfamiliar with such things as personnel record-keeping, labor legislation, and union relations (from an employer's point of view).

In small businesses, a closeness often develops rapidly between owners and their employees. This is natural. In time, employers get to know each employee fairly well. Dependency relationships on the employees' part may spring up and strengthen. However, when companies grow to the point where, let's say, there are eight or ten employees on the books, these relationships have multiplied so tremendously that much of the contact and initial closeness have begun to fade. Indeed, by this time, owners may have interposed one or two layers of intermediate management between them and their rank-and-file.

MANPOWER PLANNING FOR THE SMALL COMPANY

Like any other phase of your business, this personnel dimension requires your top administrative skills. You need to set goals, to plan and organize, and so on. At the heart of your personnel planning will lie considerations such as how to allocate your manpower resources to maximum advantage, and how to control total labor costs.

When the firm is new and small, there is little need right away for long-range thinking. People are added slowly, at least for the first year or so of operation. Thereafter, as soon as you can, devise a system for manpower planning. At that point in time, I recommend the following approach:

1. Take an inventory of your current employees. Set down on paper their present job titles and descriptions. Review and assess past performance, listing both their strong qualities and their weaknesses. (This analysis can help you to identify those who show promise and can, some day, be promoted to higher positions.)
2. Determine the organizational changes your business will require over the next few years. Project the types and numbers of people you will need to fill all niches in the organizational structure.
3. Match these positions with the people you have on hand. Decide which positions you can fill with your own people (when the time is ripe), and which will have to be filled by "new hires."

4. Anticipate some degree of necessary employee turnover and adjust future needs accordingly.

5. Bear in mind that people have to be "phased in" to new positions; they must be trained for some time before they can be expected to perform at a satisfactory level.

6. Keep a careful watch over costs.

A Word About Turnover

One fact of life you'll have to live with is employee turnover. Every business has it. Some lose people at a more accelerated rate than others but, whatever the turnover rate, it always hurts to lose a good employee (financially, as well as psychologically).

There are initial costs involved in locating, interviewing, hiring, and training an individual to the point where he or she reaches full potential. Then, there are intermediate costs of doing without that person until a replacement is found, and more expenses incur in acquiring the replacement.

People leave their jobs for a variety of reasons. Some leave unexpectedly and for unavoidable reasons: ill health, death, marriage, relocation, and deliberate terminations for due cause. Some losses are avoidable. Others are caused by poor supervisory practices on the part of owners or middle managers, by internal friction and personality clashes, by management failing to provide good incentives or an opportunity to move up the ladder, and so forth.

When any employee leaves an exit interview should be conducted and the results recorded. A review of the findings will be useful to management in taking corrective action to reduce the turnover rate. This step becomes more valuable as the company grows.

SETTING PERSONNEL POLICIES

Few small businesses can afford even a fledgling personnel department during the first few years of business operation. Nevertheless, a large mass of personnel forms and data generally accumulates rather rapidly from the very beginning. To hold problems down to a minimum, specific personnel policies should be established as early as possible. These become useful guides in all areas: recruitment and selection, compensation plan and employee benefits, training, promotions and terminations, and the like. All attendant systems and paperwork should be carefully designed and personnel files set up to hold application forms, testing and medical records, evaluation forms, changes in status, and so forth.

One practical activity which can help in policy setting is the preparation of job descriptions for every position in your firm. Analyze all positions in detail and then set down on paper the specific job title, the duties and responsibilities covered, the relationships with other segments of the business, and other relevant information. (This information will help you to write up job specifications for every opening that comes up.) In addition to the information already mentioned, add the special qualifications needed by the jobholder, such as the levels of education and experience required, familiarity with special equipment, minimum physical requirements (if these are pertinent), and so on.

As an outcome of this activity, you will be able to set up a job classification system which enables you to group the various positions by level and by function (administration, staff, supervision, maintenance, and so on). This, in turn, will have a bearing on levels of compensation.

THE STAFFING PROCESS

Broadly interpreted, the staffing process includes any activities pertinent to the recruitment and selection functions. Pinning down details and correct procedures in advance prevents errors later on that cause trouble and expense.

Personnel Sources

Over the long run, you need to explore and develop the potential of a variety of sources for future employees. Here is a listing of the more common avenues:

1. Advertising through posted announcements, window signs, and other "point-of-need" methods;
2. Recommendations from others: friends, employees, acquaintances, and the like;
3. Schools and universities: vocational, academic, technical, business;
4. Employment agencies: public, private;
5. Advertising in newspapers: classified and display advertisements;
6. Agencies which provide temporary help;
7. People who just drop by or write in for positions;
8. Unions.

The Selection of Personnel

Among the tools available to help you decide on who to hire and who to reject are: the employment application, the personal interview, the reference check, tests, and the probationary or tryout period for new employees.

The Employment Application. Prospective employees should be asked to complete an employment application. Application forms are available at your local business stationery store; they accommodate the applicant's name, address, telephone number, a history of prior work experiences, educational preparation, health and financial information, and personal data.

Generally, you can save both time and expense by using a "short form" preliminary "screening" application. This is a modified version of the larger application form, often a small, 4 x 5″ printed slip with room for only a few pertinent details—in addition to the applicant's name and address, the mandatory job specifications you've outlined in advance for a particular position. Assume, for instance, that you've run a classified ad in the local paper announcing a single opening at your place, and the ad draws twenty to twenty-five applicants. You can have them complete the shorter form quite easily (since it only requires several minutes to fill out) and then make a quick decision as to who does or doesn't have the qualifications you seek. This way you rapidly narrow down the crowd to just a few individuals who can remain for interviews. If one of the requirements is, for example, two years of previous experience in a similar position, it's simple to accomplish this preselection quickly.

The short form can also serve as a resource list for you—that is, a source of future employees if openings develop for which these individuals are more suited.

The Personnel Interview. An interview situation is usually the next step. This procedure is one of the major tools in the processing of job applicants and essentially has two aims: (1) to elicit information to supplement the facts submitted on the application form, and (2) to gain useful insights into the appearance, behavior, and personality of the prospective employees.

Because it's comparatively easy for the average interviewer to be overly influenced by an outstanding characteristic of an applicant, it's wise to develop and use an interview rating form which touches on all important areas. This helps you objectify your assessment of an individual. Of course, the more you interview people—and the more you read about how to interview in books on personnel—the better you will be at it!

Interviews can be patterned and directive: This means you plan out your approach in advance—that is, the kinds of questions you intend to ask, the order in which you'll ask them, what in particular you'll be looking for, and so forth. Interviews can also be nondirective: Here, the basic approach is to refrain from doing much talking and to encourage the interviewee to speak out at length.

Well-trained personnel interviewers often look for "knock-out factors,"the presence of certain undesirable characteristics or symptoms which in and of themselves are sufficient cause for turning down an applicant. Among the more commonly-employed "knock-out factors" are:

- evidence of frequent job-hopping in the past,
- excessive indebtedness,
- poor communicative ability,
- poor emotional control,
- too high a standard of living, and
- unexplained gaps in the employment record.

Reference Checks. As a general rule, you should make it your business to personally check all references offered by job applicants. A simple form letter and questionnaire can be devised to cover the major points you're interested in. Or you can contact former employers and other references by telephone; this method is often preferable, not only for quicker results but also because many people are reluctant to put negative comments down in writing. At times, telephone checking is useful in that any hesitancy about the individual in question can be discerned quite readily and probed diplomatically during the conversation.

Tests. On the whole, the majority of smaller firms do not resort to testing job applicants except when a position requires special aptitudes. Measures of typing speed and accuracy (or stenographic skill), arithmetic and spelling tests for clerical employees, tests of manual dexterity for certain occupations, and on-hands demonstrations of ability to run specialized equipment (such as lathes), all come under this classification.

Some firms make use of a variety of paper-and-pencil tests to aid in their selection processes. These range from intelligence tests and general knowledge measures, to personality batteries, tests of selling ability, and so forth. These tests are expensive to use and are generally not recommended until a business has grown to a substantial size. Probably their most valuable contribution is in screening out applicants with personality defects or below-average intelligence.

Medical examinations can of course be helpful, especially where a position requires frequent physical effort. In some localities, such examinations are mandated by law (food handlers, for example, must be licensed). However, when paid for by the employer, these tests can be quite expensive, especially if the number of employees is considerable.

Probationary Period. The final phase of the selection process (once an individual has been assigned to a post) should be a probationary or tryout period of a few weeks or months. This trial period is a valuable step; it will insure that you have not made an erroneous decision. During this time, the new worker should be observed and frequently rated. It's far more difficult to discharge a below-average performer after many months have elapsed, especially if your firm has been unionized.

Induction

The first few days on the job are most crucial to your new employee. This is when favorable or unfavorable work-related attitudes are formed, and when the worker is either turned on or off. Of course, when you assign an individual to his or her section, you must make sure the person receives some initial instruction—namely, about the company itself, the particular department, and the nature of the work. In addition, a helpful move is to appoint an experienced member of the department to act as a "big brother/sister" to the new employee.

In this same context, a well-prepared employee handbook can be extremely valuable. One of the free booklets available from the Small Business Administration ("Pointers on Preparing an Employee Handbook," No. 197) explains the advantages of having such an internal aid and provides suggestions for preparing your own. The "Sample Table of Contents" (in Figure 18–1) from the SBA booklet is a range of topics which you could include in your firm's handbook.

TRAINING

The training function is a vital, ongoing activity which requires your attention as the owner of a small business. Employees need and want training not only for performing their jobs satisfactorily but also as preparation for eventual promotion. Indeed, you

```
┌─────────────────────────────────────────────────────────┐
│                     Employee Handbook:                  │
│              SAMPLE  TABLE  OF  CONTENTS                 │
│                                                         │
│        1—WELCOME MESSAGE                                 │
│                                                         │
│        2—HISTORY OF THE COMPANY                          │
│                                                         │
│        3—THIS IS OUR BUSINESS                            │
│                                                         │
│        4—YOU AND YOUR FUTURE                             │
│                                                         │
│        5—WHAT YOU WILL NEED TO KNOW                      │
│                                                         │
│             Working Hours                               │
│             Reporting To Work                           │
│             "Time Clock"                                │
│             Rest Periods                                │
│             Absence From Work                           │
│             Reporting Absences                          │
│             Employment Record                           │
│             Pay Period                                  │
│             Shift Premiums                              │
│             Safety and Accident Prevention              │
│             Use of Telephones                           │
│             How To Air Complaints                       │
│                                                         │
│        6—THESE ARE YOUR BENEFITS                         │
│                                                         │
│             Vacations                                   │
│             Holidays                                    │
│             Group Insurance                             │
│             Hospitalization & Surgical Benefits         │
│             Free Parking                                │
│             Training Program                            │
│             Christmas Bonus                             │
│             Savings Plan                                │
│             Profit-Sharing Plan                         │
│             Suggestion Awards                           │
│             Jury Duty                                   │
│             Military Leave                              │
│             U.S. Old Age Benefits                       │
│             Unemployment Compensation                   │
│             Equal Employment Opportunity                │
│                                                         │
│        7—THESE SPECIAL SERVICES ARE FOR YOU              │
│                                                         │
│             Credit Union                                │
│             Education Plans                             │
│             Medical Dispensary                          │
│             Employee Purchases                          │
│             Company Cafeteria                           │
│             Monthly Magazine                            │
│             Annual Outing                               │
│             Bowling League                              │
│             Baseball Team                               │
│                                                         │
│        8—INDEX or TABLE of CONTENTS                      │
└─────────────────────────────────────────────────────────┘
```

FIGURE 18–1

Reproduced from "Pointers on Preparing an Employee Handbook" (Management Aids No. 197) (Washington, D.C.: Small Business Administration, 1975), p.3.

owe it to yourself even more than to your employees to make sure they are well trained. Well trained personnel alleviates a good many unnecessary headaches.

Here are a few of the advantages which can result when people are trained:

- better employee morale
- increased sales
- less waste
- lower turnover rate
- more production
- reduced operational costs
- speedier employee development

Usually, a new employee receives adequate initial training, and is expected to "go it alone" from then on. In a good business operation, training ought to be continuous. No clerical, sales-person, bookkeeper, or machine operator ever attains 100 percent efficiency or output at his or her specific job; there's always room for improvement. Moreover, every individual should have the opportunity to move up the ladder. This implies training for a new and higher position. Frankly, there can be a whale of a difference between satisfactory performance and performance that is outstanding. We are not necessarily talking here about a 5 percent or 10 percent difference; in some cases, productivity can be doubled (or even tripled). As a case in point, there are always a few star performers in any sizeable sales force who far outstrip the others in the production of sales.

In a small new enterprise, most training occurs on-the-job—that is, the immediate supervisor is held responsible for training the worker. But as a business grows, the need for a more thorough and professional training becomes evident. It's never too early to begin making plans for the future, if only to fill additional niches as they open up in the organizational hierarchy. This is preferable to hiring supervisors and managers from the outside, usually at a higher cost.

A careful "needs analysis" of your organization and all the people in it should be the first step in coordinating your training efforts.

A Checklist for Your Training Program

According to the Small Business Administration, there are a number of factors to consider when establishing a major training program:

1. Make a needs assessment of your company on a departmental, section, and unit basis.
2. Set the objectives to be accomplished through your training efforts.
3. Determine the curriculum (subject matter). Make certain you include not only product, company, and customer knowledge but also skills development and personal adjustment training.
4. Select the types of training which best serve your purposes.
5. Select the training methods to be used.
6. Set up a timetable and schedule for your program.
7. Select the instructor(s).
8. Watch your costs.

Training Methods and Techniques

A wide variety of training methods and techniques are available for your purposes. (Some of the books listed at the end of this chapter can help you in this area.) Among the more frequently employed approaches are formal classroom lectures, small-group discussions, seminars, conferences, the study of cases, programmed instruction, committee work, and role-playing. Of course, the most frequently found method is on-the-job training; variations of this approach include apprenticeships and internships.

For employees pegged for eventual promotion to management positions, there are other techniques available (in addition to those listed above) including job rotation, in-basket methods, special project assignments, management games, sensitivity training, and outside training (at local universities or trade associations).

WAGE AND SALARY ADMINISTRATION

Wage and salary administration is another significant segment within the personnel sphere. This area involves setting up and then overseeing the operation of a comprehensive compensation plan to cover all of your employees.

As a point of information only, the term "wages" is usually applied to payment for employee services rendered on an hourly, daily, or piecework basis. It is frequently used is connection with the earnings of day laborers, other manual workers, and workers on factory production belts. On the other hand, "salary" generally refers to compensation paid out on a weekly (or semimonthly, monthly, and so on) basis, and describes the earnings of office personnel, supervisors, and other "white collar" employees.

An employee's pay of course depends on the levels of education and experience, the skills, and the knowledges needed to do the job. In a large organization, all positions are generally grouped according to different types and levels of work and then arranged in a hierarchy according to levels of authority and responsibility. Following this alignment, the jobs are then compared with similar positions in the particular industry; pay scales are then set at the average prevailing rates for those positions. In a small new enterprise, however, the prevalent approach is to simply "meet the competition" (which, if you think about it, is much the same thing!).

Of course, people do expect to earn more over time. Everyone wants an occasional raise. It's therefore a good idea to establish a fixed compensation range for each and every position in the company—that is, a minimum (starting) rate and a maximum (or "cap"). It would also be helpful to set up a personnel evaluation program where all employees are reviewed periodically, and where pay increases are contingent on satisfactory performance.

Compensating Employees

The major compensation plans—straight salary, straight commission, and combination—were discussed earlier in Chapter 13. Consequently, their pros and cons need not be repeated at this point. However, some consideration might be given to the use of incentives, in combination with one of the major plans, to increase employee productivity. As a rule, most small businesses conform to the straight salary (or hourly wage) approach.

Fringe Benefits. All the "extras" which firms have added to the basic compensation of their employees over the years, amount to a sizeable cost factor today. For the average firm, these "fringe benefits" which are now expected by employees can add another 20 percent to wages and salaries. (Note that we're not discussing those costs required by law, such as a company's contribution to the Social Security System, and so on). Small firms are cautioned against adopting these fringes too quickly and too freely. Some are practically necessary if a company is to effectively compete for personnel against other firms in the industry; other fringe benefits, while perhaps desirable, should be postponed until a firm is in a strong and healthy position.

A representative listing of some of these benefits appears below (in no particular order):

vacation with pay	health insurance
paid holidays	awards and prizes
pay for jury duty	retirement plan

life insurance special recreational events accident insurance use of company car bonuses medical examinations severance pay profit-sharing pension plan reimbursement for educational costs

FEDERAL LABOR LEGISLATION

Since the mid-1930s, a number of important federal laws have been enacted on behalf of employees. As a result, business owners need to make sure their personnel approaches conform to all regulations affecting their labor contingent. A list of these laws follows:

1935—The Wagner Act (also called The National Labor Relations Act)—Designed to counter unfair practices on the part of employers (in those Depression years) and to reduce industrial unrest, this act gave employees the right to organize and to engage in collective bargaining. It also established the National Labor Relations Board.

1938—The Federal Wages and Hours Law (now referred to as The Fair Labor Standards Act).—This established federal regulation of wages and hours, a minimum wage, provision for overtime pay, and constraints upon child labor. A notable exemption here is administrative and executive personnel.

1963—The Equal Pay Act.—This law prohibits discrimination by the employer because of sex.

1964—The Civil Rights Act.—This piece of legislation created the Equal Employment Opportunity Commission. It prohibits discrimination among employees in hiring practices, compensation levels, or advancement opportunities that is based on race, color, religion, sex, or national origin.

1967—The Age Discrimination in Employment Act.—Similar to the Civil Rights Act in its intent, this law bars discrimination in businesses engaged in interstate commerce against people between the ages of 40 and 65 because of age. It applies to firms employing a minimum of 25 people.

1970—The Occupational Safety and Health Act.—This law seeks to assure safe working conditions for employees. Businesses must comply with safety and health standards and keep accurate records pertinent to this area. They are also subject to unannounced inspections designed to monitor compliance with the provisions of the act.

1972—The Equal Employment Opportunity Act.—An amendment to the Civil Rights Act of 1964, this legislation extended its provisions to include employees of local and state governments, educational institutions (both public and private), and others.

1974—The Pension Reform Act.—This law was designed to regulate pension, profit-sharing, and retirement plans, and to obviate deficiencies therein.

MANAGING UNION RELATIONS

Like it or not, unions are a fact of life—a fact which you will face, sooner or later.

It's true that the average small business owner looks askance on the unionization situation. Indeed, many entrepreneurs are suspicious of and resent employees who seek union affiliation, feeling that these people are ingrates and even disloyal, at the very least.

Probably, this kind of attitude can be traced to the belief that any unionization initiative will encroach on an owner's absolute control over a business.

This does appear to pose a threat. A visit by the union local's business agent carries with it the weight of a far more powerful organization than the one the entrepreneur administers. Moreover, the small business owner is at a total disadvantage in that he or she usually has little knowledge of unions and of management-union relations.

Estimates have placed the number of union members today (excluding agricultural workers) at well over one-fifth of the nation's labor force. Most locals are affiliated with either a national or international labor organization; seventy-five percent of them are tied into (and backed by) the giant AFL-CIO. So, the power is certainly there!

A small business may be able to continue operating for some time before attracting the attention of a union. It helps, too, if you pay your employees decently and treat them like people. When a union representative does finally make a call, however, he or she will be looking to talk with your employees about representing them in labor negotiations. At that time, any resistance on your part can lead to unpleasant action. Imagine the effects of a line of individuals parading to and fro in front of your building entrance and chanting "Pass them by! Pass them by!" Imagine them carrying posters which read, in bold black letters, "DO NOT PATRONIZE! THIS IS A NON-UNION SHOP!"

Collective Bargaining

A healthy attitude to maintain toward union endeavors is one of understanding and tolerance. Unions do have a place in our economy. Workers (as well as employers) do have the right to organize. Consequently, there can be no logical reason for any hostility on your part. In today's climate, management-union relations can be open and aboveboard, businesslike and even friendly, and mature. Bear in mind that the union has almost as much at stake in the continued prosperity and growth of your business as you do.

What happens eventually is that the local representing your employees will want to negotiate a labor contract with you. The process by which the contract is agreed on is called "collective bargaining."

Activities during contract negotiations resemble the kind of dickering and bargaining which takes place when a firm or an individual attempts to sell an expensive property to a shrewd buyer. Each of the two principals approaches the bargaining table well prepared; each has a clear idea as to what it's prepared to offer and what it is looking for; each has plotted its strategy and its tactics in advance. A period of give-and-take almost always characterizes the pre-agreement phase.

The contract spells out all the agreed-upon details: the new wage agreement, a listing of the conditions under which the union members will be expected to work, the procedure for handling employee grievances, a no-strike pledge, the length of time the contract will be in effect, and the like. Today, most contracts also include an "escalator" clause which guarantees a wage increase when the cost-of-living index goes up by a certain percentage.

FOR FURTHER INFORMATION

Books

Anthony, William P., and Nicholson, Edward A., Jr. *Management of Human Resources: A Systems Approach to Personnel Management.* Columbus: Grid Publishing, 1977.

Beach, Dale S. *Personnel: The Managment of People at Work,* 3rd ed. New York: Macmillan, 1974.

Chruden, Herbert J., and Sherman, Arthur W., Jr. *Personnel Management,* 5th ed. Cincinnati: South-Western, 1976.

Glueck, William F. *Personnel: A Diagnostic Approach,* rev. ed. Dallas: Business Publications, 1978.

Hamblin, A. C. *Evaluation and Control of Training.* New York: McGraw-Hill, 1974.

Hicks, H. G., and Gullett, C. R. *The Management of Organizations,* 3rd ed. New York: McGraw-Hill, 1976.

Klatt, Lawrence A., Murdick, Robert G., and Schuster, Fred A. *Human Resources Management: A Behavioral Systems Approach.* Homewood, Ill.: Irwin, 1978.

Lopez, Felix M. *Personnel Interviewing,* 2nd ed. New York: McGraw-Hill, 1975.

Pigors, Paul, and Myers, Charles A. *Personnel Administration,* 8th ed. New York: McGraw-Hill, 1977.

Sibson, Robert E. *Increasing Employee Productivity.* New York: American Management, 1976.

Strauss, G., and Sayles, L.R. *Personnel: The Human Problems of Management,* 3rd ed. Englewood Cliffs, N.J.: Prentice-Hall, 1972.

Free Materials from the Small Business Administration

Management Aids:
   # 171—"How to Write a Job Description"

   # 195—"Setting Pay for Your Management Jobs"

   # 197—"Pointers on Preparing an Employee Handbook"

   # 205—"Pointers on Using Temporary-Help Services"

   # 209—"Preventing Employee Pilferage"

Small Business Bibliographies:
   # 72—"Personnel Management"

Small Marketers' Aids:
   # 132—"The Federal Wage-Hour Law in Small Firms"

   # 135—"Arbitration: Peace-Maker in Small Business"

Small Business Managment Series:
   #   1—"An Employee Suggestion System for Small Companies," Stock #045-000-00020-6, 18 pp., $.45.

   #   3—"Human Relations in Small Business," Stock #045-000-00036-2, 38 pp., $1.60.

   # 26—"Personnel Managment Guides for Small Business," Stock #045-000-00126-1, 79 pp., $1.10.

   # 29—"Management Audit for Small Manufacturers," Stock #045-000-00035-4, 58 pp., $.75.

   # 31—"Management Audit for Small Retailers," Stock #045-000-00149-1, 50 pp., $1.80.

   # 38—"Management Audit for Small Service Firms," Stock #045-000-00143-1, 67 pp., $.90.

IV

Special Areas for Improving Operations

Hopefully, you have managed by now to get your business off to a good start and it may even be showing a profit, however small. You've become acquainted with the fundamentals of business administration and are somewhat knowledgeable about production, marketing and sales, promotion, personnel, finances, and other components of management. Now the time approaches when you ought to start thinking about "toning up" your operation, whatever type it may be.

There are many things you can do to improve your profit picture; to help you accomplish this objective specific suggestions are presented in this next section of the book. An entire chapter is devoted to each of the four most popular types of enterprises: manufacturing, wholesaling, retailing, and the service business.

19

Improving Results in Your Manufacturing Plant

As a conservative estimate, at least eight out of ten small factories operate well below their optimum capability.

Why this dire situation? For one thing, so long as a plant is producing and the operation profitable, the factory manager is usually quite content. Handicapped by the lack of a more sophisticated level of knowledge of plant operations, the manager does not realize things could be better. Other factors which contribute to manufacturing inefficiency often include improper costing practices, machine operators who are not well trained, inadequately maintained or obsolescing equipment, lack of familiarity with the use of variance analysis techniques, untidy purchasing practices, and a host of other possibilities.

These days, in the face of spiraling costs and intensified competition, the name of the manufacturing game is no longer production but *productivity*.

To improve plant productivity, no magical "open sesame" need be evoked; the pathway to improvement in manufacturing is as simple as counting 1–2–3:

1. buy better,
2. produce better, and
3. sell better.

Actually, entries 1 and 3 are ancillary problem areas; the central problem in manufacturing is that number 2—*How to Produce Better*.

It has been pointed out repeatedly in this book that good business administration involves skillfully planning, organizing, directing, and controlling all of the elements which combine to comprise the business. In short, it calls for more efficient deployment and use of all company resources—namely, the now-familiar "M's": machinery, manpower, methods, materials, and money. Moreover, efficiency in manipulating the various "M's" is inextricably tied to costs. Producing better (for that matter, buying or selling better) implies that output will be increased while cost factors representing the input will be held steady (if not reduced).

STANDARDS: THE BASES FOR IMPROVEMENT

To increase productivity, you must know exactly where you are at a particular moment in your plant, decide in a logical manner on goals which are higher than today's outputs, and then figure out ways to attain those goals. In short, measurements need to be taken—today, tomorrow, and beyond tomorrow. Only by recording and comparing those measurements over time can you ascertain whether or not plant productivity is trending upwards.

Such measurements are referred to as standards; these are based on averages obtained through observing and recording what transpires in the plant. Of course, standards are established for control purposes and, more importantly, as points of departure for improvement. They can be set up in every division of your manufacturing enterprise, not only within the production process itself but also in purchasing, sales, and even office administration. They provide answers to dozens of questions, for example:

● How much of material A goes into each unit of product B?
● How long does it take an operator to perform task C?

- How many widgets roll off machine D each hour, each week?
- What is the yield in pounds of compound Z when 50 pounds of material X are mixed with 25 pounds of material Y?
- If this piece of equipment is in operation eight hours each day on a five-day-week basis, how much electricity will be used?

In the area of production, standards such as the following should be established:

- direct labor cost/product unit,
- number of man-hours needed/unit of work,
- number of machine-hours needed/operation,
- set-up time/operation,
- amount of materials used/product,
- power usage/machine,
- number of products produced/day, and so on.

The standards which might prove useful in the sales area include: the number of new accounts opened per salesperson, the average monthly sales per salesperson, the cost of sales per sales dollar, the gross margin contribution per territory, and so forth.

Setting Standards

In efficient plant management, standards such as those mentioned above are developed and monitored regularly, perhaps with the aid of industrial engineers or consultants. These standards, of course, represent averages which are real. By definition, then, they are not ideal averages. So your next move is to work out ideal standards; in other words, strive to project the company's output if operating at maximum efficiency. Then, somewhere between the ideal and the real, there's a spot where you can pinpoint an attainable level of performance which is higher than the one your plant now evidences.

Time and motion studies are techniques available to help you maximize efficiency. The first approach records the time it takes to perform each task in a factory, in order to set up time standards for every job. Motion studies analyze all movements made in accomplishing each task and arrive at the most effective sequence of motions for each.

As a final comment on standards, remember that the ratios derived from analyzing the basic accounting statements (balance sheets, income statements) serve as standards for comparison, control, and further improvement. (See the section on "ratio analysis" in Chapter 17.)

Variances are simply differences or deviations from the norm or average. After you've worked up your initial standards, the averages you've calculated from daily plant operations will appear to fluctuate. In manufacturing, you can expect all sorts of variances: labor variances, materials variances, overhead variances. As an illustration, those standards you have developed for materials used in production can vary because of poor handling and storage, changes in the purchase price, inadequately serviced equipment, fluctuations in quality, and the like.

For each of the major cost areas (labor being often the most significant) you will have to decide just how much tolerance, or deviation from the standard you can permit. When variances are analyzed—compared to the standards you've decided are acceptable—those which exceed tolerable limits must be investigated thoroughly and corrective action taken at once. Often, better production planning and flow control, improved maintenance, and more training for factory personnel can be helpful here. Techniques such as PERT (Program Evaluation and Review Techniques) or CPM (Critical Path Method) can also be of assistance.

Major moves for improving plant productivity include upgrading the quality of the labor component (through further training, better hiring practices, more skilled supervision); moving in the direction of semi-automation through the purchase of additional machinery and equipment (and introducing the computer); and making sizable capital expenditures for plant expansion or improvement, additional personnel, and so forth.

RANDOM THOUGHTS FOR UPGRADING PLANT PRODUCTIVITY

Production

In a healthy factory operation, production planning is accomplished well in advance. Better planning means increasing the exactitude of your sales forecasting. Devote lots of good thinking to this thorny problem; involve your best people in the process. Among the methods to use are: the jury of executive opinion, customers' estimates of future purchases, salespeople's projections, and past sales. Narrow down and reconcile discrepancies in the data you collect, and then employ trend extension techniques.

Prepare your production budget just as carefully as you prepare every other component of the master budget. Consider your budgets for labor, for materials, for manufacturing overhead, for maintenance, and so on.

Plot your production with great care every step of the way. Set up a foolproof production reporting system. Involve your senior people in planning, preparing work orders, routing, scheduling, expediting, and other activities.

Set specific objectives: Your quickest route to process improvement is "production-by-objectives." Indeed, fuller utilization of all production resources leads to a higher return on investment.

Work on moving away from intermittent production and towards longer, uninterrupted machine runs. Gang orders where possible during slack periods. If your products are branded, investigate the benefits of running private label merchandise. Build up your finished goods inventories in advance of selling seasons.

If inventory levels exceed sales or if you can foresee the need for more cash in the near future, offer "early-bird" discounts inducing your customers to place orders earlier than usual.

In the production process, two or more pieces of equipment are often used in sequence. The machines usually operate at different speeds; this raises the strong possibility that bottlenecks will form. Bottlenecks can be avoided by balancing the flow lines—use flow process charts and flow diagrams to work out the ideal flow of materials. Additional machinery, proper scheduling, and the application of queueing theory can all be of assistance in this problem area.

Apply cost accounting techniques to all manufacturing operations; watch variances from all standards; take action whenever indicated, and use ratio analysis to improve efficiency.

Layout

Many small manufacturing establishments use the process type of layout; this enables plants to manufacture different products on the same equipment, thus insuring flexibility. However, there are some drawbacks: excessive materials handling costs, inefficient utilization of both machinery and labor, unnecessary delays, and so forth. By combining or anticipating orders (and by writing more business!) you may be able to introduce some line production, or "product layout," into your manufacturing. This will give you the best of both types of processes—namely, lower-cost production line output and the flexibility you need to handle job lots.

Plan all layout changes yourself with the aid of a qualified consultant. Always consider your future requirements (three to five years hence); think in terms of additional facilities, offices, new electrical wiring, plumbing, waste lines, and the like. Use drawings, plans, renderings. Machinery can be represented by templates of cardboard or other materials and dimensions indicated on these. Scale models are also useful.

Many smaller plants have a U-shaped layout where both the shipping and receiving departments are at the same end of the factory. This way, the same loading area and single bay can be used for both purposes; these set-ups are often supervised by one individual.

Machinery and Equipment

Survey all machinery: check performance records, purchase dates, warrantees. Replace antiquated equipment or machines of below-par performance with newer models of higher capacity. Remember that used equipment is often costlier in the long term.

When new machinery is considered, strive for trouble-free operation, good quality workmanship and materials, reliable performance, and a good service set-up with the manufacturer. Where possible, deal directly with the maker and not with the distributor.

If not already in existence, a strict preventive maintenance program should be instituted, including regular inspections, prompt repairs, spare parts on hand for important equipment, and so forth. Work out procedures and even backup equipment for floods, power failures, fires, and other major events which could affect production.

Leasing arrangements are at times more beneficial than outright purchases of equipment, especially those which provide options to buy.

All maintenance supplies and tools should be controlled with a careful record system. Maintenance personnel should represent various skills, such as electricians, carpenters, machinists, mechanics, and the like (depending upon the particular needs of your plant).

Materials Handling

Where possible, contract for six months' or a year's supply of materials which you use in large quantities. Make sure that the

SPECIAL AREAS FOR IMPROVING OPERATIONS

price you pay is guaranteed for the life of the contract and that quantity discounts apply. Have deliveries made to your plant as they are needed.

Materials are forever being moved about within a factory. All types of power equipment and conveyors are available for this purpose. Various proposals will be submitted to you over the year; evaluate all of them with an eye to economizing on movement and thereby increasing plant efficiency.

Follow both the "straight-line" and the "unit load" principles which an experienced warehouseman is thoroughly familiar with. The former teaches you to minimize the distances materials must travel within the plant (not adhering slavishly to straight lines but avoiding sideways or backwards movements); the latter refers to the fact that the greater the quantity of merchandise moved at the same time, the less each individual item in the load (usually palletized) costs to move.

Many kinds of materials used in manufacturing require special handling precautions, proper storage containers, temperature-controlled and/or moisture-free atmosphere, ventilation (or lack of it), specially built tanks or drums, and so forth. Proper attention to these needs prevents deterioration, spoilage, and other "wastage" of materials.

In this connection, plastic and fibre containers can be frequently used to replace more expensive and heavier items such as steel drums.

Personnel

Productivity improvement in a manufacturing plant should begin with your employees. Having the right people, with the right skills and the proper training, in the right positions within your organization, lays a strong foundation for eventual improvement.

If your company does not already have them on hand, written and detailed job specifications should be prepared for all jobs. New hires should be matched against those specifications. If at all possible, try to hire people who are proficient in two or more skill areas; this way, you can build valuable flexibility into the personnel component.

Set up an operations manual as a guide for your people. Seek a professional personnel specialist to help you produce this guide.

At all times, train your employees in good work habits. Then, insist on careful adherence to rules and instructions. Do not tolerate sloppy performance.

Strive for good management-worker relations, safe and comfortable working conditions. Encourage worker input and suggestions.

If yours is a one-shift operation which runs for five days each week, this means that your machines are lying idle for sixteen hours a day on weekdays and twenty-four hours per day over the weekend. Aim at building up business to the point where two shifts are needed (perhaps 8 AM to 4 PM, 4PM to 12 midnight); this will bring your per-item overhead costs down sharply.

Quality Control

The quality control function in manufacturing is an essential one. Ordinarily, its foremost application is to the product or products being made. It is used to detect inferior or defective work in sufficient time so that adjustments can be made quickly in production. Indeed, quality control should embrace all purchased raw, semi-finished, or finished materials used in the plant, and equipment, machinery, and supplies as well.

In a small plant, there's often no quality control department per se, simply one or several technicians who perform necessary tests and report the results to the production head.

It's not unusual for a small manufacturer to request that suppliers conduct quality control tests on their materials before shipping them in. This is a helpful type of arrangement which will save you time and money. (It's wise to verify the results from time to time yourself.)

IMPROVING YOUR SALES EFFORTS

At the beginning, a new manufacturer may rely upon his or her own efforts (or those of partners) to obtain the company's first regular customers. Later on, the firm will most likely select one or more manufacturer's representatives to take charge of the selling end of the business, thus leaving the owner(s) more time to concentrate on manufacturing. (Note: See Chapter 13, "Promotion Management.")

Eventually, a sales force can be initiated. While the salient details of managing a sales force have already been treated (again,

Chapter 13), the following description of the selling process itself may provide small plant managers with insights leading to improved results in the direct selling area.

Good selling is based on the well-known "AIDA Principle"; in this case, the name of an opera is employed as a mnemonic to help you remember the following key words:

*A*TTENTION Your first task is to secure the attention of your prospect.

*I*NTEREST Next, you must arouse his or her interest in knowing more about what you're selling.

*D*ESIRE You then begin to build desire on the prospect's part to have what you're selling.

*A*CTION Finally, you get action by securing the order.

To a large extent, good selling is also based on what's called the "needs-satisfaction" approach. Simply put, this means that you (1) ascertain the customer's wants and needs, (2) match the proper selection of merchandise to meet those needs, (3) show the prospect what those products can do for him or her, and (4) convince the person to buy.

The Selling Process

The job of personal or direct selling can be more easily understood if it's broken down into a series of steps. Then, by applying both analytical and creative thinking to each of these steps in succession, a new salesperson can develop a professionalism and skill which will improve his or her sales results.

1. *Prospecting.* Knowing how to look for potential customers; knowing where to hunt for them.

2. *Qualifying.* Also known as the "pre-approach"; during this particular step the salesperson tries to find out as much as he or she can about the prospect, so that the presentation can be tailored to the prospect's needs.

3. *The Approach.* First contact with the prospect; normally conceived of as the first minute or so after meeting the prospect. Among the better-known approaches (and rather easy to comprehend, just from the titles) are: the introductory approach, the referral approach, and the product approach.

4. *The Presentation.* The main exposition regarding the product (or service) being sold. Here is where the salesperson will show the prospect what the product or service can do for him or her, bring out all of its selling points, involve the prospect in the

presentation (touching and feeling the materials, trying out the item, and so on), and try to answer all the questions raised during the sales interview.

5. *Meeting Objections*. Almost always, the prospect will raise several objections during the presentation. A crucial factor in the selling process is the proper handling of such objections—how you handle them can make or break the sale. The majority of objections fall into one of the following classifications: objections to price, objections to the quality or workmanship of the product, objections about the firm which the salesperson represents, and, perhaps, objections to the salesperson him or herself. A large percentage of intermediate or advanced training time is devoted to teaching salespeople how to counter the more common objections.

6. *The Close*. The culmination of the presentation; the point at which the order is written. There are any number of closings to use in different situations; any good book on salesmanship will familiarize you with at least half a dozen.

7. *The Follow-Up*. Writing up the order does not end the selling process. Before departing, the experienced salesperson will be sure to thank the customer for the order, and promise to call the customer shortly after the order has been delivered to check that everything is satisfactory. In the final analysis, the key to sales success is repeat business over the long term.

MANUFACTURING AND EDP

Much has been written about the value of installing electronic data processing equipment in manufacturing plants. Indeed, you'll probably be visited by zealous systems salespeople who'll try to convince you that their equipment will work wonders for your company. Don't be convinced easily; wait until your new business is firmly established and shows steady growth.

It's true that data processing is generally much faster and more accurate than clerical processing. But there are two ways for a small operation to go—namely, a service bureau or a time-sharing arrangement.

The service bureau has both trained computer operators and programmers on its staff. For a small business, records such as journals, check registers, accounts receivable, accounts payable, and major financial statements can be computerized. Even reports such as payrolls and inventory can be put out. Two types of charges are made by the bureau: One is for designing a program which suits your needs, the other for processing the data. (You will be required to deliver the source documents to the bureau regularly; these include items such as journal entries, receipts, sales slips, checks, and the like) The programming charge is usually a one-time charge which runs from a few hundred dollars to as high as one thousand dollars. The bureau might offer you a standard programming package in which case you'll have to adapt your recordkeeping system to the required format. The typical processing charge for a small company runs about two or three hundred dollars a month.

In time-sharing, a terminal is installed on your premises and connected to a computer over telephone wires. Operating this terminal does not require the assistance of a computer specialist. Costs are moderate—they depend upon the amount of computer time used, plus a relatively small rental charge (usually, less than one hundred dollars a month).

Your accountant, banker, or trade association can put you in touch with either type of arrangement.

FOR FURTHER INFORMATION

Books

Ballou, Ronald H. *Basic Business Logistics: Transportation, Materials Management, Physical Distribution*. Englewood Cliffs, N.J.: Prentice-Hall, 1978.

Beyer, Robert, and Trawicki, Donald J. *Profitability Accounting for Planning and Control*, 2nd ed. New York: Ronald Press, 1972.

Eisenberg, Joseph. *Turnaround Management: A Manual for Profit Improvement and Growth*. New York: McGraw-Hill, 1972.

Gage, W. L. *Value Analysis*. London: McGraw-Hill, 1967.

Hedrick, Floyd D. *Purchasing Management in the Smaller Company*. New York: American Management Associations, 1971.

Higgins, Lindley R. and Stidger, Ruth W., eds. *Cost Reduction from A to Z*. New York: McGraw-Hill, 1977.

Lee, Lamar, Jr., and Dobler, Donald W. *Purchasing and Materials Management*, 3rd ed. New York: McGraw-Hill, 1977.

Lester, Ronald H., Enrick, Norbert L., and Mottley, Harry E. *Quality Control for Profit*. New York: Industrial Press, 1977.

Lock, Dennis. *Factory Administration Handbook*. New York: Beekman, 1976.

Mali, Paul. *Improving Total Productivity*. New York: Wiley, 1978.

Russell, Frederic A., Beach, Frank H., and Buskirk, Richard H. *Textbook of Salesmanship*, 10th ed. New York: McGraw-Hill, 1978.

Stroh, Thomas F. *Managing the Sales Function*. New York: McGraw-Hill, 1978.

Wilson, R.M.S. *Cost Control Handbook*. New York: Wiley, 1975.

Wolfe, Harry Deane, and Twedt, Dik Warren. *Essentials of the Promotional Mix*. New York: Appleton-Century-Crofts, 1970.

Free Materials from the Small Business Administration

Management Aids:
   #199—"Expand Overseas Sales with Commerce Department Help"
   #200—"Is the Independent Sales Agent for You?"
   #212—"The Equipment Replacement Decision"

Small Business Bibliographies:
   #58—"Automation for Small Offices"
   #75—"Inventory Management"
   #80—"Data Processing for Small Businesses"
   #85—"Purchasing for Owners of Small Plants"

Available from the Superintendent of Documents

Small Business Management Series:
   #4—"Improving Material Handling in Small Business," Stock #045-000-00041-9, 42 pp., $.75.

   #7—"Better Communication in Small Business," Stock #045-000-00102-4, 37 pp., $.75.

   #9—"Cost Accounting for Small Manufacturers," Stock #045-000-00115-6, 163 pp., $1.60.

   #15—"Handbook of Small Business Finance," Stock #045-000-00139-3, 63 pp., $.75.

   #21—"Profitable Small Plant Layout," Stock #045-000-00029-0, 48 pp., $.80.

   #28—"Small Business and Government Research and Development," Stock #045-000-00130-0; 41 pp., $.75.

   #29—"Management Audit for Small Manufacturers," Stock #045-000-00035-4, 58 pp., $.75.

   #36—"Training Salesmen to Serve Industrial Markets," Stock #045-000-00133-4, 85 pp., $1.15.

Nonseries Publications:
   "Export Marketing for Smaller Firms," Stock #045-000-00112-1, 134 pp., $1.65.

20

Improving Results in Your Wholesale Business

As you will recall from the discussion of marketing channels in Chapter 14, two out of every three wholesaling establishments in the country are classified as "merchant wholesalers." The remainder fall into four different categories: manufacturers' sales branches and offices, petroleum bulk terminals, merchandise agents and brokers, and assemblers of farm products. Since these latter types make up only one-third of all wholesalers, the improvements suggested in this chapter are oriented toward the more prevalent type—the merchant wholesaler. Nevertheless, much of the information presented here can be of value to the four other kinds of wholesalers as well.

Let's begin with a typical organizational chart for a small merchant wholesaler operation. Figure 20–1 is fairly representative of this type of company in the grocery, automotive equipment, hardware, electrical supplies, or other line of business:

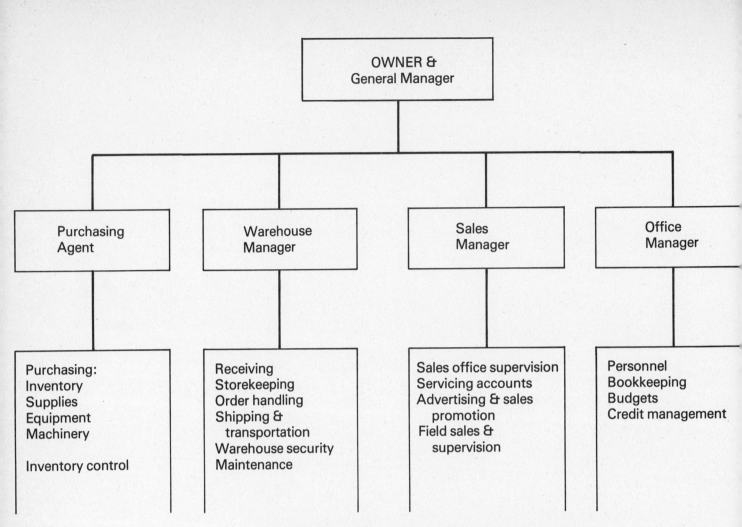

FIGURE 20–1. Small merchant wholesaler organization chart.

Improvement, then, may logically be sought within all four of the major areas of activity: purchasing, warehouse operations, sales, and office management.

Put more succinctly, in order to show a better operating statement, you must:

- buy better,
- sell better, and
- improve internal operations.

Since both purchasing and sales have been extensively treated in earlier chapters (13, 16, 19), little more will be added here on those two subjects. (However, you are advised to reread the appropriate sections of those chapters on techniques for improving the purchasing and sales aspects of your business.) The concentration here is on improving internal operations, for this

SPECIAL AREAS FOR IMPROVING OPERATIONS

is the one area where able management, better procedures and systems, and improved controls can really work wonders.

INTERNAL OPERATIONS REVOLVE AROUND ORDERS

To maximize productivity and minimize costs, all internal operations should be designed for the sole purpose of facilitating the delivery of goods to the wholesaler's accounts. There are, then, two primary components to be coordinated: (1) the entire order flow system and (2) those auxiliary structures—such as departments and the warehouse itself—which enable the order flow system to operate.

THE ORDER FLOW SYSTEM

Except for assemblers of farm products, most wholesale companies purchase their merchandise in large quantities and then break down their stock into smaller lots for resale to other businesses. Since these latter types (retailers, service enterprises, and the like) require frequent, repeat deliveries, the typical wholesaler can count on receiving hundreds of orders every month—if not every week—of the year.

All the more reason why the successful merchant wholesaler gives prompt attention to incoming orders and quick, dependable service. Ideally, every incoming order ought to be filled and the merchandise on its way to its destination within forty-eight hours. However, delays and bottlenecks are characteristically encountered; this is expecially true when orders come into the house in heavy quantities, as before a season or certain holidays, or when there is not enough manpower available to fill them, or when the customary transportation facilities are overburdened.

Another fairly common problem among wholesaling firms is occasionally losing track of orders as they are processed through the internal system. When customers phone in to inquire about the current status of their orders or to add or subtract items, the result is confusion and upsetting delay for both customer and supplier.

These and other problems can be avoided 95 percent of the time, if you give the situation some time, diligent study, and careful thought. To help you streamline your order flow system, consider the following breakdown of its various stages and apply some thought to each one:

The Order Form. A lot of time can be saved and careless omissions or errors avoided when the order form itself is carefully tailored to the needs of your organization. Preferably, it should be prepared (or revised) with the assistance of a specialist in business forms. Preprinted snap-out carbon sets will effect substantial savings for you.

Order Writing. All salespeople must be thoroughly trained to properly complete the order form. This applies not only to the field sales force but also to any inside salespeople. Terms, discounts, names and addresses, delivery information, and all special instructions must be written legibly. Poorly written out order forms, or forms with mistakes, should be acted on immediately; salespeople should be called in such instances and reproved. You must constantly keep on top of this kind of carelessness if you want to stop it.

Forwarding Orders. It is essential that orders gathered by the field salespeople are transmitted as quickly as possible to the home office. A delay of even a day or two can result in customer dissatisfaction. If the salesperson's territory is within an hour's drive of the office, a good procedure is to have that salesperson deliver the day's orders in person, either immediately after completing rounds or early the next morning before starting out again.

Of course, if the sales force operates at substantial distances from the home office, this cannot be done. Indeed, many companies prefer to keep their salespeople constantly in the field in order to maximize selling time. With this method, orders must be mailed in each evening. An even better procedure is to assign specific "call-in times" to individual salespeople during the evening hours; they can then telephone their orders to a night clerk or, preferably, to a recording machine. The actual order forms are then mailed in the next morning.

Receiving Orders. Regardless of the method employed in getting the orders to the office (in-person, mail, or telephone) there should be a central clerk to receive all orders. It's this individual's responsibility to check all orders for accuracy, clarity, conformance with company policy, and so forth; those which contain mistakes or omissions should be put aside for re-checking later. This clerk must be taught to record every order on a "daily order sheet" (which can be mimeographed or printed). Each day's sheets should have columns for writing in the order number, the time received, the customer name, and perhaps the salesperson's initials. Additional columns should be used to indicate the "routing" of the order (including the time sent) to its next stop along the system.

Processing Orders.   If additional copies of the order are needed (other than the set forwarded by the salesperson), avoid transcribing the information. A good office copier speeds up your operation; this fact plus the convenience of the machine for copying other documents more than offsets the purchase cost. Usually, all copies go first to the internal sales department where prices are checked, then to the credit desk for an okay. After approval, they are sent on to the warehouse for filling.

Filling Orders.   On receiving the order, the warehouse supervisor should register it in a log book, and then check over its details. At this point, priorities and routing considerations need to be taken into account. With respect to routing, transportation "runs" to different areas are usually scheduled for different days of the week or month; orders destined for those areas can accumulate in different boxes or trays.

Orders are distributed as the order pickers become available. These pickers then select the merchandise called for in the order. Various types of handling equipment—dollies, carts of different kinds, conveyors, even moving belts—can facilitate movement of the merchandise from the warehouse proper to the staging area. (Therefore, good warehouse layout and proper utilization of space can be of value in increasing the pickers' speed in filling orders.)

Work tables, corrugated cartons, tape, and other materials must be conveniently available when special packing arrangements are called for.

All outgoing orders, of course, should be carefully double checked before loading.

ENABLING ACTIVITIES

Chapter 16 goes into detail regarding facets of wholesale operations such as receiving, storekeeping, shipping, and traffic management; Chapter 8 contains useful information about protecting the premises. Here are just a few additional pointers on transportation and warehouse security.

Transportation

It's well worth your while to conduct a review of the entire area of transportation with the assistance of a physical distribution specialist. Investigate the pros and cons of using your own trucks versus common carriers or leased equipment. Are transportation costs adequately reflected in your current prices? Are your terms

F.O.B. (Free on Board) warehouse or destination? You may consider geographical zoning in setting up your prices or arrange a flat charge per shipment (based either on total weight or a percentage of the total invoice cost).

Warehouse Security

You can always brush up on security arrangements for your premises, especially with regard to doors, locks and keys control, lighting, and the like. Review the last section of Chapter 8 on methods for maintaining tight security.

Unhappily, employee stealing ("pilferage" is much too weak a term in this case) is all too common in wholesale operations. Often, this type of theft involves collusion on the part of two or more individuals. Sometimes one of them is a supervisor. Tight controls must be instituted in order to contain this type of problem. No merchandise should be moved—from the warehouse proper to the ready stocks area to the shipping department—without attendant paperwork. Moreover, those records should be carefully scrutinized on a daily basis by office personnel. If stealing is suspected, you might consider planting an undercover detective in the warehouse to work alongside the others, perhaps as an order picker.

Instruct all warehouse employees to both enter and leave the premises through the same doorway, and station a security guard at that location at all times; this will help curtail the amount of merchandise that "walks out" with the help. Needless to say, security checks should be run on all workers before they are hired; this too will help hold down your rate of shrinkage.

Other preventative measures include: fencing off the receiving and shipping areas, keeping unauthorized people out of those departments, making certain truck bays are well illuminated both inside and outside of the building, and spot checking incoming shipments and outgoing deliveries at different times (both day and night) and on different days of the week.

INVENTORY CONTROL

The order flow system can be adequately fueled and kept in continuous motion only if inventory levels are skillfully controlled. This means you must at all times maintain as complete an inventory as is needed to meet your customers' requirements. As you know, this is no simple feat.

Especially in the wholesale trades, inventory represents a major financial commitment. An overloaded inventory poses a serious threat to your cash position. Hence, the continued stress is on buying merchandise at the most economical prices and under the most favorable terms. Yet, it's not only the actual purchase costs which tie up your capital but also expenses like insurance, storage, handling, damage or spoilage, taxes, and so forth, as well as the very cost of maintaining good inventory records. For these reasons, you should decide right now to weed out and liquidate all slow-selling items so you'll end up about six months from now with a lean, yet sturdy stock of fast-moving merchandise.

This kind of product line review ought to be conducted every year; the end result will surely be appreciably faster turnover and more profit. It's true that a wholesaler is often reluctant to drop certain items from the line which it has supplied for years only out of courtesy, for fear of losing some customers' business altogether. While this attitude is understandable, it does not stand up very well in the face of logical business acumen.

Referring back to the now-familiar "80-20 Principle" (Chapter 11), if you carry as many as 2,000 different items in your warehouse, it's likely that fewer than 400 of them account for 80 percent of your yearly sales. Logically extended, this means that you now maintain an inventory of around 1,600 products just to produce one-fifth of your current sales.

Seems wasteful, doesn't it?

Your inventory control system should be organized to provide you with all the information you need to make sensible product line decisions.

A helpful suggestion might be to classify your products by merchandise type (for example, staple goods, seasonal items, perishable merchandise) as well as by dollar value. Then, you can examine your turnover records for the past year and divide each of these categories into three groups, according to sales movement—fast, moderate, and slow movers. You want to keep close tabs on the first group of items (fast movers) in each classification by maintaining a perpetual inventory of them. There is little practical value in doing the same for the second group, and none whatsoever for the slow-selling merchandise. Indeed, these last two are best handled by occasional inventory checks.

In this regard, a government leaflet which deals with inventory control in wholesaling provides a method for classification.[1] It

[1]See Small Marketers Aids No. 122 in the "For Further Information" section at the end of this chapter.

suggests you initiate a card file and prepare a classification card for every item you carry. In addition to room at the top for both item number and description, the card should contain three columns for filling in (1) the annual quantity used of that item, (2) the cost per unit, and (3) the "dollar usage-value" (the unit cost multiplied by the annual quantity used).

The leaflet explains the technique further:

> After you have cards for all items, put them in a file box according to dollar usage. Put those with the highest dollar usage-value in front as though you were counting from 100 down to 1.
>
> Now, you are ready to divide your inventory according to dollar usage. Start from the high usage-value end of the stack and measure off 15 percent of the length of the stack. Pull up a card for an indicator. From that indicator measure off another 20 percent of the length of the stack. The remainder of the stack is, of course, 65 percent.
>
> The first segment (15 percent) of the cards represents items which account for the bulk of your annual sales volume. The next segment (20 percent) is your medium usage-value items. The remainder of the stock (65 percent) represents items which add little to your sales volume but a lot to your inventory costs.

Other valuable information is contained in this Small Marketers Aid including data on perpetual inventory records, bin reserve, when (and how much) to order, and so forth.

SALES ANALYSES AND EXPENSE CONTROL

Regular, even frequent sales analyses ought to be part of your *modus operandi*. These are vital for effective stock planning and control, for generating recommendations for increasing sales volume, and for holding down expenses.

In the area of merchandising, I've already touched on the merits of analyzing inventory movement item by item, both by unit and by total dollar contribution to sales. The sales area is where a perceptive and aggressive management can make the most headway.

A number of different tactics can be taken here. Sales and expenses may be investigated from a variety of vantage points; those of the customer, the salespeople, company finances, and geography are among the most common.

Typically, the customer list may be broken down by type of firm, size (in assets value), annual volume of purchases placed with the wholesaler, location, and other characteristics. The results of such analyses are useful in the decision-making process, in establishing objectives, and in setting plans for business growth. (This also holds true for other types of sales analyses.) You can take steps to measure the relative performances of all salespeople (individually as well as collectively) in the number of new accounts opened each month, average size of orders taken, total contribution to gross profit (or to sales), expenses incurred, dollar value of orders returned, and the like. Or you can analyze the "territorial yield," that is, obtain the same data indicated above but examine the results emanating from the various sales territories instead of from the individual salespeople.

PUSHING UP SALES

In Chapter 13, the three vital ingredients of the promotion mix—advertising, personal (direct) selling, and sales promotion—were explored in considerable depth. More specifics on direct selling appeared subsequently in Chapter 19; more details are yet to come, in the very next chapter. Despite this rather extensive treatment of the entire promotion area, there are still additional steps to be taken which are singularly appropriate for the wholesale enterprise.

At the very core of these approaches lies the *raison d'etre* of your operation: *to render services to your customers*. Indeed, you ought to adopt this simple concept as your motto. Internalize the thought; make it part and parcel of every action you take; accept it as your prime directive. If you can convince your customers—and new prospects as well—that you can be of more value than your competitors, you'll have little difficulty boosting that sales curve of yours!

This is within your grasp *if* you broaden the list of services you now offer, either by adding to that list or by improving on the quality of those services. You should preferably aim at doing both.

As an illustration, here's a representative list of services which may be offered by the merchant wholesaler. Match them against your current offerings, one by one:

- Introduce your customers to modern methods of stock control.
- Provide them with instructional materials on all phases of retail operations management.
- Once or twice each year, run problem-solving clinics where your customers can talk over mutual business problems.
- If you make use of EDP equipment, offer assistance in stock-planning and inventory counts.

- Furnish stands, display racks, signs, and other point-of-purchase materials at nominal cost or (if possible) free of charge.

- Keep your customers abreast of newer methods and techniques which they can apply in their stores, through your salespeople and perhaps through a monthly newsletter.

- Offer more favorable payment terms and (without going overboard) higher credit limits than your competitors.

- As a service, offer free newspaper mats of professionally-prepared advertisements, making sure to leave space for the individual store's name and address. (The same treatment, incidentally, can be accorded to brochures, flyers, and catalogs.)

- Give extended terms and small loans to financially-troubled businesses; this kind of service can help cement long-term relationships.

- Organize occasional contest promotions; they can create both retailer and consumer excitement and boost sales. "Demonstrators" and "PMs" are also helpful.

- Customers outside your territorial coverage can be serviced by mail through your wholesale catalog and order form. It's sometimes worthwhile to open a "cash-and-carry" branch in a distant city where there's sufficient demand for your products to warrant such an outlet.

As a final thought, don't overlook the public relations value of maintaining close contact with your customers. You can build rapport with them via newsletter, but it's far better to get out of your office as often as you can to visit with them in person.

BETTER OFFICE MANAGEMENT

As concerned citizens, we chafe against the sluggishness of bureaucracy. We rant about the red tape which ties its operations into knots. More recently, we applaud the ongoing efforts to extricate government agencies from the mountainous paper blitz which practically immobilizes their activity, wishing ever so strongly that those agencies could be run more like private enterprise.

Sometimes it seems that the merchant wholesaler is the private sector's counterpart to a government agency. For there are mounds of paperwork in a wholesale operation. Some of it is necessary; other paperwork can and should be discarded. Not only are there customary accounts to keep track of (like payables, and the larger number of receivables) but the whole, intricate affair of controlling both merchandise and order flow is in and of itself an inordinate task. In addition, the operation requires bounteous correspondence, and collection letters *ad infinitum* for delinquent accounts.

Other than the obvious techniques of good personnel administration, the answers to better office management lie in the study, systematization, and elimination of paperwork, and the introduction of specialized office equipment to save time and labor. (Review the section on electronic data processing in the preceding chapter.)

Paperwork

Errors in paperwork can be costly. Here I'm not only referring to typographical errors but also to errors in manual writing, beginning with the initial order written by the salespeople, through the transcription and processing of the orders to all the internal forms used for conducting business. Delays too can be costly. So can an office with too many typists, stenographers, and other clerical help for the quantity of work present. You need a capable office manager well versed in "Organization and Methods" to set objectives (together with the employees), to uphold performance standards, and to monitor output. If necessary, an outside consulting firm might be brought in to help in the process.

The following factors, among others, can affect the output of your office staff:

The working environment—poor ventilation, heating, or lighting; uncomfortable chairs, desks; poor sanitary conditions; too much noise or activity and so on.

The management itself—unclear company goals; little or no supervision; faulty management attitudes and poor personnel relations; incapable management; poor personnel recruitment and selection policies, and the like.

The employees themselves—lack of experience; poor training; ineptitude at mathematics or poor writing skills; personal and emotional problems, and the like.

The system—improperly worked-out methods; badly designed forms; poorly functioning office equipment; a predominance of "rush jobs," and so on.

There you have some of the areas which may be clamoring for improvement. Now is the time to start—today!

FOR FURTHER INFORMATION

Books

Ballou, Ronald H. *Basic Business Logistics: Transportation, Materials Management, Physical Distribution*. Englewood Cliffs, N.J.: Prentice-Hall, 1978.

Beyer, Robert and Trawicki, Donald J. *Profitability Accounting for Planning and Control*, 2nd ed. New York: Ronald Press, 1972.

Danenburg, William P., Moncrief, Russell L., and Taylor, William E. *Introduction to Wholesale Distribution*. Englewood Cliffs, N.J.: Prentice-Hall, 1978.

Hedrick, Floyd D. *Purchasing Management in the Smaller Company*. New York: American Management Associations, 1971.

Heinritz, Stuart F., and Farrell, Paul V. *Purchasing: Principles and Applications*, 5th ed. Engelwood Cliffs, N.J.: Prentice-Hall, 1971.

Johnson, H. Webster. *Sales Management: Operations, Administration, Marketing*. Columbus: Merrill, 1976.

Kudrna, Dennis A. *Purchasing Manager's Decision Handbook*. Boston: Cahners, 1975.

Stanton, William J., and Buskirk, Richard H. *Management of the Sales Force*, 5th ed. Homewood, Ill.: Irwin, 1978.

Wilson, R.M.S. *Cost Control Handbook*. New York: Wiley, 1975.

Free Materials from the Small Business Administration

Small Marketers Aids:
#122—"Controlling Inventory in Small Wholesale Firms"

21

Improving Results in Your Retail Store

The average retail shop is shaped very much like a shoe box with a top, bottom, and sides, except that it's open at one end (for the entrance and display window) and its inner surfaces are attractively lined with ceiling, flooring, and wall coverings. It also has in it fixtures, merchandise, displays, store people and, hopefully, shoppers.

This description is true whether the store is located on a busy thoroughfare in downtown Philadelphia or midtown Manhattan, on a neighborhood shopping street, in a strip or regional shopping center, or in an off-street location.

In brief, your store and all its sundry parts combine to make up a system. When you think about improving your business, then, it's helpful to maintain a conceptual view of your retail shop. As with any other system (or machine), if you improve one or more of its parts, chances are excellent that the total output of the system will improve. To help you with your conceptual overview of your business, study the chart in Figure 21–1.

If you are serious about improving your retail operation (which means that you want to net more profit by the end of the year), then a good approach is to tackle each of the seven major areas indicated in the chart, preferably one at a time.

There are two "prime directives" that you'll need to constantly bear in mind. Improvement can only come from two directions:

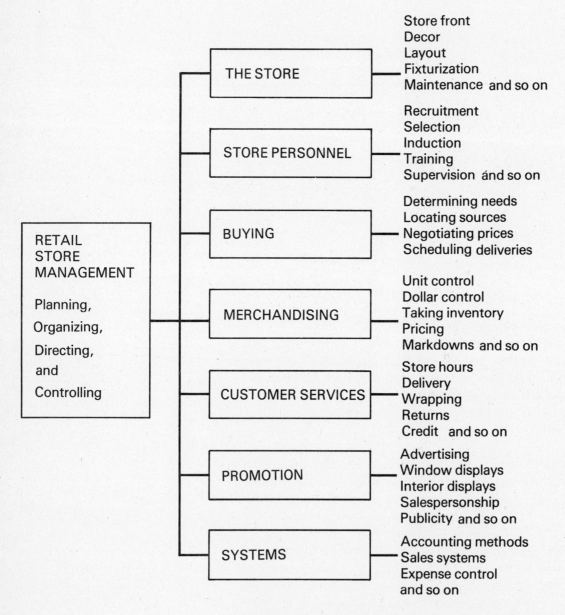

FIGURE 21–1. Organizing the retail store operation.

- increasing your sales, and
- lowering your costs.

Frankly, a combination of the two produces the best results. Yet, as you know, the second direction is by far the less important of the two. Certain expenses, such as rent, cannot be reduced; among the "reducible expenses," you'll only be able to go so far and no further. This doesn't mean you shouldn't try to hold down your controllable expenses!

Controlling your costs does indeed increase your net profit, assuming your sales remain intact. Yet, what about the following year? If you want to g-r-o-w, then obviously you need to increase sales.

Logic should tell you that when it comes down to reality, there are only two ways to increase sales (that is, to take in more sales dollars): Either you sell to more customers than you presently have or you sell more to your present customers. (For the sake of simplicity, let's set aside the strategic use of pricing as a device for increasing sales volume.)

Although all aspects of store operations touch on this business of aiding sales, several aspects are more crucial than others in this connection. Selling more is primarily the outcome of improvements made in the following areas of your business:

- buying
- merchandising, and
- promotion and personal selling.

These then, are the major topics for discussion in the balance of this chapter.

BETTER BUYING FOR MORE PROFITS

As the owner of a small retail business, you have to plan, organize, direct, and evaluate all activities in the buying area. You have to decide *what* to buy, *when* to buy, from *where* to buy, and *how much* to buy. Some of the attendant activities include:

- ascertaining the needs of your customers,
- forecasting sales,
- selecting merchandise,
- deciding upon the breadth and depth of your merchandise assortment,
- receiving and marking, and
- pricing.

Usually, it is you the owner who must do the buying, for your business has not yet grown to the point where you can afford a specialist. Yet, you are a busy individual. Probably, you are tied to your store and find you can't spare much time away from it in search of new sources of supply. Moreover, if you're not located in New York, Chicago, or Los Angeles, you can't afford to make too many long-distance trips to visit showrooms there. Instead, you must rely for the most part on wholesalers' salesmen who drop in to see you, or, in some cases, on catalogs from wholesale supply houses.

Buying Offices

One alternative existing in many retail lines is the independent buying office. There are hundreds of such firms in business to assist retailers, large and small. Most are located in New York and several other major metropolitan centers.

The independent buying office operates as your market representative. Among other things, they:

- send their buyers out to shop around for you,
- provide a steady stream of advice on new items, new sources, new promotions, and the like,
- place orders for you,
- keep you abreast of changing consumer preferences, fashions, and so forth,
- provide you with desk space and telephone when you do come into town, and
- notify suppliers of your pending arrival.

Two types of buying offices are available to the small retail operation. The more common type is the independent buying office, described above. The usual charge for their services runs about ½ of 1 percent of your store's annual sales, most often payable in monthly installments. However, if your sales are too low, they may request a minimum fee, payable monthly. Usually, they will require a signed agreement for the term of one year, cancellable by either party.

The second type of buying office available to you is the commission or merchandise broker. These firms are far fewer in number than the independents. Their basic contributions are to place orders on your behalf and (to that end) keep you informed of the latest market information. There is no charge whatsoever to the retailer; the merchandise broker earns commissions from the manufacturers who receive the orders. (Commissions run generally from 2 to 5 percent.)

There is a tendency to be attracted to the merchandise broker because the services are free. This might be a shortsighted view for two reasons: (1) the services offered are far fewer than those offered by independent buying offices, and (2) the broker's primary motive is to sell merchandise for the companies which he or she represents.

After all, wouldn't it be worth ½ of 1 percent of your sales to have competent, experienced buyers—and a whole supporting staff behind them—working on your behalf?

To locate a buying office suited to your needs, check with your local Small Business Administration office, trade association, National Retail Merchants Association (New York City), or leaf through the yellow pages of the Manhattan telephone directory.

The Art of Negotiating

While you may not be able to do too much about the prices of merchandise offered to you for resale (simply because yours is a small operation and you buy in limited quantities), there are ways to improve your cost of goods. Other than the price itself, you can do better frequently in areas such as discounts, special allowances, terms, job lots, and so forth.

Buy directly from the manufacturer, if this is at all possible; it will save you money. More likely than not, however, most of your purchases will come from wholesalers. Bear in mind that the wholesaler is vitally interested in keeping your business alive, hale and hearty, in order to retain you as a good customer. Some wholesalers offer valuable services which others do not. Examples include advanced dating of invoices, special allowances, providing information about market conditions, special point-of-purchase materials, preticketing of merchandise, free delivery, and the like. One good approach in your buying endeavors is to work up a simplified rating plan for your suppliers; this can be used to compare sources of similar merchandise not only on the quality of merchandise carried, but also the variety carried, dependability of service, prices, production capacity, special services offered, and so forth. Use simple ratings, such as:

    1 = Poor,
    2 = Fair,
    3 = Good,
    4 = Very Good, and
    5 = Excellent.

Of course, you may wish to "weight" some of the criteria used more heavily than others.

As to negotiating your purchases, you should have a clear idea before you even begin your "bargaining" process, as to the overall average markup necessary to cover all store expenses and to provide at least a modest profit by the year's end. If you have done your planning and maintained good stock turnover records, you will know whether or not you've been maintaining the necessary markup. If you need to "pull it up" somewhat, then you should look for a higher-than-usual gross margin on your new purchases.

In considering merchandise offered to you, your first decision must be to ascertain whether or not it is merchandise which you can comfortably integrate with your present stock, which your customers would want to buy, and which is within the price range your customers are willing to pay. Only if you can answer "yes" to these questions should you begin weighing the markup needed against the price asked by the supplier. If there's a considerable discrepancy between the price asked and the price you need to pay, the need for bargaining becomes apparent. In the bargaining process itself, be open and honest with the sales representative. Say the price is too high and that you can't sell the particular items to your customers because you won't be earning enough of a markup.

He or she may attempt to convince you that your judgment is faulty, and assure you that you'll be able to sell the merchandise easily at prices higher than you believe you can get. Be careful. Do not be swayed by clever, persuasive sales talk. You might even suggest that the rep's company let you try out the merchandise on a small scale—placing it in your store on consignment. Sometimes this works.

After you've settled on the price, you then have an opportunity to garner all available extras which will help you to not only reduce your overall costs but to also increase your store's sales. Explore with the sales representative the terms you will obtain. Will the goods be shipped directly to your store at supplier's cost or will you have to pay for transportation, F.O.B. his warehouse? How much time will you have before you must pay the bill—30 days from invoice date, 45 days, 60 days? If you pay your bill early, how many points can you count on earning as a cash discount? What about repeat orders—will the same prices and terms still be valid? What about quantity discounts, either noncumulative or cumulative—that is, if you buy a certain quantity within a six-month period, can you get a discount in the form of a rebate?

Also find out whether the supplier offers any advertising aids, such as mats for reproducing newspaper ads, copy for radio commercials, signs or posters you can display in your store, special contests or promotions you can tie into, cooperative advertising monies, and so on.

Job Lots, etc.

From time to time, you will receive offers of closeout or job lot merchandise. Generally, this represents stock which the vendors have been unable to sell or which has been left over toward the end of a particular season. This merchandise is offered at attractively reduced prices; consequently, the temptation is great to "seize the opportunity" to increase your store's average gross margin.

You must exercise caution in this context. Often, this kind of merchandise does not reflect the proper balance you need in selection appeal. There may be too many of the less common sizes and not enough of the popular ones; the mixture of colors may not be in proportion to your own customers' needs; the styles may be currently in vogue or in a downtrend. This does not mean you ought to ignore these offers. In considering the purchase of such goods, try to separate the merchandise into three groups: (1) items you'll have no trouble selling in your regular price lines, (2) merchandise you might be able to sell at higher prices, and (3) items you know will have to be sold off at marked-down prices. If you then tally up the total amount of sales you hope to derive (quite easily) from the entire lot, you'll be in a good position to know whether or not you should make the purchase.

The best time for you to buy such merchandise is probably right after the peak of each season. However, you must be careful in your judgment of anticipated sales; obviously, you don't want to carry any merchandise over for a full year.

Occasionally you'll come across merchandise which is not entirely perfect; these items are referred to as "irregulars" or "seconds." (Never bother with "thirds"!) Some retailers prefer to avoid such products at all costs, believing that to carry seconds would cheapen their store image in the consumers' minds. Other retailers do put them out on display and find they enjoy brisk sales on these items. This latter approach certainly would not damage store image at all if: (1) such merchandise is clearly identified as seconds or irregulars, (2) the total supply of such goods represents only a small percentage of store merchandise, and (3) such goods are offered only occasionally throughout the year.

MERCHANDISE MANAGEMENT

Initial success and steady growth in your retail enterprise is contingent on having the right merchandise at the right time in the right quantities at the right prices. The control of the ebb-

and-flow of the goods you offer for sale is not a simple matter. Indeed, improper merchandise management practices are commonplace in small-scale retailing.

The average storekeeper uses what has been termed "eyeball controls" to keep track of the store's merchandise. For the most part, he or she depends on a practiced eye to ascertain whether or not there's enough on hand of any particular item, if more should be ordered, or if there is an overstocked condition. Over time, this elementary form of stock supervision usually leads to an inventory much heavier than what's called for, and the carrying of outmoded, shopworn, or otherwise unsaleable merchandise.

Furthermore, unless an owner maintains a sensible inventory control system and good stock movement records, he or she will have little factual knowledge of the sales enjoyed by each classification of goods relative to the overall sales picture.

Take Inventory Regularly

One essential ingredient of good stock control is the taking of physical inventory, preferably on a regular monthly basis. To accomplish this properly, you need to prepare an inventory sheet on which you list all items carried in your store, grouped according to merchandise classifications. For example, a men's haberdashery shop might find it convenient to use such categories as shirts, sweaters, pajamas, slacks, underwear, neckties, and the like; a grocery store might use classifications such as breakfast cereals, dairy products, canned fruits and vegetables, cookies, salad dressings, and so forth.

Descriptions (including names, brands, sizes, and other variants) and prices of the individual items should be detailed out underneath each of the major headings. Ample space must be provided for writing in the various amounts of each product found in the bins, on the shelves, in the back room, and so on. A column for totals should be provided, and another for indicating how many (if any) should be ordered.

By reviewing your monthly inventory sheets and your delivery records, after a while you'll be able to determine approximately how much you sold of every item in stock and its average rate of movement per week, month, or season.

Your Basic Stock List

In managing your merchandise, it's helpful to think in terms of a basic list of goods which must be stocked at all times. This list should be broken down into kinds, types, and quantities. In

SPECIAL AREAS FOR IMPROVING OPERATIONS

most retail lines, the majority of items handled by the typical store unit are considered "staple goods." These are products for which people ask repeatedly; demand for such products is said to be of a continuous nature. Examples in the grocery field include sugar, salt, flour, eggs, butter, bacon, ham, other luncheon meats, baby foods, and canned vegetables.

Even within these common categories there are some products not properly classified as staple goods but rather as "selection type" or "non-staple" merchandise. In the grocery business, for instance, items such as new type of breakfast cereal, an imported French cheese, a new brand of pancake syrup, and the like are regarded as non-staples. In the apparel and related fields, selection type products are referred to as "fashion goods." Naturally, the demand for such merchandise is not continuous; indeed, it's often characterized by wide fluctuations.

Items for which there is regular, repeat business are easily controlled through setting up a basic stock list and establishing a simple replenishment system. If an entrepreneur takes inventory on a monthly basis, he or she will be able to accumulate enough information within a few months to figure out the average weekly rate of sale for all such items. Regular reorders are tied to the inventory (except, perhaps, for fast-moving merchandise where a telephone order may have to be placed with the jobber).

The entrepreneur can work with the following formula in order to maintain an in-stock position:

$$0 = (a + b)R - I$$

Where:

0 = the quantity of the item to be ordered;

a = the amount of time between inventory counts (expressed in weeks);

b = the amount of time that will elapse between placement of the order and the actual delivery of the merchandise into your selling stock (also expressed in weeks);

R = the average weekly rate of sale of the item; and

I = how many you have in stock (plus coming in) at inventory time.

To illustrate, let's assume you take inventory on a monthly basis (every 4 weeks or so); you have on hand in your store 18 pieces of Item X; another dozen is due to arrive within a day or two; delivery from the particular supplier usually takes two weeks, and you sell about 36 pieces each week of Item X. Now let's apply the formula:

(Step 1) $0 = (a + b)R - I$

(Step 2) $0 = (4 + 2)36 - 30$

(Step 3) $0 = (6 \times 36) - 30 = 216 - 30 = 186$ pieces.

Obviously, you would then need to order approximately 186 pieces to make sure you'll have enough of the particular product. Just as obviously, you won't need to have all 186 pieces on hand at one time, since these will be sold over a period of four weeks. If you lay in one month's stock for every item you carry, this could unnecessarily tie up a sizeable chunk of your operating capital. It's more prudent to phase in your deliveries, perhaps one or two weeks apart, if this can be done.

Perhaps a simpler approach (once you've got the hand of things) might be to determine both a minimum and a maximum stock figure for every staple item in your line, and order only when the inventoried amounts approach miminum levels.

After six months' or a year's experience with this nearly automatic replenishment system, the basic formula can be somewhat improved by building in a reserve factor which will take care of chance fluctuations in demand.

As an example, consider this dilemma faced by the owner of a men's store: Ordinarily, the shopkeeper maintains in stock at all times six pieces of each commonly-asked-for size of a particular brand and style shirt, in each of four basic colors: white, blue, tan, and grey. Generally, the owner has found that these quantities are sufficient to take care of his customers for at least one month. One afternoon, a customer drops by, likes the particular shirt, and decides to purchase six, all of the same dimensions (16½ neck, 33 sleeves). He selects three blue and three white, thus depleting the store's month's supply of the two colors by 50 percent.

Chances are good that, unless the store owner can have more of the same delivered rather quickly, he will be out-of-stock on the two varieties before the end of the month.

To reduce drastically the number of "stockouts" in your store, you'll need to make a slight adjustment in the basic formula:

$$0 = (a + b)R - I + r$$

The small r which has been added represents the amount of reserve stock needed to take care of about 99 percent of all

SPECIAL AREAS FOR IMPROVING OPERATIONS

extraordinary fluctuations in demand due to chance factors. To calculate r use the following formula:

$$r = 2.3 \sqrt{(a + b)R}$$

In the earlier example using Item X, r is worked out in the following manner:

(Step 1) $r = 2.3 \sqrt{(a + b)R}$

(Step 2) $r = 2.3 \sqrt{(4 + 2) \times 36}$

(Step 3) $r = 2.3 \sqrt{216}$

(Step 4) $r = 2.3 \times 14.7 = \underline{33.8}$

To build in this reserve factor the owner should add 34 pieces to the order, which then would total 220 pieces of Item X.

Controlling Nonstaples

This regular, fill-in approach used for your staple goods is not applicable to the control of nonstaple or fashion merchandise. Here it's better to think in terms of setting up model stocks on a twice-yearly basis (Spring-Summer; Fall-Winter) or, ideally, on a quarterly basis. Here, you plan your stock in advance, using merchandise classifications and breaking down each class according to its selection factors (brand, style, color, size, material, and the like).

For the sake of illustration, assume that one component of your model stock is the classification *sweaters*. After you've studied the records of last year's performance in this category and also taken into consideration any trends you may have perceived (in your store, in the trade literature, from knowledgeable suppliers), you then prepare your projections for the coming season. Of course, you should initially make an estimate of the total dollar volume you expect to reach in this classification during the Fall-Winter season, then break this down into two more manageable three-month periods.

Dollars are then easily translated into units by dividing the total dollars for each basic sweater style by the price points you've set. Additionally, total dollars for those styles are derived by approximating how much of the total sweater business is enjoyed by each style (percentage-wise).

Now let's assume you have worked through your dollar estimates for the three-month period September through November, and you estimate you'll need about 300 sweaters of all types for that period. You stock four basic styles: v-necks, cardigans, turtlenecks, and pullovers. (For simplicity's sake, we're not at this point concerned with either brands or materials.) Your planning indicates that the four different styles will enjoy the percentages of total sweater sales shown below along with the percentages translated into units:

Type of Sweater	Percent of Total	Number Needed
V-necks	30%	90
Cardigans	25%	75
Turtlenecks	10%	30
Pullovers	35%	105
Totals	100%	300

Of course, you've not finished with your homework as yet. The "number needed" for each of the four types of sweaters must be analyzed further—by sizes (small, medium, large, extra-large) and by colors. When it's finally worked out, your resulting plan for the *sweaters* classification might look something like the chart in Figure 21–2.

HOW TO IMPROVE RETAIL SELLING

You *can* Compete with the Larger Stores!

Having a capable, well-trained sales staff is one decided advantage which the small store can enjoy over department stores, discount outlets, and large chains. For many years, the trend toward self-service and self-selection has been clearly in evidence among mass merchandisers. This trend shows an effort to control operating expenses where the single biggest cost factor, other than the cost of goods itself, has been and still is the payroll expense.

As a rule, the larger retailers rely more often on stacked shelves, massed displays, and an overall "impersonal" approach to sales. Thus, the singular potential of the small store lies in the caliber of its personal selling efforts.

Shopping "Types"

An interesting tidbit from a now-classic study conducted several decades back may prove illuminating in this context. In his investigation, the researcher queried women shoppers on their

Period __Sept.-Nov., 1979__   CLASSIFICATION __Sweaters__   Total Needed __300__

Types Carried	SIZES			COLORS			
	Size	%	No.	Blue 25%	Gray 25%	Tan 20%	White 30%
1. __V-Necks__ __% 30%__ __No. 90__	S	10%	9	2	2	2	3
	M	30%	27	7	7	5	8
	L	40%	36	9	9	7	11
	XL	20%	18	4	5	4	5
TOTALS:		100%	90	22	25	18	27
2. __Cardigans__ __% 25%__ __No. 75__	S	10%	7	2	2	1	2
	M	30%	23	5	6	5	7
	L	40%	30	8	7	6	9
	XL	20%	15	3	4	3	5
TOTALS:		100%	75	18	19	15	23
3. __Turtlenecks__ __% 10%__ __No. 30__	S	10%	3	1	1	0	1
	M	30%	9	2	2	2	3
	L	40%	12	3	3	3	3
	XL	20%	6	2	1	1	2
TOTALS:		100%	30	8	7	6	9
4. __Pullovers__ __% 35%__ __No. 105__	S	10%	10	2	3	2	3
	M	30%	32	8	8	6	10
	L	40%	42	11	10	8	13
	XL	20%	21	5	5	5	6
TOTALS:		100%	105	26	26	21	32

FIGURE 21-2. Estimate sheet.

Adapted from Albert P. Kneider, *Mathematics of Merchandising* (Englewood Cliffs, N.J.: Prentice-Hall, Inc., 1974).

attitudes toward store shopping.[1] An analysis of their responses enabled him to group the women into four major categories: economic shoppers (33 percent of the total), personalizing shoppers (28 percent), ethical shoppers (18 percent), and apathetic shoppers (17 percent). (There were about 4 percent who could not be assigned to any of the four listed categories.)

The key features of the four groups follow:

- *Economic shoppers.* More interested in prices, values, quality of merchandise, and other "economic" considerations than in other store aspects (including sales personnel).
- *Personalizing shoppers.* Apparently enjoy personal relationships with salespeople, preferring to shop where they are recognized and feel welcome.
- *Ethical shoppers.* Avoid large stores and the chains because they feel that such firms are cold and impersonal; they prefer to do business with the independent merchant since they believe that this person also needs to earn a livelihood.
- *Apathetic shoppers.* Dislike shopping and only shop because they must; for them, the most important store attribute is its convenient location.

Now, here's food for thought. Set aside for the moment that one-third of "economic" women shoppers who may be attracted elsewhere by better prices/quality/values than your shop offers. (We'll return to these people later on.)

Wouldn't you agree that those 18 percent called "ethical shoppers" would almost automatically favor your store, given the right degree of "warmth" emanating from your sales personnel? Moreover, with good treatment, prompt and courteous attention, and excellent interpersonal relations, there should be no doubt but that the 28 percent in the "personalizing" category would respond quite well, too!

So, there you already have nearly one-half of all the shoppers in your area as potential customers; you should have little difficulty "stealing" them away from your competition.

You can even count on some of the "apathetic" shoppers in your neighborhood. After all, your location must be more convenient to some percentage of them than the location of your next nearest competitor!

As a final point, let's return to that one-third that we discounted at the very beginning of this discussion—the "economic" shoppers. It's completely up to you to garner some of those individ-

---

[1]Gregory P. Stone, "City Shoppers and Urban Identification: Observations on the Social Psychology of City Life," *American Journal of Sociology,* 60 (July, 1954), 36–45.

uals by monitoring your prices, quality of goods, and assortment mix. No reason why you can't do some competitive merchandising!

Are you convinced by now that you ought to take a good hard look at your current sales staff and your selling methods?

Retail Selling

No matter how fortunate you've been in selecting, training, and retraining your salesclerks, and no matter how good a job you've done in this area, your people probably haven't yet reached their peak efficiency. (No one ever does!) Consequently, you'll have to admit there's still room for improvement.

The basic way to improve your staff's selling performance is through a planned, continuous program. The keys to mastery here are:

- training,
- training,
- training, and
- more training.

An integral portion of your success in training your employees resides in your attitude toward them. Salespeople are not simply "hands and feet." So many retailers wrongly think of their sales personnel only in terms of "coverage"—that is, how many salesclerks ought to be on the floor at which hours of the day or night to take proper care of the customer traffic.

These are people and not robots that process orders for you. Truthfully, they can make or break your business.

Among the more desirable personal attributes your people should possess are:

- a good appearance (including good posture and cleanliness),
- a pleasant personality,
- courtesy and tact,
- an enjoyment of selling, and
- an understanding of psychology (practical, not theoretical).

Usually, a small business owner makes certain that he or she teaches the salesclerks about all of the following topics:

- the merchandise carried in the store,
- where to locate the merchandise,
- the prices of the goods,

- how to ring the register and make change,
- store policies,
- wrapping merchandise, and
- how to keep things neat.

Rarely does the average retail storekeeper spend much time in teaching employees *how* to sell other than advising the new salesclerk to greet the incoming customer with a prompt "May I help you, sir (or Ma'am)?" and thanking the customer after the purchase has been rung up.

The small store owner isn't alone in this respect. In an analysis of (among other things) the initial formal training programs of department stores in New York and California, I discovered that the median time allotted to the training of sales personnel in a classroom setting came to only 12.5 hours; The topics covered were as follows:

Company knowledge	1 hour
Product knowledge	1.5 hours
Store knowledge	2 hours
Customer knowledge	1 hour
Art of selling	1 hour
Register/policies/systems	6 hours[2]

Only *one hour* on "The Art of Selling"????

The Selling Process Analyzed

Retail selling follows along much the same lines as the personal selling process described earlier in Chapter 19, except that the salesclerk does not have to do any prospecting. Your store windows, the interior displays, your advertising and sales promotion take care of this. Happily, prospects are drawn to and into your shop.

It might be advantageous to take apart this personal selling process, step by step, with an eye to study and improvement. If you, the owner, spend some time mulling over each step, you'll doubtlessly come up with at least two or three usable ideas in each case. Only a few comments are made below; they are designed to set you thinking:

The Approach. Salespeople often confuse this first step with the salutation or greeting, for example, "Good morning, sir!" or "How can I help you?" All the Greeting does is initiate a

[2]Irving Burstiner, "Current Personnel Practices in Department Stores," *Journal of Retailing,* 50 (Winter, 1975), 3–14, 86.

conversation; this has little or nothing to do with selling. Actually, the approach ought to be the beginning of the sales presentation, for what goes on in that first minute or so of contact should facilitate the presentation.

Give customers time to "get into" the store. Neither lurch at nor pounce on them. If they know what they want, they'll most likely walk directly to you (or another salesperson); if they're not sure what they want, they might enter hesitatingly, look around at the displays, or glance perplexedly toward the salesclerk. If the salesperson is approached directly, he or she should smile, greet the customer cordially (preferably by name), and ask, "How may I help you?" This, of course, implies that you have trained your employees to recall customers' names; this technique could be especially valuable if yours is a shopping or specialty goods store. (A "guest register" in which your customers can record their names and addresses would be helpful here. It can also come in handy when you run occasional special promotions for "favored customers.")

When shoppers seem to be "just looking" or appear otherwise not ready for service, the salesclerk should at least comment on the fact that she is available if the customer needs assistance (after greeting the customer, naturally!).

Where a shopper is evidently interested in a displayed item, your employee ought to approach the person and point out some interesting feature of the product or, better still, some benefit which the item can bring to the customer.

Where there are several customers (and not enough sales help), the experienced salesperson will assure those who are waiting that they will be waited on shortly.

The Presentation.   Having learned of the customer's needs during the approach, perhaps with several well-chosen questions, the salesperson then makes a smooth transition into the presentation itself. Here, the object is to arouse the interest of the prospect, build desire on his or her part to purchase the item, and then "close" the sale. In reality, people buy benefits, not products per se; therefore, concentrate on what the merchandise can do or will do for the prospect. Try to involve the customer in touching the material, holding the item, putting it on if it is a garment, and so on.

To make a good presentation, the salesclerk must:

(1) know the selling points of the merchandise, (2) be familiar with its qualities and characteristics, (3) know how to care for it and, (4) if it's a mechanical thing, how it's operated.

A good salesperson is also familiar with your competitor's merchandise, and how your products compare.

Objections. As in any type of direct or personal selling, the majority of prospective customers raise all sorts of issues during the presentation. These are obstacles to be expected by the salesclerk; obstacles to making the sale. As such, they challenge the imagination of the good salesperson. Some comments may be simply excuses which people present so that they don't seem like easy targets for sales pitches. Others are real objections: to price; to style, quality or other features; to the store's service policies; and so forth. Sometimes, these objections are not spoken aloud; in such cases, it's up to the salesclerk to determine why the customer is reluctant, perhaps by asking several probing (though tactful) questions, perhaps by observation alone.

A variety of techniques are available which can be used effectively in meeting customer objections. Sometimes, these can be "turned around" so that what has been proposed as a negative by the customer can be made into a positive selling point. Another method, called the "Yes, but . . ." technique, enables the salesclerk to appear to agree gracefully with what the customer has been saying while, at the same time, giving him or her the opportunity to point out one or more additional, positive facts which may help to clear up the problem.

There are other methods, too. The bibliography at the end of this chapter, as well as those in Chapters 13 and 19, can assist you in your selling efforts.

The Close and Suggestive Selling. The "close" or "closing" represents the culmination of your sales effort; at this point, you take down the customer's order (if you use the sales slip method), ring up the register (if you do not), and deliver the merchandise to your customer (or arrange for its delivery). However, knowing *when* and *how* to close a sale is perhaps a more difficult feat for the salesclerk. Again, a good book on retail selling methods (such as the one by Buskirk mentioned at the end of this chapter) should help tremendously.

Of course, suggestive selling may be used during the sales presentation itself. However, its most commonly recognized form is probably the closing suggestion.

All too often, the salesclerk will ask, "Will there be anything else?" before proceeding with the bagging or wrapping of the merchandise selected. How superfluous can a question be? "Anything else?" is a phrase which marks a lazy, inefficient salesperson. Unless a customer intends to buy something additional—in which case it would have already been mentioned—a negative response is certain.

On the other hand, statements such as the following may elicit a completely different sort of response:

- *At a confectionery shop:* "Did you know that our salted cashews are on sale for this week only, at thirty cents less than the regular price?"
- *At a gift shop:* "We're now taking orders for delivery on Mother's Day. May I show you a display of unusual gifts for Mother?"
- *At a men's store:* "I believe we have just the right necktie for the shirt you have selected. May I show it to you?"
- *At a hardware store:* "That's a fine pair of pliers you've picked out. Would you be interested in a quality hammer?"
- *At a bakery:* "Here's a sample of our chocolate chip cookies. I'd like you to taste one to see just how delicious it is."

Concrete suggestions do pay off. When you suggest an additional item, you implant an idea in the customer's mind, thus confronting the person with the necessity of making a decision. While the response may still be "No, thank you" in many cases, there's a fair chance of an occasional affirmative answer. Remember that old adage "Nothing ventured, nothing gained."

Closing suggestions are aided by a display of the item suggested located close to the register so that the salesclerk can point to the merchandise while talking about it. These kinds of suggestions are particularly effective with inexpensive items of the "pick-up" variety, or with products which are timely, on sale, or related to the merchandise the customer has already selected.

Experienced salespeople claim they can sell additional merchandise to at least three out of every ten customers.

PROMOTIONAL CREATIVITY

It was pointed out in Chapter 13 that there are essentially three facets to the "promotion mix": direct (personal) selling, advertising, and sales promotion. The first area has just been treated in more detail in this chapter; the remaining two facets were discussed in some depth in the earlier chapter on "Promotion Management." As to advertising, it is true that the average small retail shop does little of this throughout the year; when it does advertise, it does so generally in the busy season or around holiday times. In view of these facts, little more need be said on this subject other than: (1) Refer back to what has been presented in Chapter 13. (2) Strive for more "creativity" in your ads. (3) Try to make your advertising dollars go further.

Here are just a few "hints" in this connection:

1. Doubling the size of your ad will not double the number of people who read it.
2. Don't overwrite. Layout and copy should be simple, clear, and understandable.
3. Feature the right merchandise in your advertising.
4. A photo or illustration is much more compelling than straight text.
5. Your store name, address, and telephone number should be easily discernible.
6. A series of advertisements will have a more powerful effect on your public than an occasional, one-shot ad. (Continuity!)
7. Exercise care in media selection.
8. An advertiser can often obtain free publicity (in the form of a news write-up) from a local or area newspaper.

A Word or Two About Services

The department stores and other sophisticated retailers call it "nonprice competition"; this term refers to the strategic use of a variety of customer services as a major method of differentiating a store from its competitors.

What a fine attitude for you to formulate with respect to your own store! Try to think about the services you can offer to your customers which will make your store stand out from the rest. You might consider this type of orientation as a "merchandising of services," rather than goods.

Of course, some services are expected by shoppers today, and they expect storekeepers to provide them completely free of charge. Some of these services are: convenient store hours (for the customer, not for you), courteous salesclerk attention, wrapping (or bagging) purchases, and prompt and satisfactory handling of complaints and adjustments.

There are other services to be considered. Some you may decide to offer without charge; others, you may feel require a minimal charge. (Today's consumer recognizes that business overhead costs have been increasing over the years; consequently, people may not be averse to you charging a small fee for some services.)

Here's a brief listing of services which you can consider offering:

- alterations and repairs,
- credit,
- making local deliveries,
- telephone and mail orders,
- parking arrangements,

- rest rooms,
- renting equipment,
- gift wrapping,
- serving free coffee, and the like,
- chairs for resting,
- bulletin boards for customer notices,
- special discounts to groups, and quantity discounts,
- check cashing, and
- water fountain.

SALES PROMOTION

The majority of small, independent retailers apparently do not exercise much creativity in their promotional efforts. To convince yourself that this is indeed the case, simply take a stroll some afternoon along any shopping street in the city. Look into all the shop windows you pass. How many of them manifest colorful, striking window treatments or backgrounds, or airy displays with obvious center features, or motion in the window, or interesting posters and signtickets which "talk up" the displayed merchandise? (At this point, it would be worthwhile to review the section on "Displays" in Chapter 13.)

You need to do some very creative thinking in order to come up with promotions which really produce traffic and increase sales volume. The techniques involved in new product development (outlined in Chapter 11) will really be helpful to you in this respect.

The "Promotion Calendar"

One of the most valuable approaches to improving your promotional efforts is the preparation in advance of a detailed six-month promotion calendar.

Draw six columns on a large sheet of paper. At the top of each column write the name of each of the next six months; then breakdown each column into four or five sections—for example, Week I, II, III, IV, and perhaps V. From your regular yearly calendar, enter in all the holidays for which you normally plan promotions.

Right away you'll see that there are many open weeks for which there is no ready-made theme. So, your task is to fill in all those empty spots on your promotion calendar, choosing from a wide range of possibilities, including the more obvious back-to-school promotion (in September), "warm weather" or vacation theme in June or July, "after-Christmas" sale, and the like. But you should really go beyond these promotions and dig into the potential here; try to set up some truly distinctive promotions.

You know about Mother's Day and Father's Day and that your business will probably be brisk on both occasions. What about some rarer themes, like "Grandma's Day," "Secretaries' Week," "Latin-America Week," "Goin' Fishin'?" "Travel Time," "Hobby Time," "Do-It-Yourself Month," and a zillion others?

Incidentally, if you lack ideas, your trade association or the National Retail Merchants Association in New York City (which does have a promotional calendar) will have some good ideas for you.

Once you've determined your themes, the next step is to fill in all the details: the amount of money to be spent on each promotion, the merchandise you will feature, the advertising (if any) you will do and where it will be done, when you'll bring in the necessary stock, when the displays go up (and come down), instructions for your salespeople, and so forth.

Out of all this effort and activity comes a solid promotional blueprint for boosting your sales. If it's all down on paper well in advance, you'll have excellent direction to follow. Moreover, it isn't rigid; you can change things and add to things as you go along!

For instance, you can use one or two traffic-building contest promotions during the half-year; these can be based around simple ideas like "count the number of jelly beans in this jar," or a "sweepstakes" drawing, an art contest, a "prettiest baby" contest, a "roving photographer," and more.

As a final thought, early, thorough planning and coordination of all elements in each promotion are the keys to promotional success.

FOR FURTHER INFORMATION

Books

Bodle, Yvonne Gallegos, and Corey, Joseph A. *Retail Selling*. New York: McGraw-Hill, 1972.

Bolan, William H. *Contemporary Retailing*. Englewood Cliffs, N.J.: Prentice-Hall, 1978.

Buskirk, Richard H. *Retail Selling: A Vital Approach*. San Francisco: Canfield Press, 1975.

Diamond, Jay, and Pintel, Gerald. *Retail Buying*. Englewood Cliffs, N.J.: Prentice-Hall, 1976.

Duncan, Delbert J., and Hollander, Stanley C. *Modern Retailing Management: Basic Concepts and Practices,* 9th ed. Homewood, Ill.: Irwin, 1977.

Gillespie, Karen R., and Hecht, Joseph C. *Retail Business Management,* 2nd ed. New York: McGraw-Hill, 1977.

Gold, Annalee, *How to Sell Fashion.* New York: Fairchild Publications, 1968.

Jacobs, Lawrence W. *Advertising and Promotion for Retailing: Text and Cases.* Glenview, Ill.: Scott, Foresman, 1972.

Mason, J. Barry, and Mayer, Morris L. *Modern Retailing: Theory and Practice.* Dallas: Business Publications, 1978.

Mills, Kenneth H., and Paul, Judith Edison. *Create Distinctive Displays.* Englewood Cliffs, N.J.: Prentice-Hall, 1974.

Shipp, Ralph D., Jr. *Retail Merchandising: Principles and Applications.* Boston: Houghton Mifflin, 1976.

Rachman, David J. *Retail Strategy and Structure,* 2nd ed. Englewood Cliffs, N.J.: Prentice-Hall, 1975.

Wingate, John W., and Friedlander, Joseph S. *The Management of Retail Buying,* 2nd ed. Englewood Cliffs, N.J.: Prentice-Hall, 1978.

Free Materials from the Small Business Administration

Small Business Bibliographies:
- # 20—"Advertising—Retail Store"
- # 37—"Buying for Retail Stores"
- # 75—"Inventory Management"

Small Marketers Aids:
- # 111—"Interior Display: A Way to Increase Sales"
- # 116—"How to Select a Resident Buying Office"
- # 121—"Measuring the Results of Advertising"
- # 123—"Stock Control for Small Stores"
- # 124—"Knowing Your Image"
- # 127—"Six Methods for Success in a Small Store"
- # 130—"Analyze Your Records to Reduce Costs"
- # 140—"Profit by Your Wholesalers' Services"
- # 147—"Sound Cash Management and Borrowing"
- # 158—"A Pricing Checklist for Small Retailers"
- # 159—"Improving Personal Selling in Small Retail Stores"

Available from the Superintendent of Documents

Small Business Management Series:
- # 31—"Management Audit for Small Retailers." Stock #045-000-00149-1, 50 pp., $1.80.

22

Improving Results in Your Service Business

The service sector of our economy includes so many varied business types that it's difficult to generalize about reducing expenses or improving sales and profits, or to specify other than the customary approaches. For service firms range the entire spectrum: from tiny, one-person enterprises founded mainly on the specialized skills or knowledge of the owner, to substantial corporations which operate advertising agencies, hotels, universities, laundries, and other multi-employee institutions.

Nevertheless, in addition to good overall management and plain common sense, there are other guidelines for improving results in your service business which merit your attention. They are just as applicable to the small service business (tutoring, typing service, dance or crafts school, dry cleaners, and so on) as to the large corporations mentioned above. They are, in fact, useful keys to successful business growth, aids which will help you build a loyal clientele.

1. *Make a fetish of honesty.*   Customer confidence and loyalty are logical outcomes of equitable, ethical treatment. Don't try to fool other people. Never embroider the truth. Never oversell yourself, your capabilities, or your service.

2. *Practice good human relations.*   Treat others as you would yourself be treated. Be responsive to community problems; join in local activities. Never, never lose control of your emotions.

3. *Become the epitome of dependability.*   Never make promises you cannot fulfill. Have things ready for the dates promised. Keep your word; become known by others as someone on whom they can rely.

4. *Take pride in your work.*   Demonstrate a professional, proprietary attitude in whatever you do. Craftmanship and technical skill should characterize your service operation.

5. *Don't stint on materials.*   Always use the best quality parts, materials, and equipment. Don't be penny wise and pound foolish; be willing to spend more on better materials than your competition does.

6. *Give freely of your time.*   The service business is unique in that customers often ask endless questions (as in the tool or equipment rental service) and present a variety of complaints. Be patient. Spend time explaining and giving advice. This kind of personal service can only enhance your firm's reputation.

7. *Know your trade.*   More than in any other type of business, the service enterprise demands mastery of the area of specialization. Learn all you can about your craft through reading, attending seminars and conventions, from your trade association, or wherever.

8. *Train your personnel well.*   Customers will come to judge your business by the way they are treated at the hands of your employees. Courtesy and tact are always expected; no doubt, you have already inculcated these two traits in your personnel. However, it's equally as important to the service business to make certain your people are knowledgeable, continually informed, and technically proficient. Training ought to be a continuous process.

9. *Offer better guarantees than your competitors.*   Find out the details of your competition's guarantees/warranties. Then, set your own standards, going well beyond theirs. Where others offer a six-months' guarantee, for instance, offer yours for a full year.

10. *Improve all internal systems.* Work-in-process, materials and supplies, and schedules must all flow smoothly in your operation. Accompanying paperwork and records should be detailed and exact to assist this flow. Cut down excess reports; simplify the forms you use; substitute office equipment for manual clerical operations.

MAKE THE MOST OF YOUR FACILITIES

Your premises may be just right for your current needs. On the other hand, they might be inadequate, or even more than adequate. If you are like most owners of service enterprises, you feel that your premises are too "tight" and that if you had larger quarters you would be able to enjoy more business. Yet you may feel a sense of helplessness about all of this because you are most likely tied into your present location with a lease that still has a few years to go.

What to do?

The answer may lie in making a thorough appraisal of your present layout. Hire a consulting firm with experience in your line of business to help you do it properly. Often by rearranging your stock and work areas, and by updating your equipment, you can gain extra space. Reserve stock, for example, can be relegated to a basement, office, the second floor of a taxpayer, or other nearby site.

The ideal layout depends on the type of business you are in. Some types require a great deal of space for customer contact (beauty salons, dance studios, and the like, come readily to mind). In other kinds of businesses, working space is at a premium—for example, pet care establishments, auto repair shops, upholsterers, laundries, and so forth.

In all these firms, some space is needed for meeting and serving the customer. Whatever your business, the surroundings for "customer contact space" should be attractive. They don't have to be in high fashion design; neither should the decor or furnishings reflect cheap or shabby characteristics. It's not always necessary or desirable to convey too expensive-looking an atmosphere. New, attractive wall covering or even a good paint job can work wonders for your place of business. The interior can easily be enhanced by better lighting or a new floor. These relatively minor actions can have a positive effect on upgrading the public's image of your business.

You should also check both entrances and exits to make certain they are clear and inviting, so that traffic won't be impeded in any way. Make sure doors are easy to open and close, and that company identification (signing, lettering) is completely legible.

Incidentally, the terms of your present lease should not preclude you from planning seriously for an eventual move to larger quarters. Such preparation should be started well beforehand so that you can, together with experienced advisors, project not only your long-term space requirements but also the optimum layout, placement of fixtures, and even the exact equipment you'll need.

REFINE OPERATIONS

Just as with all other types of business, your service enterprise can benefit by your probing into various fundamental aspects of your operation. With some thought and application, you can refine your approaches and techniques to all of the following areas:

- the purchasing of materials, supplies, and equipment,
- inventory methods and inventory control,
- advertising and sales promotion,
- personal selling (salesmanship),
- budgets and other financial controls,
- personnel, and
- the internal work flow and other systems.

All of these have been amply discussed in earlier chapters; you can locate detailed information on these areas by checking the Index at the back of this book. However, the advertising and sales promotion area merits more extended treatment here, in the following section.

INCREASING YOUR SALES VOLUME THROUGH PROMOTION

Word-of-mouth advertising is the cheapest of all forms of promotion. It costs nothing, yet it's the most effective of all. The ten keys to repeat sales mentioned earlier in this chapter, if followed, will generate plenty of this kind of advertising; you can precipitate even more of it by being more active—visit offices, retail shops, and factories in the vicinity to introduce yourself, to talk about your business, and to outline the services you offer. Carry along business cards and leave one with everyone you speak to. Better still, distribute a 4 × 6 index card printed with all the necessary details. The cost of a thousand such cards is minimal.

Many supermarkets make bulletin boards available for local notices; put up an eye-catching flyer in your neighborhood store. A special offer on the flyer will bring results, and so will delivering the same flyer to all residents in the area. (The benefits of using this technique for one service firm are mentioned in the section on "Advertising" in Chapter 13.)

A valuable little booklet put out by the Small Business Administration suggests that you "let people know" about your service shop:[1]

> Customer confidence is of little value if people don't know that your shop is there and ready to serve them. Keep reminding people. A small ad in the classified section of the telephone directory won't do the job if your competitors are constantly reminding people about the advantages of their offerings.

> Some repair shops let people know what they offer by using direct mail advertising. Such flyers, designed by a local print shop, can also be delivered door-to-door.

> Other repair shops promote themsleves by mailing out a small item which can be used in the home. A list of emergency telephone numbers—such as the fire station and police station and your own number, of course—makes a good item. Customers can attach it to their telephones. . . .

> Sometimes a shop's location can be used for promotion. The owner-manager offers his basement or other space as a community meeting room. He announces its availability with a sign in the window. As people use the meeting room, the shop becomes an unofficial community center instead of just another small service shop.

> Special contests are another promotional tool. One radio repair shop holds an annual contest for the best "homemade" radio built by teenagers. Besides the goodwill, the contest helps the sale of radio parts, and it may help you to spot individuals who would make good part-time employees. An auto repair, hardware, hifi or appliance shop may be able to do the same thing. Sometimes the owner-manager can interest newspapers and radio and television stations in doing a feature story about the contest.

In the very same booklet, the SBA suggests that you prominently display a framed copy of your industry's code of ethics, in your shop.

A listing in the yellow pages of the telephone directory is essential for a service firm. Paying for a bold type listing and a small advertisement would be even better. Costs for these are quite reasonable.

[1]Small Marketers Aid #128 —*Building Customer Confidence in Your Service Shop.*

Ask your customers to register in the "Guest Register" book when they come in; the book should have columns for names, addresses, and telephone numbers. This will help you build and maintain an up-to-date customer file, a valuable list which you can periodically "milk."

Keep your clientele posted on upcoming specials either by mail or by telephone. In fact, you should make more use of the telephone: to call people when their repaired items are ready, to discuss with them any problems that come up, to give them advice, and so forth. Ask your customers for recommendations; work out an inexpensive giveaway promotion to encourage them.

If you have a store front and some selling space, do a little retailing to help pay the rent. Put in a display of fast-selling items which will appeal to your customers. (Beauty salons have profited from this technique.)

Finally, look over your list of services. Do you make deliveries in the neighborhood free of charge? How about credit? Can you make a promotion tool out of extending credit by publicizing it? Can you furnish an appropriate substitute for your customers' use while their appliances, tools, and the like are in the shop for repairs? Can you afford to finance large purchases? Apply some of the creative thinking approaches to the problem of how you can successfully distinguish your business from those of your competitors.

FOR FURTHER INFORMATION

Books

Foster, D. *The Marketing of Services.* Elmsford, N.Y.: Pergamon, 1977.

Kalt, Nathan. *Introduction to the Hospitality Industry.* Indianapolis: Bobbs-Merrill, 1971.

Sibson, Robert E. *Managing Professional Services Enterprises.* New York: Pitman, 1971.

Witt, Scott. *How to Make Big Profits in Service Businesses.* West Nyack, N.Y.: Parker Publishing, 1977.

Witzky, Herbert K. *Modern Hotel-Motel Management Methods,* 2nd ed. Rochelle Park, N.J.: Hayden, 1976.

Free Materials from the Small Business Administration

Small Marketing Aids:
   # 126—"Accounting Services for Small Service Firms"
   # 128—"Building Customer Confidence in Your Service Shop"

146—"Budgeting in a Small Service Firm"

Available from the Superintendent of Documents

Small Business Management Series:
   # 38—"Management Audit for Small Service Firms," Stock #034-000-
      00143-1, 67 pp., $.90.

V

The Future of Your Business

Your gamble has finally paid off.

Because you planned so carefully and managed all aspects so well, you have succeeded in establishing a flourishing business of your own. Your customer ranks are growing; you keep an iron-tight lid on expenses; your end-of-year bottom line looks better each year. Quite naturally, then, you look eagerly forward to many years of prosperous operations. But it may not be all that easy, for growth is always accompanied by new challenges.

What about five, ten, or twenty years from today? Do you believe that your business will remain healthy throughout? How much will conditions change over the years: neighborhood characteristics, competitive forces, economic conditions, legal regulations and taxation, the very customers you are now catering to? What about your own firm— what changes will it undergo?

Will you have the necessary capital to grow? The manpower? The managerial talent?

Are acquisitions or mergers in your future? Should you think ahead to a public offering?

Finally, what will happen to your business when you retire? How can you insure its continuance?

In the next and final chapter, you will find some useful answers to these and other questions.

23

Growth and Continuity

Do you recall back in Chapter 11, the discussion of the "product life cycle" concept? Businesses—like products and like people— evidence several different stages during their life spans. A business is conceived and born to the world; it grows and goes through a perhaps turbulent adolescence; it attains maturity; and then, eventually, it fades away.

It's during the initial, or introductory, stage that the entrepreneur starts up operations, hoping to carve out the beginnings of a niche in a particular industry. This is the most perilous stage; success or failure lies in the offing. If the enterprise is viable in the first place, well-managed in the second place, (and if the owner is lucky), the end-of-year bottom-line figure will be registered in black ink instead of in red. In this stage, all the major business functions are under the direct control of the owner. Sales thereafter will continue to grow, albeit perhaps slowly. If tight reins are held on spending, the business will continue to prosper.

Several employees (part-time or full-time) may be added thereafter, and profits are repeatedly ploughed back into the business, but this is more of a holding operation or a clinging to survival than real business growth. This type of situation may prevail for a year or two, sometimes longer. Indeed, some businesses may never fully attain the next stage.

The growth stage is characterized by more accelerated progress, the consolidation and strengthening of the business' position relative to its industry, an ascending sales curve, and a growing number of employees. More capital equipment is purchased; the value of the firm's assets increases sharply. More capital may be brought in, perhaps through the original owner taking on one or more partners, borrowing substantial sums from a financial institution, or selling some of the corporation's stock. Supervision is gradually given over to employees; several layers of management now exist between owner and rank-and-file. Profits during this stage are excellent. Expansion begins. Indeed, some companies at this stage begin to consider such moves as acquisitions and mergers in addition to internal growth and relocation.

Eventually, the company appears to reach its limits in size and performance. No one knows, of course, how many years this will take for any particular firm. The firm has matured; it may have by now a sizable share of market. It no longer can be considered a small business. When growth slows down to a mere crawl, the future cannot look promising. Any no-growth situation will inevitably lead to decay, to that fourth and last stage of the "business life cycle"—decline and eventual demise.

For any one enterprise, each stage in the cycle may be lengthened or shortened. In the final analysis, it is management's vision (or lack or it) that is responsible for the pacing.

Growth is essential to the well-being of your business. So is continuity in management. Both of these ideas are developed further in the balance of this chapter.

Typical Examples of Initial Small Business Growth

Greeting-Card Stores   In a metropolitan area on the West coast, two competitive greeting-card shops are located within three blocks of each other. Both started in business seven or eight years ago. The owner of one store decided to expand his business by leasing the stores on either side of his location, breaking through the walls, and thus quadrupling the size of his original establishment. He added several new merchandise lines (records, stereo equipment, quality chocolates) and departmentalized the premises. The owner of the other store took in two partners, along with their additional investment capital. They found desirable locations in several neighboring towns, initiated a small chain over the next several years. Today, only three of their six current stores are profitable; leases for the other three will not be renewed.

Hardware Distributor   A hardware wholesaler expanded his operation into a contiguous state. He advertised for, interviewed, hired, and trained three additional salespeople for the new territory. Subsequently, a new compensation plan was prepared for the entire miniature sales force, and both a sales manager and a "trainer" were employed. Within two years, the new territory had been built up substantially and the company went on to "attack" a neighboring state.

Gift Shop   A middle-aged couple, successful operators for twenty-three years of a gift and souvenir shop in a New England resort area, sought a warm climate in which to spend their winters and their eventual retirement. They opened another outlet in South Florida, an almost exact copy of their northern store down to layout, fixturization, and items carried in stock. Unhappily, the newer store does less than half of the sales volume which the older store enjoys. They cannot manage to reach their breakeven point. Nevertheless, the couple decides to use the profits of the first store to carry along the second one, hoping to build it up over time.

Land Developer   A small land developer placed a down payment on some wooded acreage in the mountains of Pennsylvania, bulldozed roads through the property, then subdivided the land into homesites. The property was offered in its semideveloped state, one lot at a time, for vacation or retirement homes. Within two years after start-up, more than $10 million worth of land had been sold through television, direct mail, and telephone solicitation. Meanwhile, the company expanded to the point where several hundred salaried employees and commission salespeople were on the books.

Soft-Drink Stand   After registering an instant, sound success with their first soft drink-and-frankfurter stand, three partners managed to open up two more outlets within the next six months. This way, they reasoned, each stand could be operated and tightly controlled by a partner. All three units enjoyed brisk sales. Soon thereafter, the owners decided to go the franchise route. They hired a franchise director on a commission basis, worked out all details of the franchise "package" with his assistance, and succeeded in blanketing the state with fourteen additional stores.

Manufacturer of Kitchen Furniture An Arizona firm that manufactured kitchen dinette sets perceived the profitability of installing a similar plant in the Midwest close to several of its major, though long-distance customers. This way, not only are they better able to service these accounts and add new customers to their books, but they'll save considerably on transportation costs.

CONTROLLED VERSUS EXPLOSIVE BUSINESS GROWTH

A distinction needs to be made between deliberate, planned growth, and unchecked, even explosive growth. The first is cautious and carefully charted—carried along through regular planning sessions, periodic progress reviews, and program modifications. The second embraces a substantial element of peril which may actually destroy the potential of the budding company. Unprecendented initial success often leads to serious complications. In those firms which experience runaway growth patterns, we see many of the following symptoms:

- an excessive number of employees,
- the proliferation of departments,
- confused lines of authority,
- runaway costs,
- a lack of coordination and thus a loss of control,
- improperly-trained department heads and supervisors,
- a climbing turnover rate, and
- general dissatisfaction and even dissension.

PLANNING FOR GROWTH

Planned growth is by far the more sensible approach. This planning, incidentally, may be even more vital to a small company than to a large firm simply because the former cannot afford to make many errors. It does not have the financial reserves to make amends for mistakes.

Growth means expansion. It creates additional profit. It must be planned for, organized for, then guided and nurtured. To have growth, top management must covet growth. Moreover, they must be highly motivated in this direction and possess the ability to grow.

An organization is primed for growth when:

1. the company manufactures or purchases for resale good quality products and offers them at reasonable prices;
2. the firm takes pride in its operations;
3. internal lines of communication are unimpeded;
4. management is growth-minded, flexible, and oriented toward innovation and change;
5. sales are trending steadily upwards;
6. costs are carefully monitored and kept under control;
7. employee morale is high—and they are well motivated;
8. there exists considerable talent at all levels of management; and
9. the company is both people- and marketing-oriented.

How to Develop Your Company Growth Plan

Once top management has made the commitment to pursue a growth pattern, the very next step ought to be the preparation of a "master plan" for growth. This document should embrace all of the required elements: the specific targets set (including objectives such as desired return-on-investment, the number of additional units to be opened, new plants or warehouses to be set up, the sales levels to be attained, and the like); the schedule for organizing and putting into operation the successive stages of the plan; how all company resources are to be gathered and allocated (manpower, methods, materials, management, merchandise, and so forth); the arranging for required financing; the setting up of checks and balances to insure that all activities are on track; and so on.

At the very least, a plan coordinator (or even better, a two- or three-person committee) should be charged with overseeing the neccessary coordination for developing the plan. Responsibility must be assigned since day-to-day activities need to continue uninterruptedly throughout.

WAYS TO GO

Planned growth may be either an internal or an external affair, or perhaps a combination of the two. By ploughing back each year's profits, acquiring one or two new partners, selling stock to friends and relatives (if a corporation), or securing a large bank loan, the small firm can generate sufficient capital to finance an appreciable degree of internal growth. Such growth is usually accomplished through new product development, the purchase of additional machinery, innovation, product line expansion, automation, promotional creativity, different methods of distribution, and a variety of other approaches.

However, external growth can be made to proceed at a more rapid pace; this is sometimes more expedient for the healthy young firm. Management's attention may be directed toward going public, becoming franchisors, acquiring another company, or merging with some other firm. All of which generally takes more capital than can be generated by reinvestment of profits or borrowing.

Because of stock market conditions these past few years, there has been a slowdown in the number of companies going public. Today, only a firm which has demonstrated steady growth over a period of five or more years, has reached an annual sales volume of at least $20–25 million, and has demonstrated a good net earnings record of, say, 5 percent, should consider this route. If you are thinking of floating a stock issue for your corporation, discuss the pros and cons with a responsible accounting firm.

With respect to franchising, you'll need a top-notch franchiseable "package," substantial monies for advertising and promotion, capable and trustworthy salespeople, legal advice, and other vital components. In addition to some pretty heavy competition, you'll have to combat the public apathy and even suspicion surrounding the franchise field, both of which have been engendered by shoddy practices and shady operators. Combinations, however, are another story altogether; these are described in the next section.

MERGERS AND ACQUISITIONS

In the typical merger, two companies of roughly equal market strength and asset value decide to combine. This "marriage" usually results in a new and stronger entity, with all of the resources of the original two at its command. In the acquisition situation, the two firms are unequal in net worth, sales volume, and so forth. The larger one buys over the smaller—lock, stock, and barrel. Payment may be made entirely in cash (this is true of about one-quarter of all such cases) or in some combination of cash plus common stock, bonds, etc.

The majority of combinations are of the so-called *horizontal* type; this is where companies conducting similar business operations combine, such as two supermarket chains, two hotels, two appliance manufacturers, and the like. Other types include the *vertical combination,* (where companies integrate backwards or forwards along the marketing channels—as when a large wholesaler acquires a manufacturing plant or a manufacturer opens retail outlets for its own products, and the *conglomerate,* where a company will buy up other firms in entirely different industries in order to diversify its holdings).

For the interested firm, the names of prospective candidates for acquisition may be obtained from banks, management consultants, investment bankers, CPAs, business brokers, law firms, and other sources.

Many of the potential advantages of mergers and acquisitions are indicated in this quotation from a current management text:

(a) Marketing: increased turnover; more intensive use of existing markets, adding new markets, perhaps expanding from local or regional markets to national markets; access to new market-research information; adding new products or services to the product line to help existing customers and/or add new customers with associated needs; offsetting any seasonal or cyclical fluctuations related to the existing product line; acquiring brand names and any special market reputation.

(b) Production: new products and/or markets making greater use of existing plant and machinery, thus leading to increased economies of scale; acquiring patent rights, licenses, etc., and additional R. and D. facilities; augmenting or complementing productive capacity, additional factory buildings, plant and equipment; new manufacturing processes; vertical integration, acquiring sources of raw materials and /or customer outlets.

(c) Finance: better utilization of joint resources, employing idle capital or gaining additional funds (as, for example, a progressive company acquiring a dormant company having little ambition, but ample cash or marketable securities); taking advantage of a tax loss situation; spreading the business risk; minimizing stockheld balances; increasing the market value of shares; exploiting large-scale opportunities; enhanced profits and reserves.

(d) Management and Personnel: outlet for excess managerial capacity; acquiring additional management skills, key workers, trained staff, etc.; access to training facilities, management development plans, etc.[1]

MANAGEMENT SUCCESSION

Along with growth and expansion, there is mounting pressure on top management to devise a strong talent acquisition program. Additional specialists are needed to fill the new supervisory and executive slots even as they are created in the developing organization, and to replace those managers who leave or are weeded out due to incompetence. Managerial talent is

[1]W.F. Coventry, and Irving Burstiner, *Management: A Basic Handbook.* Englewood Cliffs, N.J.: Prentice-Hall, Inc,, 1977, p. 399.

difficult to locate; in this country there has been a serious shortage of executives for years.

Usually, management that is sophisticated enough to embark on an expansion program rises to the challenge by initiating needs assessment for five or more years into the future. Simultaneously, a personnel talent inventory is prepared. Promising employees, those adjudged to have the potential for growth and promotion, are identified; a comprehensive training and development program is begun; the management skills of the selected candidates are nurtured through a variety of methods, including university courses, job rotation, committee work, and project assignments.

Strangely though, while the entrepreneur provides for this continuity of management talent long into the future, he or she rarely applies this concept to him or herself. In the entrepreneurial personality, an owner is not only regarded as indefatigable but as indestructible. Personal soul-searching questions such as "What will happen to my business if I become ill and am unable to carry on my duties?" and "Who will take over the reins later on?" are shunted off into the distant future. Yet, as the key in the entire business, the owner should realize that more than anyone, he or she needs a backup—for eventual replacement. Certainly the firm would suffer most if his or her services were to be lost.

The Family-Owned Business

Often, one or more family members are active in the business. This leads the founder(s) to look forward to the time when sons or daughters—or perhaps sisters or brothers—will take over at the helm. Several friction-generating possibilities accrue to this type of situation:

1. No one else in the family may possess the vision, requisite skills, desire, or self-direction to someday manage the business;
2. Personality clashes between owner(s) and relatives—or among the latter alone—will probably occur from time to time; and
3. Jealousy and rivalry among family members can ruin their relationships, if not the business itself.

Frequently, it is wiser to think of hiring a capable administrator, perhaps someone with an excellent track record as president or executive vice-president of another company. This is preferred to designating one of the family as your eventual successor.

In any event, that new executive should be brought into your business as early in the game as possible despite the fact that it's an expensive move. More likely than not, several years of thorough training and hands-on application will go by before this manager will acquire mastery of your operations. You will also want to maintain close supervision over this individual and make frequent evaluations before deciding that you have sufficient confidence in his or her capabilities to turn over the major portion of your own responsibilities when it becomes necessary.

FOR FURTHER INFORMATION

Books

Berman, Daniel S. *Going Public: A Practical Handbook of Procedures and Forms.* Englewood Cliffs, N.J.: Prentice-Hall, 1974.

Cohen, Theodore, and Lindberg, Roy A. *Survival and Growth: Management Strategies for the Small Firm.* New York: American Management Associations, 1974.

Harvey, John L., and Newgarden, Albert, eds. *Management Guides to Mergers and Acquisitions.* New York: Wiley, 1969.

Hilton, Peter. *Planning Corporate Growth and Diversification.* New York: McGraw-Hill, 1970.

Linowes, David F. *Managing Growth through Acquisition.* New York: American Management Associations, 1968.

Mahler, Walter R., and Wrightnour, William F. *Effective Continuity: How to Build and Retain an Effective Management Team.* Homewood, Ill.: Dow Jones-Irwin, 1973.

Scharf, Charles A. *Acquisitions, Mergers, Sales, and Takeovers.* Englewood Cliffs, N.J.: Prentice-Hall, 1971.

Vignola, Leonard, Jr. *Strategic Divestment.* New York: American Management Associations, 1974.

Wyatt, Arthur R., and Kieso, Donald E. *Business Combinations: Planning and Action.* Scranton, Pa.: International Textbook, 1969.

Free Materials from the Small Business Administration

Management Aids:
> #198—"How to Find a Likely Successor"
> #208—"Problems in Managing a Family-owned Business"

Available from the Superintendent of Documents

Small Business Management Series:
> #33—"Small Store Planning for Growth", Stock #045–000–00039–7, 99 pp., $1.80.

Index

Retail (*cont.*)
  store types, 28
Retailing, 26-30, 34
  financial data, 29-30, 34
  improving results in, 293-315
  in America, 28
  increasing sales in, 295
  system, 294
Return:
  on assets, 242
  on investment, 55, 74
  on investment pricing, 184
  on net worth, 242
  -through-profits method, 55-56
Rifle approach, 38
Risk, 116-118
  management, 117-118
  pure, 117
  speculative, 116-117
  transfer of, 117
Risks, 7-9
Robbery, 122, 126
Role-playing, 260
Route:
  salesman, 190
  sheets, 230-231
Routing, 231
  shipments, 233
"Running the alphabet," 169-171
Runs, interrupted, 228

S

S-type corporation, 108
Safes, 128
Safety needs, 156, 157
Salary, 260-261
Sale, rate of, 301-302
Sales:
  analyses, 288-289
  branch, 25
  force, 167-168, 190-191
  forecasting, 272
  historical data, 218
  improving, 276-278
  management, 190-197
  office, 25, 191
  organization, 191
  performance, 195-197
  productivity, 190, 276-278
  promotion, 200-202, 289-290, 313-314
  ratios and indices, 195
  representative, 189-190
  research, 217
  target, 72
  taxes, 115
  territories, 194
  training, 194-195
Salesman, route, 190
Salesmanship, 277-278
  retail, 304-311
Salespersons, 190-191
Salutation, 308-309
Scale, rating, 64
Scheduling, 231
  shipments, 233
SCORE, 31
Score card, 65
Screening, 172
  application, 255

"Searching" stage, 216
Seasonal discount, 184
Secondary:
  business districts, 61
  data, 217-219
Seconds, 299
Security, warehouse, 286
Segmentation, forms of, 38-40
Selecting personnel, 255-257
Self-actualization, 156, 157
Self-analysis, 11-19
Self-selection, 304
Self-service, 304
Selling, 139, 189-190, 277-278, 308-311
  agent, 189, 209
  direct, 189-190
  "needs-satisfaction" approach, 277
  personal, 189-190
  positions, 190
  price, 185
  process, 277-278, 308-311
  retail, 189, 304-311
  suggestive, 310-311
Semantic differential, 220-225
Semi-finished goods, 228
Seminars, 260
Semi-processed goods, 228
Sensitivity training, 260
Sequence, new product development, 171-172
Sequences, operations, 230
Service bureau, 278-279
Service businesses, 28, 30-32, 316-322
  improving results in, 316-322
  ten keys to repeat sales, 317-318
  types of, 30-32
Service Corps of Retired Executives, 31
Services:
  customer, 312-313
  of merchant wholesaler, 289-290
Setting standards, 144
Shareholders, 78
Shares of stock, 77-78
Sheet:
  balance, 78-80
  route, 230-231
Shifts, 276
Shipment, 69
Shippers' associations, 210
Shipping, 69, 231, 232-233
  department, 69, 211, 231, 232-233
Shoplifting, 126
Shoppers, types of, 304, 306-307
Shopping:
  centers, 61-62
  community centers, 61-62
  goods, 163, 164
  regional centers, 61-62
  strip centers, 61
Short form, 255
Shotgun approach, 38
Signs, 200, 201
Simulation, 159
Single-line wholesaler, 208
Skids, 211
Skimming, 177
  price, 185
Small Business Administration, 22, 31, 58-59
Small business corporation, 22, 108

Small Business Investment Act, 31
Small Business Investment Corporations (SBICs), 31
Social:
  environment, 42-43
  security taxes, 113
Sole proprietorship (*see* Proprietorship)
Solid Waste Disposal Act, 42
Sources:
  of capital, 74-78
  of personnel, 254
Space productivity, 73
Span of control, 143
Special packing, 233
Specia project assignments, 260
Specialization, 139, 229
Specialty:
  goods, 163, 164-165
  wholesaler, 208
Specials, 177
Speculative risk, 116-117
Sprinkler system, 126
Staffing, 254-258
Standard Industrial Classification System, 22, 37
Standards, 230, 270-271
  setting, 144, 271
Staple goods, 163, 165, 301
State:
  development agency, 63
  taxes, 114-115
Statement:
  income, 80-81
  operating, 80-81
  profit-and-loss, 80-81
Statistical Abstract, 218
Statistics, government, 218
Steps, 67
Stock:
  control, 299-305
  issuing, 77-78
  market, 330
  model, 303
  ratios, 242
  replenishment, 301-303
Stocks, buffer, 235
Stockholders, 93
  meetings of, 94
Stockkeeping, 69, 230, 234
Stockturn, 242
Storage, 69, 70, 205
Storekeeper, 234
Storekeeper's Burglary and Robbery Policy, 122
Straight-life insurance, 124
"Straight-line" principle, 275
Strip shopping centers, 61
Structure, organizational, 134-135, 229-230
Stuckeys, 50
Study:
  motion, 271
  time, 245, 271
Success, personal qualities needed for, 9-10
Succession, 331-333
Suggested price, 185
Suggestion box system, 168
Suggestive selling, 310-311
Supervision, 157-158